EMANCIPATION AFTER HEGEL

Emancipation After Hegel

ACHIEVING A CONTRADICTORY REVOLUTION

Todd McGowan

Columbia University Press
New York

Columbia University Press
Publishers Since 1893
New York   Chichester, West Sussex
cup.columbia.edu
Copyright © 2019 Columbia University Press
All rights reserved

Library of Congress Cataloging-in-Publication Data
Names: McGowan, Todd, author.
Title: Emancipation after Hegel : achieving a contradictory revolution / Todd McGowan.
Description: New York : Columbia University Press, 2019. | Includes bibliographical
references and index.
Identifiers: LCCN 2018048909 | ISBN 9780231192705 (cloth) |
ISBN 9780231549929 (ebook)
Subjects: LCSH: Hegel, Georg Wilhelm Friedrich, 1770–1831.
Classification: LCC B2948 .M3175 2019 | DDC 193—dc23
LC record available at https://lccn.loc.gov/2018048909

Cover design: Mary Ann Smith

For Richard Boothby,
the disciple of unknowing

CONTENTS

ACKNOWLEDGMENTS

Chapters 5, 7, and 8 contain work revised from earlier publications. I am grateful to Rowman and Littlefield for the permission to reprint portions of "Hegel in Love," in *Can Philosophy Love? Reflections and Encounters*, ed. Cindy Zeiher and Todd McGowan (London: Rowman and Littlefield, 2017), 3–26. Thanks also to *Continental Thought and Theory* for permission to reprint some of "The End of Resistance: Hegel's Insubstantial Freedom," *Continental Thought and Theory* 1, no. 1 (2016): 100–27, and to *Crisis and Critique* for permission to reprint part of "Learning to Love the End of History: Freedom Through Logic," *Crisis and Critique* 4, no. 1 (2017).

Thanks to Wendy Lochner at Columbia University Press. She is the most philosophically adept and brutally kind editor imaginable. I am grateful that she believes in alchemy when it comes to what I send her. Thanks also to Susan Pensak for her generous work editing the manuscript.

Dashiell and Theo Neroni, my twin sons, acted out difficult portions of the *Phenomenology of Spirit* for me when I found myself unable to understand what Hegel was getting at.

Thanks to my mother, Sandi McGowan, who read Hegel to me instead of children's books when I was a small boy, despite my pleas for a normal childhood.

I am grateful for the help of Emily Bernard and Andrew Barnaby, who introduce the dialectical cut to a world allergic to it.

Thanks to Jill Delaney-Shal for giving me an early lesson in Hegel by placing me in the dialectic of master and servant in the form of a love relationship.

This project would have taken much longer if not for the generous gift of time from Dean William Falls at the University of Vermont. Bill is the only administrator I've ever seen who could do the impossible—successfully bringing the law of the heart into power.

The Theory Reading Group—Joseph Acquisto, Sarah Alexander, Bea Bookchin, Hilary Neroni, John Waldron, and Hyon Joo Yoo—makes the University of Vermont habitable, despite the best efforts of those who run the place.

Thanks to Clint Burnham, Danny Cho, Joan Copjec, Jennifer Friedlander, Mattew Flisfeder, Henry Krips, Donald Kunze, Juan Pablo Lucchelli, Hugh Manon, Quentin Martin, Jonathan Mulrooney, Ken Reinhard, Frances Restuccia, Molly Rothenberg, Mari Ruti, Russell Sibriglia, Fabio Vighi, Louis-Paul Willis, and Jean Wyatt, who have always followed Hegel's example, sacrificing their particularity for the sake of the universal.

Sarah Alexander generously read multiple chapters of this book and provided invaluable advice. Unfortunately, the quality of the book's argument drove her from Hegel to Marx.

Slavoj Žižek's epochal rereading of Hegel will never be surpassed. His work is the condition of possibility for this book. He claimed that mine couldn't possibly be as long as his, which turned out to be correct.

Thanks to Adrian Johnston, whose thoughtful reading showed how I might better hide the book's many errors. He pointed out just where to adjust the disguise.

Ryan Engley worked through many of the ideas in this book with me. He gained absolute knowledge by working at Wal-Mart, a laboratory of Left Hegelianism.

Thanks to Sheila Kunkle, who constantly reminds me that contradictions hide paradoxes.

Anna Kornbluh's incisive reading cut this book down to size. She was able to see the trees that the forest was hiding. Without her suggestions for reduction, it would have been even more overweight.

Walter Davis read the whole book twice, providing extensive commentary each time. I appreciate the implacability of his demands, which are those of a relentless friend.

ACKNOWLEDGMENTS

This book would be unimaginable without Richard Boothby. Rick never failed to be astonished, even when the insights should have been ordinary. He made time for the book even when he was stuck in the middle of the ocean.

Finally, thanks to Paul Eisenstein, Walter Davis, and Hilary Neroni. I learned Hegel with Paul, struggled with Mac about what Hegel said, and was able to marry Hilary only because Hegel was unavailable.

EMANCIPATION AFTER HEGEL

DIVIDED HE FALLS

A POSTHUMOUS CATASTROPHE

Philosophers inevitably endure catastrophes in their afterlives. It is difficult to come up with a major thinker who has escaped this fate entirely. The Catholic Church adopted Aristotle as its theological foundation during its hegemony over Europe; tyrants took up the mantle of Karl Marx; Nazis erected Friedrich Nietzsche's *Übermensch* as their ideal; and American ego psychologists proclaimed that they were practicing Freudian psychoanalysis. In the light of these catastrophes, Hegel seems to have gotten off easily. The catastrophe that befell his philosophy didn't lead to mass extermination, but it did preclude the possibility for a fair estimation of his philosophical importance.

Hegel's philosophy had its catastrophe very soon after his death with the split between Left and Right Hegelians.[1] Each side in this conflict, as one would expect, advocated a specific interpretation of Hegel. But they also portioned out the parts of the philosophy between them. The Left Hegelians took the dialectical method and focus on the historical development of subjectivity, while the Right Hegelians guarded for themselves Hegel's Christianity and his embrace of the state.[2] As the Right Hegelians disappeared into history and the Left Hegelians prevailed (primarily through

Karl Marx and subsequent Marxists), Hegel's legacy ceased to bear the marks of his Christian theology or his enthusiasm for the state.

For over a century, this split seemed beneficent. It appeared as if the Left Hegelians had taken the fruit of Hegel's thought and left behind nothing but the chaff. Not only did Left Hegelianism lead to Marxist revolutions across the planet that liberated people from oppressive situations, but it also produced some of the most important philosophers of the twentieth century, like György Lukács, Alexandre Kojève, Theodor Adorno, Jean-Paul Sartre, Simone de Beauvoir, and Frantz Fanon, among many others. Seen in this light, it is difficult to label the split that overran Hegel's philosophy a "catastrophe."[3]

But in the aftermath of the twentieth century, the verdict ceases to be so decisive. All of the Marxist revolutions have failed, and the philosophical terrain opened up by Hegel's followers has become infertile. Few still adhere to the Hegelian Marxism of Lukács or the existentialism of Sartre. Even Adorno's critical theory appears outdated in an epoch that no longer has a place for his form of theoretical resistance to the hegemony of the popular. If Hegel's only legacy were that of the Left Hegelians, we would have to proclaim him a dead dog. But the failure of the nineteenth and twentieth century's Left Hegelianism creates a contemporary opening for the rediscovery of a new version of Hegel. This is a propitious moment for returning to Hegel.

There can be no question of resuscitating Right Hegelianism in response to the end of its leftist counterpart, since it distorted Hegel's thought beyond recognition. Its demise was merited. But when we look at what has resulted from the triumph of the Left Hegelians, we must revisit the evaluation of the split itself. Though the Left Hegelians got all the good stuff (dialectics, history, subjectivity) and threw out the apparently ideological baggage (Christianity and the state), this baggage was in fact a necessary part of the radicality of Hegel's philosophy. Left Hegelian Ludwig Feuerbach thinks that he is improving on Hegel by reducing God to a projection of humanity, but in the act of jettisoning Christianity he also unknowingly throws out Hegel's conception of freedom.[4] Marx believes that the state is nothing but the ideological arm of the capitalist class, but by dismissing it he reintroduces a substantial authority into the social order. It turns out that the apparently retrograde aspects of Hegel's philosophy are integral to its theoretical importance.

Hegel's posthumous situation parallels that of Captain Kirk (William Shatner) in an episode of the original *Star Trek* television series entitled "The Enemy Within." In this episode, a malfunction with the device that teleports Kirk back from a planet to the starship causes him to split into two separate beings—one embodying his kindness, generosity, and sense of justice, the other embodying his aggression, cruelty, and lust. The incident occurs unbeknownst to the other members of the crew and even to Kirk himself. Each version of him experiences himself as Kirk, just as both Left and Right Hegelianism experience themselves as the real Hegelianism. When the split becomes evident, the members of the crew treat the gentle Kirk as the authentic version and the violent one as a counterfeit. But it soon becomes clear that Kirk cannot function as the captain of the ship without this capacity for violence. The most unappealing traits are precisely those that render him an effective starship captain.[5]

Left Hegelianism emerged in an event akin to a transporter malfunction. It subtracted the worst traits of Hegel's philosophy in order to make it more presentable for the modern world. This version of his philosophy would no longer bow before God or the state. But, like Kirk, Hegel loses his effectiveness without his unappealing traits. What seems outdated in Hegel's thought is actually crucial to its radicality. Left Hegelianism did not just throw out the baby with the bathwater but mistook some of the baby's essential organs for the bathwater. Though his investment in Christianity and the state has the veneer of conformism, it provides the linchpin for Hegel's theory of emancipation. Once one subtracts Christianity and the state from Hegel's thought, one loses sight of the freedom that his philosophy offers.

Christianity is not a conservative remnant of the premodern world that Hegel has passively retained in his philosophy. Instead, it is this philosophy at its most modern. From Christian love, Hegel discovers the structure of the concept as the identity of identity and difference. Hegel's logic commences with Christian love, which enables Hegel to move beyond Immanuel Kant's philosophy of duty. But the real importance of Christianity for Hegel concerns what it does to God.

Christianity, for Hegel, is not the religion of salvation or divine providence. It is instead the first religion to reveal the divine as a divided subject, when God appears in the figure of Christ and dies on the cross. As he states in the *Philosophy of Religion*, "The highest estrangement of the divine idea . . . is expressed: God has died, God himself is dead—is a monstrous, fearful representation, which brings before the imagination the deepest abyss of cleavage."[6] The cleavage that Hegel announces here occurs not between God and humanity but within God: it is God's self-division. The event of this self-division—Christ's crucifixion—represents a monstrous moment for the believer because it strips away the idea of God as a substantial divine authority, but it is for this same reason also a moment of emancipation.

With the advent of Christianity, the God of the beyond, the substantial God, reveals itself succumbing to the same contradictions that humanity endures. God ceases to be one and becomes a subject with the death of Christ. This Christian event frees us from the image of a substantial Other, a divinity that has a harmonious self-identity. The subject who experiences the death of God through Christ's crucifixion is a free subject, though most Christians retain the idea of a substantial and indecipherable God located in the beyond who survives this crucifixion. This is how the majority of Christians avoid the freedom that Christ's death grants them.

When we think about the centuries of oppression and ignorance perpetuated by the Christian church, it makes perfect sense to view the abandonment of Christianity as a progressive step. Christian belief attests not only to a cultural chauvinism but, even worse, to a fundamental intellectual backwardness. This is the case not just for the Catholic Church during its centuries of controlling Europe but also for contemporary Christianity. True believing Christians are the ones opposing the rights of women, rejecting gay sexuality, promulgating militant nationalism, and denying the fact of evolution, among other sins. If one were to create a global balance sheet, one would have to conclude that, in the final accounting, Christianity is doing more damage than it is helping. If Hegel were alive today, it is tempting to say that even he would have followed Marx and subtracted Christianity from his system.

But Christianity is not these retrograde political positions that various self-proclaimed Christians take up. These positions are heresies, betrayals of the radicality of the Christian event, which is the moment at which the God of the beyond becomes a divided subject, when the infinite shows that it must appear as finite. It is this event that Hegel cannot abandon without destroying his entire system. When one removes Christianity, as Marx does, one ends up erecting a new substantial form of the divine with tragic consequences.

In the case of Marxism, this new substance takes the form of a substantial future free from contradiction. This future justifies everything, like the substantial God of the beyond prior to the Christian event. The substantiality of the future realm of freedom after the proletarian revolution enables one to commit any atrocity for the sake of ushering it in. The rise of Stalinism is inextricable from an investment in the substantiality of this future that emerges from Marx's abandonment of Hegel's Christianity.

Like Christianity, the state plays a crucial role in the subject's freedom. Hegel believes that the state or some similar collective structure is a necessary condition for the subject's freedom. But according to those who conceive of freedom as a natural fact of human existence, the state is the antithesis of freedom. Though we might accept some state power in order to avoid violent death at the hands of our neighbors, its restrictions nonetheless function as a limitation on our freedom and a burden that we would prefer to do without. The state seems like an unfortunate necessity, which is why Marx proposes its eventual withering away.

When we look at the abuses of state power since Hegel's death, Marx seems to have a point. In addition to the role that power has played in oppressing people within states, it has also been responsible for a series of wars destroying millions of lives. Through a single gesture on August 6, 1945, one state killed over a hundred thousand people instantly. What's more, this was an act perpetuated by the democratic side in the war, not the fascists. If the verdict on Christianity is negative on the balance, the verdict on the state is much more overwhelmingly so.

And yet subtracting the state from Hegel's philosophy has effects just as pernicious as removing Christianity. The state or some form akin to it is necessary to rip subjects out of their attachment to the illusions of their private world. Through the encounter with the state, the subject recognizes the logical priority of its public being. The state provides the form through which the subject sees that it is a public being before it is a private one. Hegel doesn't value the state for the mutual protection that it offers subjects—to his mind, this is an impoverished view of the state—but for the constitutive role that it plays in subjectivity. Without the state, the subject cannot recognize its freedom because it cannot recognize its dependence on the public.

Left Hegelianism's act of getting rid of Christianity and the state had the effect of producing a more straightforward Hegelianism. No one would deny that reading Ludwig Feuerbach, Friedrich Engels, and Karl Marx is less of a slog than reading Hegel. Understanding Left Hegelianism is easier than understanding Hegel because the surgery that it enacted on Hegel's philosophy transformed the position that contradiction had within the system. With the Left Hegelians, philosophy became the struggle to overcome contradiction rather than the effort to further it.[7]

PARIS, TEXAS

The split into Left Hegelians and Right Hegelians obscures what I argue is the central contention of Hegel's philosophy—that being itself is contradictory and that we have the capacity to apprehend this contradiction by thinking. Rather than trying to eliminate contradiction, subjects attempt to sustain and further it. Contradiction is not anathema to thought but what animates both thought and being. Hegel's primary philosophical contribution is to reverse the historical judgment on contradiction. It is the driving force of his philosophy.

The role of contradiction in Hegel's philosophy calls into question two pillars of traditional logic—the law of identity and the principle of noncontradiction. Though many attribute both of these laws to Aristotle (along with the law of the excluded middle), it isn't entirely clear that he formulates the law of identity.[8] Or at least he never explicitly says "each thing is what it is" or "A is A" as Gottfried Leibniz does in the *New Essays on Human Understanding*.[9] Leibniz takes self-identity as banally true, as one of the primary truths of reason. It is so obvious that it is not informative, but one cannot dispute this law while remaining on the terrain of reason.

Though Aristotle is reticent about the law of identity, he is much more forthcoming about the principle of noncontradiction. In the *Metaphysics*, he provides the canonical definition of this principle. He states, "obviously it is impossible for the same man at the same time to believe the same thing to be and not to be; for if a man were mistaken in this point he would have contrary opinions at the same time. It is for this reason that all who are carrying out a demonstration refer it to this as an ultimate belief; for this is naturally the starting-point even for all the other axioms."[10] Aristotle sees the problem with the rejection of the principle: one would be able to say anything and thus would say nothing of significance. Sense seems to require adhere to the principle of noncontradiction, which is just the negative version of the law of identity. If one violates the law of identity by saying an apple is not an apple, one falls into contradiction.

Hegel's position on the law of identity is straightforward. The propositional form in which the law of identity is articulated reveals this law's self-refutation. The attempt to formulate an identity through a proposition inadvertently reveals how the identity is not purely itself. In the *Science of Logic*, Hegel states, "Such talk of *identity . . . contradicts itself.*" It does so because the propositional form entails a "movement of reflection in the course of which there emerges the other."[11] The redoubling of the entity being identified in the proposition shows that it is not purely self-identical. Even if otherness is not acknowledged, it is nonetheless involved as a vanishing moment in the constitution of identity. Otherness emerges through the very articulation of the law. Identity depends on what negates it. In this sense, Hegel's challenge to the law of identity is inseparable from his questioning of the principle of noncontradiction.

Commentators on Hegel are divided about his relationship to the principle of noncontradiction. On one side, Béatrice Longuenesse insists that the role of contradiction in Hegel's thought in no way threatens the principle of noncontradiction nor suggests that being itself might be contradictory.[12] This position has a wide following especially among those who see Hegel as primarily an epistemologist. Slavoj Žižek, from the other side, insists that the whole point of Hegel's philosophy is that one "accepts contradiction as an internal condition of every identity."[13] The extreme opposition between Longuenesse and Žižek on this question reflects the extent to which it divides Hegel's commentators. How we answer this question about the principle of noncontradiction determines how we understand Hegel's project. Žižek puts us on the right track, but even he doesn't go far enough in the direction of contradiction. The point is not just accepting contradiction but seeing how it drives our thinking and our actions. We don't retreat from contradiction but seek it out.

That said, Hegel doesn't not simply reject the principle of noncontradiction. One cannot construct manifestly contradictory propositions like "Paris, the city in France, is in Texas." If one allows oneself to say anything, then one can say nothing. Instead, Hegel shows that the principle of noncontradiction actually refutes itself. When one follows the principle of noncontradiction through an analysis of a series of philosophical positions, one ultimately discovers that insisting on noncontradiction leads to contradiction. This is the trajectory that each of Hegel's major works follows. Utilizing the principle of noncontradiction, Hegel illustrates how a position is at odds with itself. This leads Hegel to a subsequent position that avoids the contradiction that undid the previous one but that inaugurates a new contradiction. For instance, after discovering the contradiction that unravels sense certainty at the beginning of the *Phenomenology of Spirit*, he moves on to perception, which avoids this contradiction while inadvertently creating a new one through its solution to the prior one. Hegel advances in this way until he reaches the absolute—the point at which contradiction reveals itself as intractable. It is only here, at the absolute, that Hegel rejects the principle of noncontradiction. Getting to this point enables Hegel to recognize the central role that contradiction plays in everything.

According to Hegel, if I begin with a clear opposition like the difference between being and nothing, I soon discover that the opposition is not as clear as it appears. Without its relationship to nothing that is evident in becoming, pure being is indistinguishable from pure nothing. Being requires nothing in order to be. Contradiction is the name for the necessary impurity of every identity—its inability to just be itself.

Identity is incapable of being identity without introducing some form of otherness that reveals the lack of perfect self-identity. The failure of what Hegel calls formal thinking lies in its inability to account for the necessity of contradiction. As Hegel puts it in the *Science of Logic*, "The firm principle that formal thinking lays down for itself . . . is that contradiction cannot be thought. But in fact the thought of contradiction is the essential moment of the concept. Formal thought does in fact think it, only it at once looks away from it."[14] Even formal thinking that believes itself to be free of contradiction must go through contradiction in order to perform its operations. Its formulations of identity necessarily involve the negation of this same identity, but formal thinking holds this negation as external and separate from the identity. As a result, contradiction remains repressed within formal thinking. Hegel's philosophy is the return of this repressed.

Hegel does not just confine contradiction to logic. In one of his most controversial moves, he also sees contradiction in the natural world as well. When we examine what he means by this, however, it becomes less outlandish than it initially appears. For Hegel, entities in the natural world never simply are what they are. Organic entities constantly become other than what they are by eating, growing, and eventually dying. Even the inorganic world cannot simply be what it is: ice caps melt, and stars go nova. Hegel links these changes to contradiction because he sees the same disruption at work in both logic and the world. But subjects have a much different relationship to contradiction than that of the natural world.

What Hegel calls spirit (*Geist*) is just this capacity of thought to apprehend contradiction rather than merely succumbing to it as the natural world does. Recognizing contradiction as intractable enables Hegel to reimagine the task of philosophy. Philosophy becomes the drive to uncover the intractability of contradiction through the insistence on the principle of noncontradiction. The result is not a paraconsistent logic but a logic that reveals its own moment of incapacity.

As Hegel sees it, to refuse to accept that contradiction is not only thinkable but also possible would leave us unable to account for the act of thinking itself, which requires the involvement of nonidentity within every assertion of identity. An identity free of negation would be completely immobile, isolated, and finally unable to be identified. It is through the negation that contradicts identity that identity becomes what it is. Ironically, for Hegel, rejecting the possibility of contradiction is self-contradictory. In the act of thinking anything at all, we think some form of contradiction, some movement of identity into difference.

Contradiction does not function as a transcendental a priori truth for Hegel but rather emerges out of the attempt to think through each position that Hegel confronts. Rather than trying to eliminate contradictions in the way that other thinkers do, Hegel aims at uncovering them in order to discover the constitutive status of contradiction for the subject. He sees in contradiction the site where thought comes to ruin and, paradoxically, the site of thought's fecundity. If we fail to recognize the necessity of contradiction in the last instance, we lose thinking altogether.

At every turn, contradiction manifests itself, even when one attempts to articulate the simplest proposition. If contradiction isn't just an error of thought but a prerequisite of being, then it becomes impossible to avoid. Rather than being a license to say anything, recognizing the inevitability of contradiction forces one to pay more attention to what is said. One must integrate the ultimate inevitability of contradiction into the fabric of one's thought in order to avoid betraying its constitutive role. The philosopher of contradiction need not guard against straightforwardness and strive for obscurity. Instead, this philosopher has to take the effect of contradiction into account with the formulation of each proposition.

Contradictions seem like problems to overcome, which is why both the traditional interpretation of Hegel's dialectic and Marx's materialist version are so attractive. But Hegel's significance as a thinker derives from his ability to defy common sense, as his claim in the preface to the *Phenomenology of Spirit* that "what is well known as such, because it is well known, is not *cognitively known*" makes clear.[15] By recognizing the structuring role that contradiction plays not just in our subjectivity but even in the nature of being itself, Hegel enacts a philosophical revolution that provides an ontological basis for freedom, equality, and solidarity. But Hegel's philosophy loses its revolutionary status when the Left Hegelians take away its most theoretically radical features in the name of progress.

One can never return to Hegel's philosophy before the split. The damage has already been done. But this damage is at once a possibility for encountering Hegel again, for seeing the possibilities that neither his followers nor Hegel himself could properly see. The years since Hegel's death have witnessed the spectacular failure of Left Hegelianism and the quiet disappearance of Right Hegelianism.[16] The missteps of both camps have cleared the path for a new radical Hegel. Hegel is a radical not because he eschews the traditions passed down to him but because he takes them seriously. The philosophy of contradiction has its origin in the revolutionary act of God dying on the cross. Hegel is the first thinker to see the profundity of the transformation that Christianity inaugurates. When the infinite reveals itself as ignominious, we know that nothing is free of contradiction.

Chapter One

THE PATH TO CONTRADICTION
Redefining Emancipation

SYNTHESIZING A SOLUTION

It would be nice if we could explain Hegel's philosophy by simply repeating the mantra "thesis, antithesis, synthesis." Not only does it make the notoriously difficult Hegel easier to understand, but it also provides a comforting image of how conflicts and contradictions end up working out. Unfortunately, everyone who knows anything about Hegel knows that the popular view of his thought as a movement from thesis to antithesis to synthesis is nothing but a caricature. One can understand why this misconception developed: Hegel has a profound fondness for threes, and the unfolding of his dialectic often seems to move from a one-sided claim to an opposing one-sided claim to a third claim that addresses the shortcomings of both. Thus, the image of thesis, antithesis, and synthesis takes hold.

Despite the superficial resemblance, Hegel never employs these terms to describe his own philosophy and even implicitly criticizes this way of organizing the movement of thought. Nonetheless, it is a favored image for those who want to attack Hegel because it makes it seem as if Hegel believes in tidy and necessarily progressive resolutions of oppositions in a universe that constantly gives the lie to this verdict.[1] With this image of his thought in mind, Hegel appears as a bright-eyed optimist incapable of registering the unresolved messiness of real life. Fortunately for those not ready to leave

Hegel in the dustbin of history, his philosophy takes up almost the exact opposite trajectory as the one prescribed by this formula.[2] In this sense, the misleading formula is helpful insofar as it points negatively to Hegel's actual claims.

As Hegel sees it, movement in being and thought occurs through contradiction—the inability of any identity to constitute itself without simultaneously negating itself. Contradiction is not mere opposition. It is not the assertion of a thesis and a contrary antithesis. Instead, contradiction occurs when a position follows its own logic and thereby finds itself at odds with itself. As Hegel sees it, there is no identity or position that can function as a stable thesis. A thesis is never an isolated starting point that subsequently confronts an antithesis. On the contrary, every position ultimately undermines itself by exposing its own internal division.

If I, for instance, take up a skeptical position and reject the certainty of any knowledge at all, the logic of my own position contradicts itself by establishing universal certainty about the lack of certainty. Or if I demand universal tolerance for all different belief systems, I inherently refuse to tolerate those belief systems that themselves don't allow for tolerance. If, on the other hand, I tolerate the intolerant system, then I forgo the universalization of tolerance. In each case, the thesis is at odds with itself on the basis of its own articulation, not through the emergence of an antithesis that responds with a counterpoint. These are not exceptional cases but instances of what inevitably occurs with any thesis. For Hegel, the thesis always generates its own contradiction.

Just as there is no isolated thesis for Hegel, there is no external opposing antithesis. Hegel interprets opposition through the contradiction that informs it. Contradiction is the basic ontological fact that opposition serves to obscure. When opponents of Hegel transform this internal division into the opposition of thesis and antithesis, they make his philosophy an easier target while at the same time performing the fundamental ideological gesture that this philosophy tries to combat.[3]

Ideology transforms contradictions into oppositions in order to give us an enemy on which to direct the aggression stemming from our own failure. Contradictions undermine positions from within and reveal how they fail to attain self-identity through their own logic. Oppositions provide the subject with the image of a stable self-identity that obscures this failure. They are much easier to manage and much less threatening to the subject

considering them than contradictions are. Oppositions, such as the opposition between thesis and antithesis, divide the world into friends and enemies. Hegel's philosophy represents a thoroughgoing rejection of the opposition between friend and enemy insofar as it interprets opposition not as
genuine opposition but merely as a form that contradiction takes on. Opposition expresses contradiction while obfuscating its self-destructiveness.
Though opposition might require one to go to war, it provides an external
enemy to fight and a coherent sense of identity for oneself, which is its most
important ideological function.

Today, we erect the figure of fundamentalist terrorists as oppositional
to the global capitalist universe that they attack. This opposition creates a
sense of identity for those within this universe while also giving them a target on which to pour their animus. But this opposition hides the contradictions of the global capitalist system that the mere existence of terrorism
suggests. Hegel's thought demands that we refuse the image of an opposition between a global capitalist thesis and a fundamentalist terrorist antithesis in order to see the contradiction that inhabits both positions. This is
his basic philosophical operation.

A Hegelian examination of the global capitalist system and of the terrorist would reveal that in each case their enemies follow from their own
contradictions. The global capitalist system promises universal inclusion
while relying on systematic exclusion to sustain itself. When the figure of
the terrorist emerges, this contradiction disappears into an opposition. For
their part, fundamentalist terrorists attack the system that provides the
basis for their identity. Fundamentalism promises a return to some form
of traditional values, but these values have their significance only through
their absence in the global capitalist universe. Through the act of destroying traditional values, global capitalism gives these values their significance
for the fundamentalist. Recognizing this enables us to challenge the ideology of opposition. Hegel's philosophy of contradiction deprives subjects of
their enemies, which also deprives them of their image of self-identity.

Hegel's philosophy systematically uncovers contradiction lurking within
opposition. This philosophy enables us to see that oppositions are really just
contradictions in disguise. Those we imagine as enemies most often turn
out to be versions of ourselves (which doesn't eliminate the need for fighting them but just changes the conditions of the fight). By asserting the
primacy of contradiction in relation to opposition, Hegel breaks with all

philosophies that establish identity through the contrast between self and other or between friend and enemy. As a result, the popular reading of Hegel that imagines contradiction in terms of antithesis thoroughly betrays his radicality and enables us to return to the figure of the enemy who serves as a foil for our identity.

But it is with the third term that the problems begin in earnest. *Synthesis* is at once the term most popularly associated with Hegel and the one most alien to his philosophy.[4] For Hegel, the movement that results from contradiction is not a synthetic one. What Hegel calls the resolution (*Auflösung*) of contradiction is not its elimination through a third term, as the idea of synthesis suggests. Instead, it is the reconciliation (*Versöhnung*) with contradiction, the recognition that contradiction is not a problem to be eliminated but the driving force of all movement in being. One cannot arrive at a synthesis that would eliminate contradiction because contradiction is the basic fact of all being. This is the heart of Hegel's philosophy, which the formula "thesis, antithesis, synthesis" utterly betrays.

Rather than synthesizing, the logic of the movement in Hegel's works is one of the dramatizing of a position in order to make its contradiction apparent. In the drama that his philosophy unleashes, every position reveals its own undoing, exhibiting that rather than being self-identical it is at odds with itself. Dramatization exposes each position to its own crisis. When the contradiction becomes evident, Hegel moves on to subsequent position that avoids this specific contradiction. The new position is not a synthesis but another perspective from which the earlier contradiction ceases to be contradictory. This gives rise to a more recalcitrant contradiction, not the elimination of contradiction. Through the development of Hegel's system, contradiction doesn't become increasingly easy to resolve but increasingly more difficult, until the final recognition that thought itself—and ultimately being—is contradictory.

Hegel concludes the *Science of Logic* with the absolute idea, which is the affirmation that contradiction is unsurpassable. This is what he is getting at in this discussion when he claims "in fact the thought of contradiction is the essential moment of the concept."[5] Once one sees that contradiction is not a trap to be avoided but "the essential moment of the concept," one's entire approach must change. Hegel's philosophy moves toward the recognition that contradiction is absolute by thinking through successive contradictions. This is the content of the absolute idea.

In order to work through contradictions and arrive at this recognition, Hegel must employ the same formal logic that he ultimately reveals to be contradictory. This suggests that his philosophy of contradiction undermines itself—or that Hegel espouses the inevitability of contradiction with his fingers crossed. But his use of traditional logic is not an instance of self-contradiction or philosophical hypocrisy. Despite the way that every proposition results in contradiction, we remain able to think and to formulate propositions that make sense in the terms of formal logic. In order to account for this discrepancy, Hegel distinguishes between ordinary and speculative propositions, propositions that express formal identity and those that express contradiction. Ordinary propositions obey the rules of formal logic, while speculative propositions convey identity in difference.

We can see this distinction at work in the opening chapter of the *Science of Logic*. Hegel begins with an ordinary proposition about the indeterminacy of pure being. He states, "In its indeterminate immediacy it is equal only to itself and also not unequal with respect to another; it has no difference within it, nor any outwardly."[6] Pure being is self-identical and involves no difference. But when we read this proposition in the ordinary way, it becomes impossible to distinguish pure being from nothing, which also has no difference within it. This inability to distinguish between being and nothing creates a speculative reading of the original proposition, in which we see that pure being includes its own negation within itself. Hegel then articulates the speculative version of the proposition: "*pure bring and pure nothing are therefore the same*."[7] This expression of the identity of being and nothing is simultaneously an expression of their difference. It is contradictory to claim that being and nothing are the same, but we can only arrive at this contradiction by reading the initial proposition of the purity of being as ordinary. The ordinary proposition leads us to the speculative, just as the principle of noncontradiction leads us to the necessity of contradiction. We discover contradiction on the path from the ordinary proposition to the speculative proposition.

The difference between ordinary and speculative propositions is not an objective difference. There are two different ways of approaching propositions: one reads propositions either as ordinary or as speculative. Ordinary propositions that eschew contradiction are necessary even for the speculative philosopher who aims to reveal the necessity of contradiction. One must begin by treating propositions as ordinary in order to discover that they are actually speculative. If one begins by treating all propositions as speculative (expressing contradiction), one paradoxically misses contradiction by finding it everywhere.

Hegel initially grants the validity of ordinary propositions on their own terms. Without this gesture, it would be impossible to make any claim at all. This is why, in the preface to the *Phenomenology of Spirit*, Hegel insists that "non-speculative thinking also has its rights."[8] This is not just a reluctant concession to a position that he would rather dismiss. He sees that it is only by acceding to the significance of ordinary propositions that one discovers the inevitability of contradiction. There is no direct access to contradiction or to speculative thought without this detour. Taking the ordinary proposition seriously leads the philosopher to the speculative proposition. One follows the logic of the ordinary proposition to the point at which it ultimately undermines itself and thus ceases to be ordinary. Doing so reveals that every ordinary proposition harbors the contradiction of a speculative proposition within itself.[9]

Contradiction animates Hegel's system. The point is not to eliminate contradiction but to find a path to sustain it. However, sustaining it requires thinking through all the potential avenues for its elimination. One must think through the failure of all solutions in order to recognize contradiction as unsurpassable. The only possible image for surpassing contradiction would be the heat death of the universe—the final end of all movement and change. This is the only way to conceive of noncontradictory identity. But if this event occurred, no one would be capable of thinking it. Unlike those who see contradiction as an error in thought and as an impossibility in being, Hegel views it as an unavoidable fact of thought and being.

PHILOSOPHICAL ANIMATION

As Hegel defines it, contradiction is the inability of anything to be identical with itself. The law of identity, $A = A$, does not hold in the Hegelian universe.[10] The two As in the statement cannot, as Hegel sees it, be identical. The formulation of identity inevitably undermines identity because it introduces difference, a difference not external to identity but inherent to it. Identity forms through difference, which is what the law of identity obscures. Entities gain their identity through the act of becoming what they aren't rather than remaining self-identical. It is impossible for an entity to simply remain what it is. The involvement with otherness is essential to what an entity is and to our ability to think that entity.

Hegel's embrace of contradiction stems from his recognition that no entity or thought of an entity can be isolated from otherness. As a result, perfect self-identity is impossible, and even the way that we express the law of identity, $A = A$, gives this away. As Robert Hanna points out, "Hegel is suspicious about the analyticity or tautologousness of the law of identity, because he holds that the very form of the proposition in which an identity is expressed is sufficient to imply the non-analyticity or 'syntheticity' of the proposition."[11] Whereas Kant relies on the firm distinction between analytic propositions in which the predicate is contained in the subject and synthetic propositions in which it is not, Hegel contends that all propositions are in some sense necessarily synthetic. It is impossible to affirm self-identity. Even the law of identity unknowingly gives the lie to it.

When one understands Hegel's beef with the law of identity and the principle of noncontradiction in this way, his position seems much less indefensible. But it enacts a twist of traditional logic that many nonetheless find hard to stomach. It is precisely Hegel's rejection of the law of identity and the principle of noncontradiction that renders him such a divisive figure in the history of philosophy. But this is at once the key to his importance. Hegel's intervention is divisive because he represents an absolute rupture with traditional logic and ontology. His investment in the inescapability of contradiction reveals that logic and ontology cannot be kept apart, that logic has ontological implications and vice versa.

While there is near unanimity about Kant's philosophical significance, when we get to Hegel many subsequent philosophers believe that we depart from philosophy altogether and even that we leave the ground of sense itself. Hegel divides the philosophical world into those who deem him worth reckoning with and those who dismiss him out of hand, between those who are willing to contend with contradiction and those who aren't.[12] Even if the common understanding of Hegel is that his ultimate synthesis overcomes contradiction in the end, his philosophy nonetheless moves too far in the direction of accepting contradiction as conceivable for many to accept. This is the primary source for the controversy that he arouses among subsequent thinkers.

The movement of Hegel's thought is not, as almost everyone believes, a progressive one. Or at least it is not progressive in the usual sense. He is not creating an increasingly secure position for himself through the conquest of successive contradictions. Instead, my contention is that he is serially tearing away the possibilities for escaping contradiction. Our thought moves forward not in order to escape the contradiction that confronts it but because we can no longer sustain that contradiction as a contradiction. As we engage with each contradiction and think through how it emerges, it ceases to pose enough of a problem to catch thought's interest. The resolution of each contradiction is the indication of its ultimate poverty and inadequacy for thought. Successive resolutions lead to more and more appealing contradictions. Thought advances so that it might remain engaged with contradiction. Hegel himself did not directly articulate this as his project, but if we pay attention to the structure of his thought, it becomes impossible to miss. Contradiction is even more important to Hegel than he himself thought.

We can see this at work in the broad movement that animates the *Science of Logic*. Hegel moves from a discussion of the different determinations of being in the first major section of the book to a discussion of the essence that underlies mere being in the second section. Being refers only to immediate determinations like quantity and quality, while essence includes determinations that endure and create more distinctiveness. One can more easily resolve the contradictions of being than those of essence, which is why the discussion of essence comes after that of being in the book.

Essence emerges as a category that resolves the contradictions of thinking about entities solely in terms of their being. Essence is more stable than being; it endures over time. In the first chapter of the "Doctrine of Essence," Hegel theorizes essence in relation to semblance (*Schein*), which is how essence reveals itself externally.[13] Essence begins as the determinate negation of being, but this negation requires an immediate being or semblance against which it defines itself. The differentiation is integral to essence. Semblance is not externally opposed to essence, even though we think of semblance and essence in terms of opposition. That is, we might say that this has the semblance of being a nightstand, but it is essentially a coffee table. Without the semblance, however, one cannot discover the essence. In order to posit the essence of a table, one must distinguish it from how the table seems, otherwise the distinction of essence would have no meaning.

The contradiction emerges because, according to the logic of essence, the semblance has no value. And yet, semblance is how essence manifests itself.

In order to think about the essence of the table, one must be able to contrast it with the semblance. There is no essence without the inessential semblance. The logic of essence holds the immediate semblance as nothing in itself but nonetheless necessary for the manifestation of essence. This is the contradiction that the essence confronts in its initial articulation. The resolution of this contradiction occurs through a turn to reflection, in which essence posits the immediate existence that functions as its semblance. After this turn, reflection includes semblance within the activity of essence. When we reach reflection, the fact that the coffee table seems like a nightstand is part of the coffee table's essence rather than a fact totally divorced from it. In this way, the doctrine of essence moves from semblance to what Hegel calls the determinations of reflection, in which semblance is included in essence. The resolution that reflection offers for the contradiction of semblance leads to a subsequent contradiction that is more difficult to resolve.

The *Phenomenology of Spirit* evinces the same overall structure. The book becomes increasingly difficult as one goes along because the contradictions become increasingly difficult to resolve. Hegel begins with consciousness, which has contradictions that we can easily resolve. In the opening chapter of the "Consciousness" section, sense certainty shuns universals and yet must rely on them for its claims. Here the contradiction is evident, as is its resolution through the turn to perception. "Self-Consciousness" brings more difficult contradictions, as the desire of the subject must navigate its investment in the other. The advances through "Reason" and "Spirit," the subsequent major sections, reveal the subject increasingly at odds with itself, until the final chapter of the "Religion" section. In his discussion of "Revealed Religion," Hegel describes the most extreme contradiction imaginable: God appears in the completely humiliated and debased form of Christ on the cross. This is a contradiction that we cannot overcome but must reconcile ourselves to. The trajectory of the major sections of the *Phenomenology of Spirit* leads from simple contradictions to contradictions that more and more resist resolution.

This dynamic is visible within each section as well. For instance, in his discussion of self-consciousness Hegel describes the movement from stoicism to skepticism as a changed relation to the external world. The stoic retreats from the external world and deems it valueless in relation to the internal world where the stoic invests all worth. Thus, the stoic, such as Epictetus, can be a slave and remain completely content. Epictetus views his slavery as merely external and thus insignificant. But the purportedly valueless external world actually provides all the content for the internal world. Stoicism focuses solely on what it negates and thereby gives the external world an absolute value. By focusing on how little his servitude concerns him, Epictetus inadvertently gives it significance. This mode of valuing contradicts what the stoic claims about its own position.

Just as reflection resolves the contradiction of semblance in the *Logic*, the turn to skepticism about the external world—the position that we cannot know this world—resolves the contradiction of stoicism. It puts the external world into doubt in order to break the subject's dependence on it. Unlike the stoic, the skeptic does not discover the content of its experience in the external world because it abandons any attempt to know that world. The skeptic remains preoccupied by the world it claims not to know, though this preoccupation is less evident than in the case of the stoic. The skeptic claims that the external world is unknowable rather than just turning away from it as the stoic does. As a result, a contradiction that is more difficult to resolve emerges.[14]

This movement toward increasingly stubborn contradictions becomes clearest in Hegel's discussion of art. In his analysis of the particular forms of art, Hegel begins with architecture and concludes with poetry. Architecture marks the beginning point of art not because it was historically primary—Hegel doesn't care at all about this question—but because it provides the clearest form of contradiction. It doesn't even take a philosopher to recognize it in the case of architecture. Anyone can see the self-division of the architectural work of art: as with all works of art, architects express the problem of subjectivity through the artwork, but in the case of architecture this expression occurs in a material form that is completely alien to subjectivity. The contours of the material building must manifest the immateriality of the subject.

Sculpture continues to express subjectivity in a material form. This form, however, becomes that of the subject itself, which makes the contradiction more difficult to detect and more difficult to resolve. In painting, the singularity of the subject emerges in contrast to the abstraction of sculpture. Then music eliminates the material manifestation altogether. In the progress through each of these arts, a barrier between subjectivity and its manifestation disappears. As a result, the contradiction becomes less evident and more recalcitrant.

Hegel concludes his philosophy of art with poetry. Poetry leaves no barrier between the subject and its artistic manifestation. The result is not, as one might expect, that poetry perfectly expresses subjectivity or that poetry is subjectivity. Instead, poetry enables us to recognize that the subject's alienation from itself is not the product of the artistic form it employs. The subject is divided from itself even in the form in which it is completely at home. Even in language without any material substrate, the subject remains alien to itself in the artwork. But in this form contradiction ceases to be self-evident, as it is in the case of architecture. It appears within the form itself—in the struggle between Antigone and Creon, for instance—which requires interpretation to uncover. Poetry doesn't eliminate the contradiction of architecture but reveals that contradiction as such is impossible to overcome.

A dialectical advance, as Hegel conceives it, is a step in the direction of absolute contradiction, not a progressive movement toward the elimination of contradiction. The unity that occurs at the end of each dialectical process does not do away with contradiction but enacts a reconciliation with it. Rather than synthesize two opposing positions, what Hegel calls unity involves the recognition that the position is opposed fundamentally to itself, that it involves itself in what it is not. Unity enshrines contradiction as the constitutive form that identity takes. Contradiction both undermines and defines the identity of the subject.

When thought arrives at the absolute and thereby achieves totalization, the status of contradiction undergoes a thoroughgoing transformation. At the point of the absolute, thought can no longer seek the resolution to contradiction through another dialectical movement of thought. At the end of Hegel's philosophy, there is nowhere left to go because Hegel has explored all possible logical resolutions. Though other empirical possibilities surely exist, none promises any novel pathway out of contradiction. The absolute is nothing but the affirmation that contradiction is unsurpassable. At the position of the absolute, we recognize that we cannot ever eliminate contradiction, no matter how long or how hard we strive to do so.

The absolute takes different forms in Hegel's works, but the point it announces is always the same. In the *Phenomenology*, absolute knowing is the recognition that one can never overcome contradiction because contradiction lies within being itself, that it is not just the subject's own failure but a failure of being. In the *Logic*, the absolute idea is the idea that contradiction is essential to identity. The basic deception of thought that Hegel uncovers with the absolute is that thought seeks to resolve the contradictions it encounters. Rather than seeking respite from contradiction, thought finds a way to preserve and heighten the contradiction. We misunderstand Hegel completely when we view him as a philosopher who accounts for the movement of thought through the elimination of contradiction. Thought moves in order to discover a new contradiction that will prove more resistant to resolution than the previous one. The absolute is the end of this search.

WADING AND NOT WADING IN A RIVER

Hegel's philosophy of contradiction does not emerge sui generis. Though the history of philosophy from Aristotle onward clings to the principle of noncontradiction as foundational for thought itself, Hegel finds a thinker prior to Aristotle who anticipates his own grasp of how contradiction undermines all identity and, in fact, makes thought possible. This explains why Hegel appears so overjoyed when he comes to Heraclitus in his account of the history of philosophy. Hegel announces the arrival of the philosophy of Heraclitus with an enthusiasm that he evinces for no other philosopher.

Not only does Hegel think that Heraclitus represents a leap forward beyond Parmenides and Zeno (his philosophical contemporaries), but Hegel sees him as a fecund source for the development of his own philosophical system. When he begins to discuss Heraclitus in the *History of Philosophy*, Hegel exclaims, "Here we see land: there is no proposition of Heraclitus which I have not adopted in my Logic."[15] Even though only a few fragments of his philosophy remain extant, and even though he lived over twenty-three hundred years before Hegel, Heraclitus is nonetheless a thinker who, according to Hegel, can contribute to the modern world. Heraclitus provides a model for speculative thinking—thinking that grasps the contradictory identity of identity and nonidentity—that Hegel would take up.

But in order to discover a model for his own philosophy in that of Heraclitus, Hegel has to move beyond the popular understanding of him as a thinker of universal flux. The prevalence of this understanding stems largely from the role that fragment 91 plays in our conception of Heraclitus. In the famous fragment, he states, "it is not possible to step twice into the same river."[16] The problem with taking this fragment as paradigmatic is that it appears as a simple affirmation of the flow of time, not a statement of the inevitability of contradiction. There is nothing contradictory about constant change, especially when articulated in this way. The statement seems commonsensical rather than philosophical. But when one looks at Heraclitus's other fragments that deal with this same action, the contradiction that he theorizes becomes clearer.

The celebrated fragment 91 notes but doesn't emphasize contradiction. One could read this fragment and conclude that there is simply no identity at all, that all claims of identity are simply our illusions. But in the lesser known but related fragment 49a, Heraclitus insists that there is identity, even though this identity involves itself in difference. By looking at this fragment rather than its more famous counterpart, we can gain an insight into the bond between Heraclitus and Hegel that would otherwise remain hidden. Heraclitus says, "We step and do not step into the same rivers; we are and are not."[17] Here, Heraclitus states the contradiction directly. He articulates identity through the contradiction that undermines it rather than subsuming identity completely in the flux of differences, as the better-known fragment suggests.

When Hegel talks about the way that philosophers have historically misunderstood Heraclitus, he could be talking about the misunderstanding that would come to surround his own thought. Other philosophers complain about the obscurity of Heraclitus's philosophy and the difficulty in making sense of it, just as later philosophers have complained about Hegel. Aristotle chalks up the obscurity of Heraclitus's style to the lack of proper punctuation that makes the signification difficult to decipher, while Cicero believes that Heraclitus actually strives for obscurity.[18] But for Hegel, the solution is clear. Heraclitus is obscure, like Hegel himself, because he is a speculative philosopher, a philosopher who sees the impossibility of sustaining any abstract principles that do not ultimately prove contradictory.

The great advance that Heraclitus makes is that he integrates contradiction into philosophy and thus breaks from the position of abstract identity that dominates among his fellow pre-Socratic philosophers. Rather than asserting the existence of a universal substance without qualities like Anaximander or the oneness of all being like Parmenides, Heraclitus conceives of philosophy as the recognition that contradiction animates being.[19] He has no founding principle with which his thought begins but instead pays attention to the contradictions that envelope every founding principle, a procedure that Hegel will subsequently systematize.

But for all the importance that Heraclitus has in the development of Hegel's own philosophy, he does suffer from the limitations of being a premodern thinker. Though Hegel contends that "with Heraclitus the philosophic idea is to be met with in its speculative form," he also sees that he must emend the form of Heraclitus's thought—its inability to think the concept.[20] Heraclitus fails to move from the recognition of contradiction to the recognition that this is the structure of the concept itself. There is no theorization of the subject's capacity to affirm contradiction in the philosophy of Heraclitus. This theorization becomes the starting point for Hegel's system. Hegel interprets contradiction through subjectivity rather than reading it directly in the natural world as Heraclitus does. The subject's ability to recognize contradiction distinguishes it from objects in the world. The act of recognizing contradiction changes the subject in a way that Heraclitus does not anticipate and that Hegel develops.

HEGEL'S FLIRTATION WITH IDIOCY

Hegel's insistence on the reality of contradiction leaves him open to a damning critique: it violates the foundation of logic.[21] In several different works, Bertrand Russell specifically targets Hegel for deviation from the rules of formal logic and the resulting absurdity of his claims.[22] Russell notes several errors, but one specific mistake is crucial—and it is a rudimentary one. According to Russell, Hegel's entire philosophical edifice is the result of mistaking one use of the copula (predication) for another (identification), while Russell insists on the absolute distinction between them.

Russell argues that when we use the copula to predicate a subject (like saying that Socrates is mortal), we do something completely different than when we use the copula to name an identity (like identifying Socrates as an ancient Greek philosopher). In *Our Knowledge of the External World*, Russell claims that Hegel confuses these two uses and that "owing to this confusion, he thinks that 'Socrates' and 'mortal' must be identical. Seeing that they are different, he does not infer, as others would, that there is a mistake somewhere, but that they exhibit 'identity-in-difference.'"[23] Russell places "identity-in-difference" in quotation marks not just because he is quoting Hegel but because he wants to indicate how ridiculous this way of thinking is.

Russell's anti-Hegelian logic attempts to separate predication from identity. According to Russell's formal logic, claiming that "Leonard Nimoy is mortal" is an instance of predication, whereas asserting that "Leonard Nimoy is the actor who played Spock" is a case of identification. This distinction enables Russell to avoid the contradiction that Hegel sees operating in the statement "Leonard Nimoy is mortal." For Russell, the idea that this might even be considered a contradiction bespeaks Hegel's own utter confusion about the distinct ways that the copula functions.

One might imagine a defense of Hegel that claims that every statement of predication implies a prior identification that remains presupposed. One must know what one is talking about before predicating it, and this requires identifying it. As Hegel shows in the "Sense Certainty" discussion in the *Phenomenology*, pointing at the entity in no way obviates this problem of identification that all predication presupposes. One must always know what specific object one is pointing at, which requires the act of identification. What's more, one must be able to identify the predicate that one employs.[24] Russell presupposes both identity of the entity and of the predicate, as a result of his attempt—along with all formal logic—to understand the statement outside any sociohistorical context. Predication is far from a simple matter. Its dependence on a context is an involvement in contradiction, much as Russell would like it not to be.

The problem is that simple statements of predication, despite what Russell claims, don't tell us what a thing is. This is the basis for Robert Pippin's defense of Hegel against Russell's attack. Pippin claims that statements of predication are "uninformative" and require the supplement of a statement of identity to become informative. For Pippin, the statement of identity is the necessary precondition for the statement of predication. We can only predicate what we have already identified.[25] As a result, Russell's attempt to avoid contradiction by separating predication and identity collapses.

While this defense of Hegel is compelling (and successfully fends off Russell's critique), it has the effect of minimizing the radicality of Hegel's conception of identity. For Hegel, there is no such thing as a statement that successfully expresses identity. All statements are statements of predication, even those that appear in the guise of statements of identity, because every statement refers to otherness. Or, to put it in other terms, there are no purely analytic truths.[26]

Statements of predication, unlike statements of identity, clearly involve difference. To say that "Leonard Nimoy is mortal" or "Leonard Nimoy is tall" is to introduce difference through the predicate. Mortality and height are categories that apply to entities other than Leonard Nimoy. In order to make sense of how they relate to him, we must understand them across a variety of different contexts. We think of other mortals and other tall beings, all implied in these predicates applied to Leonard Nimoy. Predication, for Hegel, is a complicated business if we really pay attention to it. The fact that the predicates must apply in other contexts in order to make sense when applied to Leonard Nimoy reveals that predication cannot avoid otherness.

When we turn to purported statements of identity, we find, according to Hegel's logic, the same dynamic. "Leonard Nimoy is the actor who plays Spock" is a standard form of the statement of identity (akin to Russell's own favorite example, "Scott is the author of *Waverly*"). Leonard Nimoy is simply the actor who plays Spock, and the statement doesn't add any additional determination to the subject Leonard Nimoy. But in fact, Nimoy's performance as Spock does involve predication and thus difference. Even though Nimoy and the actor who plays Spock are exactly the same person, the would-be statement of identity nonetheless introduces the difference of predication insofar as it implicitly relates him to other actors playing other roles. This is not just a contingent feature of this example but holds for all statements of identity, including Russell's own involving Walter Scott. For Hegel, identity cannot occur through a statement or proposition because this form fails to express adequately identity's contradictory structure.[27]

Identity emerges not as a result of a statement of identity or multiple statements of predication but through the failure of statements of predication. This is the startling conclusion of Hegel's rejection of the statement of identity. Predicates tell us the properties that an entity has, but they don't identify it.[28] An entity can share all the properties of another entity (as with perfect clones or other indiscernibles) without being identical. The specific way that predication fails gives the entity its identity. In the *Logic*, Hegel writes, "identity consists in being *separation* as such, or in being essentially *in the separation*, that is, it is *nothing for itself* but is rather *moment of separation*."[29] When predicates fail, a separation from them takes place, and identity emerges. In this sense, identity arrives only through contradiction and never through a positive statement. It is the negation of an entity's predicates.

The point is not that no predicate can capture the richness of an entity but that no entity can fully embody any of its predicates. This is why the failure of predication provides identity. One discovers what an entity is through the specific way that it fails to be what constitutes it. It is thus appropriate that when Leonard Nimoy went to identify himself to the world he did so through a book entitled *I Am Not Spock*. Nimoy's identity consists in his inability to be Spock, in his separation from this predicate.

Hegel locates identity in separation rather than in positive statements because he recognizes the limitations of all such statements. The attempt to identify an entity directly or even to describe it fully always leads down the path of misidentification. Rather than try to offer a corrective, Hegel accepts misidentification as the only possible form that identification could take. In this way, he tries to make clear that he's not just spouting nonsense, even if Russell is unable to see this.

CHOOSING YOUR WORDS MORE CAREFULLY

When one examines the logic of contradiction that Hegel develops, a basic question about terminology and method soon comes to mind. If traditional logic and formal thinking always lead to contradiction, why doesn't Hegel just invent a new logic that is not so unwieldy? In other words, maybe he should have become Gottlob Frege instead of being content with being Hegel. When Frege looks out on the vast system of traditional logic, he is, like Hegel, dissatisfied with what he sees. But rather than try to use this worn-out idiom against itself, Frege does something much more constructive: he simply builds a new idiom, one in use even today.[30] It is puzzling why Hegel does not take a similar tack. Though Hegel's *Logic* alters the results of traditional logic, it accepts its terms. Hegel is content to change this logic from the inside rather than aspire to Frege's revolutionary gesture.

Though Hegel never provides an explicit justification for this choice, one can easily imagine what it would be. Inventing a new logic that would center around Hegel's understanding of contradiction would defeat the entire point of his philosophical project. He uses formal thinking as a foil not to be perverse but to show how thought is always at odds with itself. There is no possible corrective, no new form of logic that one might create in order to avoid the self-undermining that occurs in formal thinking and traditional logic. That is not to say that certain errors of traditional logic might not be corrected, but only that contradiction will nonetheless continue to appear at new points in the new system.

Hegel sees that the invention of a new logical system will always result in Russell's paradox—that is to say, in a point at which contradiction undermines its logical consistency.[31] It is not just formal thinking that fails but all thinking. Desiring a replacement that would be able to register contradiction not as a disruption but as a normal part of the system's functioning is a fool's errand. And it is an errand that Hegel would not want to embark on. The disruptiveness of contradiction is central to its value. It must retain the status of a disruption if it is to remain the source of all activity.

But this raises another question about Hegel's terminology. Why does he call the inability of an entity to be simply self-identical *contradiction*? Wouldn't a better—and much less confusing—term for this be *vitality*? Perhaps Hegel's use of the term *contradiction* is nothing but a category error. Replacing it with *vitality* would capture the animation of thought and life without the baggage that *contradiction* brings with it. Hegel doesn't move in this direction and preserves the term *contradiction* to register the disruptiveness of all activity. Contradiction (*Widerspruch*) has the sense of speaking against oneself—a self-betrayal that every entity undergoes. In the attempt to announce their identity, subjects expose themselves as being at odds with themselves.

If I proclaim myself as a person of great humility, I reveal that I am not humble at all. Even if, in contrast, I confess that I am a braggart, this self-humiliation defies what I say about myself. What I say or do undermines what I am. I am nothing but this contradiction, this act of constantly revealing that what I am not plays a central role in my identity. The situation seems better for entities that can't speak—they don't have to worry about saying anything that contradicts what they are—but for Hegel, it's far worse.

Speaking subjects enact their own self-betrayal, whereas all other entities suffer it from the outside. Earth constantly suffers from an external violence that interrupts its self-identity. The gravitational force of the Sun constantly acts on it. Earth endures a steady barrage of meteors from space. At the same time, humans dramatically transform its surface from one moment to the next. Though Earth seems like a solid foundation for us, it is actually even more at the whim of the violence of an identity at odds with itself than we are. Hegel evokes contradiction to convey this violence.[32]

There is not just a positive vitality that expresses itself in a steady and constant fashion. Instead, all activity occurs through negation, destruction, and conflict. There is constant change, but there is no harmonious change. If Hegel had described the dynamic that animates being in terms other than those of contradiction, we would slip into vitalism, which is for him the greatest danger.

Vitalism contends that there is a pure productivity in the natural universe. It locates the source of becoming and change within this pure productivity. For the vitalist, change is a natural occurrence linked to being itself. Change doesn't occur through negation—negation doesn't exist in the vitalist universe except as a misrecognition of change—but through the positive development of being. There is a natural fecundity that constantly generates novelty in the world. The task of the vitalist thinker is to uncover this fecundity from the obfuscation that it receives by conceptual thought. With his emphasis on becoming, Hegel might have taken this path.

But Hegel clings to the term *contradiction* in order to indicate the profound violence that animates all being. *Vitality* enables us to imagine violence as external and its disruptiveness thus as avoidable. As long as we follow this path, we are lost not only in self-deception but in a fruitless search for respite from this violence. The term *contradiction* enables us to register the violence that we experience as inextricable from our vitality. It renders visible the animation that we receive from what wounds us.

THE DANGERS OF A = A

The problem with the assertion that reason has the ability to think contradiction is that the implications risk destroying reason altogether. If reason justifies contradictions, then there is nothing to stop someone from making claims about the world that are fundamentally at odds with each other. While embracing the idea that reason identifies the contradictions of being, I can say that all trees are stones or that all dogs are cats. Once I permit the introduction of contradiction into the operations of thought, the floodgates open, and all regulation of what I can claim flows away.

If I really take the inevitability of contradiction seriously, then I cannot make any claims at all—not even a claim about the inevitability of contradiction. Every claim would instantly unravel itself. No amount of vigilance would insulate my claims from this danger. If Hegel were right about contradiction, he could never convincingly say so but would instead remain adrift in a sea of mutually opposing claims. The inevitability of contradiction appears to spell the demise of philosophy.

The danger becomes clearer if one thinks of this in political arguments: one can imagine someone arguing that immigrants threaten to destroy the fabric of our society while simultaneously holding that we are a welcoming society made up of immigrants. Unfortunately, one need not even have recourse to imagination to conjure up a political figure that flouts the principle of noncontradiction for nefarious purposes. This is the basic political strategy of Donald Trump.

Throughout his campaign and presidency, Trump would constantly contradict himself and refuse to admit the contradiction. He would claim that he never supported the Iraq War despite audio evidence to the contrary. He would deny firing FBI director James Comey because of the Russia investigation after publicly admitting this was the reason. It is as if Trump took a course at the fraudulent Trump University on Hegel's philosophy that enabled him to conclude that all positions are contradictory and thus invulnerable to any critique on this count. As the case of Trump illustrates, the principle of noncontradiction is not just a logical rampart but also a political one. When Hegel rejects it, he seems to open the door to a grave danger.

But Trump is not a Hegelian. His contradictory rise was not a danger resulting from Hegel's challenge to the principle of noncontradiction. Hegel's philosophy doesn't give the subject the right to say just anything and then deny it. Though Hegel does ultimately reject the principle of noncontradiction, he does not simply make contradictory assertions or construct a contradictory system. Rather than flout the principle of noncontradiction in his philosophy, he illustrates the consequences of adhering strictly to it. Through a noncontradictory argument, it becomes evident that "contradiction is the root of all movement and vitality; it is only insofar as something has a contradiction in itself that it moves, that it has drive and activity."[33] The refusal to accept the contradictions that other philosophers accept—like the law of identity depending on nonidentity—leads Hegel to discover that contradiction is not an error of logic but a fact of being. Trump's blatant use of contradiction is actually an effort to avoid any confrontation with the disruptiveness of contradiction's intractability. Deliberately contradicting oneself blinds one to the necessity of contradiction.

We can look at an example from the opening section of the *Science of Logic*. In his discussion of the determination of a simple something (*Etwas*), Hegel notices that we can define this something only through its otherness. Without defining an otherness, a something has no distinctiveness whatsoever and blends together with everything else. The otherness intervenes in the definition of a something to create the distinction that constitutes it. But the problem is that this otherness becomes integral to the something. Something and other have a semblance of independence that masks their mutual interdependence. As a result, the otherness is no longer just otherness, and the something is no longer a distinct something opposed to the otherness. Or, as Hegel puts it, "*being-for-other* is in the unity of something with itself, identical with its *in-itself*; the being-for-other is thus *in* the something."[34] The otherness begins as merely an external point of reference and ends up as definitive for how we identify something. The seemingly clear distinction between something and other loses its clarity once Hegel examines it closely.

We can see an obvious case of this relationship between something and otherness manifest itself in the police. While the police becomes a something by distinguishing itself from its criminal other, police officers must adopt the behavior of criminals themselves in order to function effectively as what they are. They must bribe informants for leads, lie about whom they suspect, go undercover with false identities, and shoot those who resist arrest. Though there is a difference between the police officer and the criminal, the officer who never acts like a criminal could not be an effective police officer. The more one considers it, the less clear-cut the difference becomes.

It is precisely Hegel's concern for the principle of noncontradiction that enables him to discover the fact of contradiction. Other thinkers just accept the distinction between something and other as if it were commonsensical. Hegel refuses to accept the presupposition that permits the contradictions of traditional logic to pass unnoticed. He probes the foundations of the distinction between something and an other in order to reveal the point at which it contradicts itself. This does not license him to abandon the distinction between something and other altogether or to brazenly put forward contradictory claims. Instead, he must resolve the contradiction he encounters in order to discover the point at which contradiction becomes irreducible. Resolution, for Hegel, is not the complete elimination of contradiction but the movement whereby contradiction gains a more intractable position in the philosophical system and eventually becomes the animating principle of the entire system. The resolution of contradiction does not eliminate it but complicates it. There is no philosophy without contradiction, but the question concerns where contradiction resides within the philosophy. It is the failure to recognize the ontological status of contradiction that causes us unknowingly to fall into it. Hegel's great achievement is to have revealed its foundational status.

Donald Trump makes clear the political danger of giving free reign to violations of the principle of noncontradiction: one can lie with impunity. But there is an opposite danger that poses a much more ubiquitous threat. This is the danger associated with strict adherence to the law of identity, to the conviction that A = A is perfect self-identity. Ayn Rand takes the law of identity as her political starting point and shows that it licenses the most rapacious capitalism. Rand's philosophical import lies in her ability to expose this link between the law of identity and capitalism, which appear to have no intrinsic relation to each other. She shows that the law of identity is even more nefarious than the open violation of the principle of noncontradiction. One can identify Trump's contradictions and use them to discredit him, while Rand's political philosophy continues its quiet hegemony in the guise of common sense.

But in reality these positions are not opposed at all. Despite Rand's purported respect for the law of identity, she needs figures like Trump who cheerfully take up contradiction in order to advance her capitalist vision. Trump's administration brings together the overt violations of the principle of noncontradiction with Rand's embrace of the law of identity. Trump contradicts himself in order to provide cover for tax cuts for the wealthy, massive deregulation, and the dismantling of the public commons—precisely the political philosophy of Ayn Rand—that the people would not accept without lies like "we're cutting taxes on the wealthy to help the lowest workers earn more." No one can be an open Randian and garner public support. No one can politically invoke the law of identity without also relying on overt contradictions.

On the basis of the law of identity (which she attributes to Aristotle), Rand insists that capitalist producers have no responsibility at all to their employees or to the society in which they exist.[35] Each producer is an independent and isolated being that brings value into the world through the creative act. Since there is no possible contradiction, the value that the capitalist creates must belong solely to the capitalist and no one else. Capitalist production creates value without any sacrifice, just as the commodity exists in isolation from the labor that creates it. For Rand, the capitalist creation of value doesn't necessarily rely on the immiseration of workers as it does for Marx. The production of value has nothing to do with negation because $A = A$.

The title for part 3 of Rand's magnum opus *Atlas Shrugged* is "$A = A$," which provides the main through line for the lengthy radio speech that the hero John Galt gives toward the end of the novel. In his speech, Galt praises Aristotle and rejects the existence of contradiction.[36] This rejection is not just a philosophical quirk associated with Rand but the essential core of every capitalist political philosophy. Capitalism depends on subjects regarding themselves as isolated beings whose identity does not involve otherness.

Even Adam Smith, though he lacks Rand's straightforwardness, theorizes capitalism on the basis of the law of identity. Smith recognizes that labor is the source of value, but he conceptualizes the exchange between the laborer and the capitalist as an exchange between two independent self-subsistent beings. As a result, the capitalist has no responsibility for the miserable situation of the laborer. By the same token, the consumer can enjoy a commodity without any responsibility for the labor that produced it. The isolation of self-identity—the conviction that $A = A$—keeps the capitalist system operational. Rand lays this bare in a way that others do not. She reveals the hidden link between traditional logic and the justification for capitalism. Her full-throated embrace of both the law of identity and capitalism marks a stark contrast with Hegel.

Hegel's philosophy of contradiction cuts off the path for the development of Rand's political program. Granting the necessity of the contradictory role that otherness plays in identity, as Hegel insists, inoculates us to the seductions of Rand's vision. We recognize that Rand's rejection of all contradiction is really a rejection of all thought. But as long as we cling to the inviolability of the law of identity and the principle of noncontradiction, the danger of Ayn Rand will always loom. Because it hides itself in the trappings of traditional logic, it is a threat far more ominous than that represented by the open contradictions of Donald Trump. Not only does Hegel's thought not pave the way for Donald Trump, it has the added benefit of providing a refutation of Ayn Rand *avant la lettre*.

THE DIFFICULTIES OF CONTRADICTING ONESELF

By concluding that contradiction not only can be thought but has an actual existence, Hegel challenges the foundational axioms of both ancient and modern philosophy. The risk is that everything that one would say would become indistinguishable from its opposite. But Hegel finds a way to reject the principle of noncontradiction while still making sense. He does so by showing how this principle itself leads to the inevitability of contradiction.

One cannot simply abandon the principle of noncontradiction and contradict oneself, nor can one straightforwardly announce in a noncontradictory fashion that contradiction exists. Were Hegel to do so, he would implicitly accept the very principle he shows to be untenable. In short, Hegel cannot be Walt Whitman. Even though he embraces Hegel as a primary inspiration, Whitman's Hegelianism offers tacit support to the maxim that the greatest threat to a thinker are acolytes rather than enemies. Whitman attempts to articulate Hegel's opposition to the principle of noncontradiction in "Song of Myself," where he writes, "Do I contradict myself? / Very well then, I contradict myself, / (I am large, I contain multitudes)."[37] In contrast to Hegel's prose, few readers struggle to make sense of what Whitman says here. The lucidity of Whitman's position derives from his ability to take up a straightforward position on the principle of noncontradiction. While it might create a compelling poem, Whitman's unambiguous embrace of contradiction would be untenable for Hegel as a philosopher. The trick, for Hegel, is that he must embrace the principle of noncontradiction in order to show that it ultimately does not hold.

At times, Hegel will articulate straightforward claims about contradiction that serve at guideposts for his philosophy. For instance, in the *Science of Logic*, he makes clear the foundational status of contradiction when he states, "All things in themselves are contradictory."[38] This type of statement is rare, and it functions heuristically. It is an ordinary proposition necessary to help the reader to access Hegel's speculative propositions that enact contradiction. It is easy to state that entities are contradictory, but what is difficult—and what generates the misunderstandings of Hegel's thought—is demonstrating the necessity of contradiction while following the principle of noncontradiction. Though Hegel sees that he must offer occasional statements about contradiction, these statements can be, on their own, misleading. They risk fomenting the belief that one can step outside of contradiction in order to make a straightforward declarative statement about it, which is impossible. One must run the risk, otherwise one's philosophy will become completely impenetrable. For the most part, however, Hegel confines himself to the playing out of contradiction, to exposing contradiction as inescapable.[39]

This becomes evident when Hegel discusses pain. On two occasions in the *Science of Logic*, Hegel identifies pain as a privilege that living beings have and that inert matter lacks. Just claiming that pain is a privilege strikes the reader as contradictory. No one who is in pain conceives it as a privilege. But to be in pain is to find oneself immersed in contradiction, and this is a fortunate quandary when compared with the alternatives. Hegel claims, "the living being is for itself this rupture, has the feeling of this contradiction which is *pain*. Pain is therefore the prerogative of living natures. . . . It is said that contradiction cannot be thought; but in the pain of the living being it is even an actual, concrete existence."[40] Why is pain the "concrete existence" of contradiction? Hegel conceives pain here as the negation of living entity: it is a response to stimulations that damage and even threaten to destroy the entity. When a nonliving entity faces destruction (when a supernova threatens to engulf a planet, for example), this entity suffers no pain before its destruction. No planet writhes in agony in the moments during which its star explodes because the negation is completely external to it. During the experience of pain, in contrast, the living entity has an awareness of the damage it is undergoing. This awareness of undergoing damage is what it means to be alive. One is alive only at the cost of experiencing that life damaged, and this is where Hegel sees contradiction operative.

Of course, one can wish not to be in pain—this is what most living entities wish for—but the complete elimination of pain would entail the elimination of life as well. The ability to feel life being damaged points toward the end of life, but, at the same time, it is life. Without the capacity for awareness of this damage, one loses sentience. Pain provides the key to grasping how Hegel conceives contradiction because it brings together negation and creation, revealing that the experience that negates the living entity is constitutive for the living entity. Without the negation of life, one could not be alive. This is not just a metaphor for Hegel, a claim that one feels most alive when one is near death, but an actual ontological claim about the necessary role that dying plays in living.

Hegel's theory of the emergence of subjectivity out of animality focuses on the moment that animality becomes damaged. In his early Jena *Realphilosophie*, Hegel states, "the sickness of the animal is the birth of spirit."[41] It is only through some disturbance of animality that subjectivity could emerge. In this sense, the subject is a sick animal, an animal unable to live a healthy animal life. If there is a privilege in subjectivity, this privilege lies in what doesn't function properly.

Each contradiction that Hegel explores functions in the way that pain and sickness do, even when it extends beyond the living being. For Hegel, the contradictions of thought lead us to those of being. As Hegel sees it, logical contradiction implies ontological contradiction. Negation infiltrates every positive entity, not as a foreign intruder but as the necessary basis for the entity's existence. Contradiction isn't impossible. It is the absence of contradiction that is impossible to imagine.

That the predominant misunderstanding of Hegel saw him as a philosopher of synthesis is not surprising. In the same way that unconscious homosexual desire can manifest itself as heterosexual profligacy in men who cannot confront this desire, we transform a philosophy of contradiction into a philosophy bent on eliminating contradiction in order to avoid facing its traumatic consequences. Rather than arriving at the irreducibility of contradiction, we conclude with the assurance of a synthesis. In this manner, we consciously solve the problem that Hegel poses. We have accepted the distortion of Hegel's thought so as to avoid the distortion it introduces into thought.

Chapter Two

HEGEL AFTER FREUD

COMING TOO SOON

What stands out about Hegel as a philosopher is the controversy that surrounds his most basic positions. No other philosopher in the Western tradition occasions such wild divergence concerning the principal concerns of her or his philosophy, and the competition is not even close. To capture the immensity of the divergence of views concerning Hegel, one would have to imagine some readers of Marx seeing him as a champion of the capitalist system rather than its foremost opponent or envision disciples positing Friedrich Nietzsche as an advocate of Christian morality rather than its fierce critic. Though there is disagreement about the details of the philosophy of Marx, Nietzsche, and other major thinkers, a general agreement exists concerning the fundamental principles. The same cannot be said in the case of Hegel.

For many, Hegel is the philosopher of totality and closure; for others, he is the thinker of singularity and openness. There are even those who see him as the proponent of totality and openness. These are not just minor degrees of difference amid a broad agreement but categorically opposed estimations of what Hegel thinks. It is not that Hegel's opponents (like Karl Popper and Gilles Deleuze) have one idea and his advocates (like Robert Pippin and Rebecca Comay) have another. Such a situation is relatively commonplace. In the case of Hegel, neither his opponents nor his champions even agree among themselves.

There is more distance separating Pippin's conception of Hegel from Comay's than that which separates Pippin's from Deleuze's. Pippin sees Hegel as a proponent of mutual recognition, while Comay insists that, for Hegel, "what binds us to one another is precisely our failure to recognize one another, a blockage underscored by the untimeliness of the encounter."[1] Even though Deleuze is critical of Hegel's political position, he more or less agrees with Pippin about what this position is. Oddly enough, there is often disagreement among Hegel's champions and agreement between some of these champions and his most vehement detractors. The inability of thinkers following in his wake to come to even the broadest consensus about Hegel's philosophical project is perhaps the salient feature of the project. This fact demands our attention.

The failure to nail down the basic features of Hegel's philosophy cannot simply be the fault of two centuries of poor interpreters. Many of the greatest thinkers of the nineteenth and twentieth centuries devote considerable time to interpreting Hegel, and the results in almost every case are doleful. Marx sees in Hegel someone who envisions the subject's complete appropriation of objectivity at the point of absolute knowing, while Søren Kierkegaard views him as a philosopher who reduces the singular individual to the objectivity of the system. In the twentieth century, Martin Heidegger interprets Hegel's philosophy as the absolute imposition of subjectivity on being. For Jean-Paul Sartre, Hegel is a philosopher of mutual recognition. All of these appraisals of Hegel obscure what he's saying. The misreading of Hegel stretches so far among so many different types of thinkers that it must go beyond poor interpretation.

In contrast, poor interpretation can explain the subjectivist version of Kant that proliferated from time to time since the publication of the *Critique of Pure Reason* in 1781. Whenever this reduction of Kant to a subjectivist raises its head, correctives emerge to rectify the misunderstanding so that it does not linger.[2] The correction of this misinterpretation by other readers of Kant suggests that the misinterpretation is contingent rather than necessary, that we cannot fault Kant himself. In the case of Hegel, the fact that the misinterpretation remains widespread suggests that the fault lies with Hegel.

Hegel had an awareness of his inability to make himself properly understood. His purported last words indicate this awareness and paradoxically communicate the intransigence of the problem. In his apocryphal account of Hegel's final words, Heinrich Heine writes, "When Hegel was lying on his deathbed, he said, 'Only one man has understood me,' but shortly afterwards he added fretfully, 'And even he did not understand me.'"[3] It is likely that Hegel never said these words, but it's clear that they would have been an appropriate conclusion to his life. This statement nicely encapsulates the unique difficulty of grasping Hegel's philosophy: just when one understands, he seems at that moment to be saying the opposite of what one has understood.

In the face of Hegel's own dying conviction that even the one who understood him ultimately didn't, one might conclude that interpretive relativism is in order. Readers could discover in Hegel's philosophy the message particular to their own historical moment. This is the position of Daniel Berthold-Bond, who avows that "it seems appropriate that each generation should have its own discovery and appreciation of his philosophy, for each age will be animated by new historical and cultural perspectives."[4] According to this view, there is so much ambivalence in Hegel's thought that one must impose one's own decision on it in order to derive a clear position. Hegel's failure to be understood results from an inability to make up his mind, so one must do so for him. Whatever the appeal of this type of interpretation, it ends up leaving Hegel himself in the lurch. The reader's decision to cut through the ambivalence involves believing that Hegel simply errs in refusing to be clearer.[5] The obscurity becomes nothing but a misstep.

It is even more tempting to chalk up the obscurity of Hegel's prose to a simple inability to write clearly. But while Hegel struggles to articulate himself both in his lectures and in his books, poor writing alone cannot serve as the scapegoat for the various misunderstandings of his thought.[6] If that were the case, the years since his death would have produced commentaries presenting the ideas lucidly and clearing up the difficulties for readers. Instead, though there are many excellent commentaries on Hegel's philosophy, other commentaries have often exacerbated the failure to understand rather than resolving it.

This is especially apparent with a commentator like Peter Singer, who writes an introduction to Hegel guaranteed to mislead even the most diligent student. Singer characterizes Hegel's thought as a philosophy of synthesis and portrays absolute knowing as absolute solipsism, in which the mind comes to recognize that *"what it seeks is to know itself."*[7] In other words, Hegel takes a roundabout path to arrive at the philosophy of George Berkeley. Given Singer's decidedly anti-Hegelian utilitarianism, it is difficult to avoid the paranoid suspicion that he wrote this introduction to Hegel as a subversive gesture, as a way of undermining the philosophical enemy from within by poisoning young minds with the image of Hegel as a moron.

Such grievous errors create additional barriers to the comprehension of Hegel's thought rather than assisting readers in surmounting them. But even outstanding commentators, like Frederick Beiser, still misleadingly present Hegel as an optimistic philosopher of progress who believes that spirit can overcome contradiction.[8] While recently the situation has ameliorated with the interpretations proffered by Rebecca Comay, Catherine Malabou, Slavoj Žižek, and others, the misunderstandings surrounding Hegel continue to proliferate. In almost every case, it is the problem of contradiction and the role that it plays in Hegel's thought that trips up commentators.

In order to understand the misunderstandings concerning Hegel, one must see Hegel's obscure prose style not as a merely personal defect but as the result of the role that contradiction plays in his thought. One can translate this prose style into more approachable language without thereby clarifying the project itself. It is as if Hegel's thought itself produces a failure of expression, which is why it does no good simply to clarify the prose in a commentary.

Although Hegel's philosophy indicates that the driving force of the concept is the force of contradiction, he was not able to make this completely clear, even to himself. Not only did others fail to understand what Hegel was up to, but he himself couldn't lucidly see the project inherent in his philosophy. In other words, Hegel is so difficult to understand that he can't even understand himself. The difficulty stems from the effort to create a philosophy of contradiction. This is, as Hegel recognizes, the source of the obscurity in the style of Heraclitus that puts off his interpreters, and it leads Hegel to see Heraclitus as his genuine fellow traveler. But even when compared with Heraclitus, Hegel's philosophy presents greater difficulties. Why?

Because, I contend, he emerges as a thinker almost a century too soon. Writing at the turn of the nineteenth century, Hegel lacks the theoretical apparatus through which he could formulate the drive to sustain and extend contradiction. The language does not exist for him, and the result is torsion within the existing language of the time. Hegel is trying to say what cannot be said in the terms bequeathed to him by Immanuel Kant, Johann Gottlieb Fichte, Friedrich Hölderlin, and Friedrich Wilhelm Joseph Schelling, despite his great debt to all of them. The theoretical terrain does not allow for the clear formulation of Hegel's philosophy of contradiction.

A century later, a new theory arises that makes it possible to reconsider Hegel's project by highlighting contradiction as the subject's fundamental aim. According to this new way of thinking, subjects are not driven to eliminate what destroys them and achieve harmony but to find a way to sustain the self-destruction. To grasp the role that contradiction plays within Hegel's system, one must turn to Sigmund Freud, who creates the theoretical apparatus that makes it possible to understand the radicality of Hegel's project. Freud's most important insight is that subjects do not seek their own good, despite their conscious intentions. By conceiving of an unconscious that impels the subject to act against its own conscious wishes, Freud defines subjectivity through a contradiction that the subject cannot eliminate.

Freud is not a follower of Hegel. He barely mentions Hegel throughout all of his work.[9] As Mladen Dolar notes in his analysis of the theoretical links between the two, "Freud never really engages with Hegel, never considers using any of his concepts, as he does with many other philosophers, for better or worse."[10] Though we might lament this missed encounter, given the image of prevailing conception of Hegel's thought during Freud's lifetime, we should probably thank God that Freud just ignores him. Nonetheless, my argument is that Freud's formulation of the basic psychoanalytic project provides a theoretical supplement for Hegel, giving us a language that makes Hegel's otherwise misleading philosophy accessible.[11] It is only after submitting Hegel's philosophy to the structure of psychoanalytic theory that we can articulate clearly what is at stake in it.[12]

THE SUBJECT'S CIVIL WAR

The first essential term that Freud introduces is the unconscious. Armed with this concept, we can provide a more cogent explanation than Hegel himself for his philosophical project. According to psychoanalysis, the unconscious is the fundamental barrier to the subject's self-identity. To say that the subject has an unconscious is to affirm that it is inextricably out of joint with itself. No amount of self-reflection will enable the subject to get in touch with its unconscious because the unconscious shows itself in acts that evade the subject's conscious control—like dreams and slips of the tongue. As Freud sees it, it is impossible for the subject to cause the unconscious drive to align with conscious intentions. It is impossible for the subject endowed with an unconscious to live in harmony with itself. This impossibility parallels exactly Hegel's recognition of the inevitability of contradiction.

The unconscious renders the subject a contradictory entity. It subverts the subject's conscious wishes and produces satisfaction for the subject by thwarting what the subject believes that it wants. The unconscious desire and the conscious wish cannot coincide, even though both inhabit the same psyche. No amount of will power can bring the two into alignment because they follow opposed logics. Every time that the subject acts, the unconscious hijacks the subject's conscious intentions, if only to derive enjoyment for the subject from what it consciously tries to do. Even realized intentions become other than what the subject intends because of the unconscious, which adds a surplus enjoyment to the subject's plans.

The unconscious also thwarts the subject's conscious wishes, like when it causes someone to forget the day of a test at school, the birthday of a romantic partner, or the passcode to a phone. The subject's failure to realize its wishes is not just the result of the resistance that the world puts up against them but the resistance produced by the subject itself. It is always a struggle to follow one's conscious self-interest. The existence of the unconscious means that the subject is always working against itself.

When we examine just the subject's conscious intentions, it is clear that Aristotle is correct, that "everyone always acts in order to obtain that which they think good."[13] Even those who pursue evil do so out of the conscious conviction that it represents a good for them—happiness, pleasure, self-interest, health, or some other good.[14] The subject does not have the ability to consciously pursue an end that it does not deem good. However, once we take the unconscious into account, it becomes clear that the subject is not pursuing a good after all. The unconscious is not concerned with what is good but with what is satisfying. The good serves as a lure for consciousness that enables the unconscious to satisfy itself by undermining the subject's conscious intentions.[15]

This becomes evident when we consider how slips of the tongue operate. Subjects speak with the conscious intention for accomplishing some
good—advancing their own interests, serving others, or simply creating a
hospitable social space—but their unconscious desire takes advantage of
this intention to satisfy itself by undermining it. Consequently, the subject
says what it doesn't intend, though its desire resides in what it says rather
than what it intends to say. When the slip occurs, the subject finds itself in
the contradictory position of seeing that it desires what it doesn't want.

Anyone who has ever continued to desire an old romantic partner while
involved with a new one can recognize this dynamic. In this situation, one
inevitably slips up and uses the name of the former lover to address the new
partner. Such slips always occasion outrage from the new partner, who sees
clearly that the subject still desires the former lover. Though consciousness
strives to suppress the old name, the subject in the thrall of unconscious
desire continues to speak it in the form of the slip. Not only that, but the
more that the subject strives not to slip, the more prone it will be to do so.[16]
The desiring subject triumphs over the will.

The triumph of desire over the will—the marginalization of consciousness by the unconscious—becomes clearest in our deeds. Hegel's investment
in the unconscious a century before Freud's discovery of it shows itself
through his belief in the absolute revelatory power of the deed. For Hegel,
the deed is the truth of the subject. As he puts it in the *Encyclopedic Logic*,
"while a human being in an individual instance can certainly disguise and
conceal a great deal, he cannot conceal his inner make-up altogether, which
announces itself infallibly in the *decursus vitae*, such that, in this connection, it must also be said that a human being is nothing other than the series
of his acts."[17] What one thinks or claims about oneself falls aside in the face
of what one does. This is not just Hegel's critique of hypocrisy but his recognition that what we do manifests our desire in a way that our thinking
cannot. If we want to grasp our unconscious desire, we must pay attention
to what we do, which is what Hegel does.

For instance, when looking at a supposedly happily married couple, the
revelatory power of the deed can expose the indifference that often replaces
love as time goes by. When the partners occupy themselves with their own
concerns, stay late at work to avoid going home, spend time with friends
rather than the spouse, and find excuses for not having sex, these acts point
toward the disappearance of love, even though the partners can't admit

their indifference to themselves, let alone to each other. Consciously, they tell themselves that they are still in love, that all relationships go through highs and lows. But what they do gives the lie to this conscious conviction. By focusing on the deed, Hegel demonstrates his precocious understanding of how the unconscious works. The deed exposes the contradiction of subjectivity that appears in the unconscious.

UNHAPPINESS AS SYMPTOM

The contradiction between the unconscious and consciousness manifests itself most concretely in the psychoanalytic symptom. The symptom marks the point at which the subject's suffering coincides directly with its satisfaction. According to Freud, subjects develop symptoms as a result of the repression of desire that occurs in neurosis. The trauma associated with desire leads to its repression in neurotic subjects, but repressed desire doesn't just vanish from the subject's psyche. It returns in the form of the symptom.

The symptom is located on the subject's body or in what the subject does. Some might lose the ability to speak or feel pain in the throat, while others might repeatedly wash their hands or count the steps that they walk to work. In each case, the symptom disturbs the subject's conscious life. At the same time, however, it provides unconscious satisfaction for the subject. The symptom is at once the expression of the subject's desire and the indication of that desire's repression.

Consciously, the subject wants to overcome the disturbance of the symptom, a wish that might send the subject into psychoanalytic treatment. But unconsciously, the subject desires to sustain the satisfaction that the symptom offers. The unconscious satisfaction that the symptom provides for the subject explains, according to Freud, the negative therapeutic reaction—a subject's resistance to analysis not because of its failure but because of its success. Rather than accepting the psychoanalytic cure, the subject clings to the satisfaction that the symptom provides. The prospect of eliminating the suffering that the symptom generates can seem less appealing unconsciously than risking the loss of this satisfaction.

But because psychoanalysis takes the subject's unconscious satisfaction into account, it does not try to interpret away every symptom. Doing so risks precisely what the subject fears—unraveling the subject's source of satisfaction. The wager of psychoanalysis is that the subject can recognize the symptom as satisfying and thereby identify with its symptom rather than experiencing the symptom as the indication of an external disorder that has invaded its subjectivity. In doing so, the subject can relate to its satisfaction as its own.

By turning to the *Phenomenology of Spirit*, we can readily see how a reference to the unconscious and the symptom might clarify Hegel's argument. When he arrives at the final form of self-consciousness, what he calls "unhappy consciousness" (*unglückliche Bewußtsein*), Hegel describes a subjectivity divided against itself. This subjectivity desires what is unchanging but experiences itself always confined to finitude. The unhappiness of unhappy consciousness stems from a sense of its own defilement in relation to the unchanging: even though unhappy consciousness knows the unchanging as part of itself, it cannot overcome its own investment in bodily functions that separate it from this unchanging with which it strives to identify itself. The more it renounces the body, the more the body takes center stage through the act of renunciation that can never fully overcome it. As a result, unhappy consciousness cannot recognize itself and find satisfaction in its own acts.

Hegel's description of unhappy consciousness bears a remarkable resemblance to Freud's account of the obsessional neurotic. For unhappy consciousness, according to Hegel, "animal functions . . . instead of being performed without embarrassment as something that is in and for itself null and which can acquire no importance or essential significance of spirit . . . are rather the object of serious effort and become precisely matters of the utmost importance."[18] While reading Hegel's description, one can imagine Freud recounting an obsessional's rituals surrounding defecating, sleeping, or eating. Hegel details the emergence of the obsessional's symptom, though he never uses this term. The rituals imbue these animal functions with an outsized importance and reveal that they are the sites where the subject's unconscious desire expresses itself. Obsessionals can find sexual satisfaction in the apparently nonsexual act of washing their hands, which is what Hegel suggests in his portrait of unhappy consciousness treating animal functions as if they were spiritual ones.

According to Hegel's account, unhappy consciousness becomes reason at the moment when it sees itself in the absolute and ceases to consider its body as inherently debased. Because Hegel doesn't employ the theoretical apparatus of psychoanalysis, he cannot make it clear that the investment of unhappy consciousness in the body is the product of repression or that the turn from unhappy consciousness to reason is the result of the subject recognizing itself in the symptom. But this is precisely what happens. If we understand the turn to reason as the subject recognizing itself in the symptom, then it becomes clear that subjectivity pursues rather than eschews contradiction.

The attempt to surpass the body by unhappy consciousness entails the body's return in the form of repressed material. The only way to escape the torments of unhappy consciousness is to identify with the symptom, to treat the obsessional ritual as the manifestation of subjectivity rather than just as a disruption of it. This is what Hegel suggests when he envisions the resolution of unhappy consciousness as the discovery of reason, in which the subject ceases to consider itself divided from its own acts. The problem is that, lacking Freud's concepts, Hegel does not properly explicate the nature of this transition.

Transitions are the great bogey of Hegel's philosophy, especially in the *Phenomenology of Spirit*. At times, it is impossible to understand how Hegel moves from one position to another, as numerous critics have pointed out since the work's publication. Even Hegel's devotees often balk at them, as Terry Pinkard does when he proclaims that "there is no more rhyme or reason for any particular transition than that it struck Hegel that such a transition might be fun or illuminating."[19] Though other interpreters of Hegel are not as harsh as Pinkard, the view that Hegel's transitions constitute a problem is almost universal among them. The consensus is that the awkwardness of the transitions requires extreme interpretive machinations to avoid dismissing their illogic out of hand in the way that Pinkard does.[20] This is where Freud's terminology proves most useful.

In one of the major transitions of the *Phenomenology*, Hegel turns from unhappy consciousness to observing reason, reason that discovers itself in the world rather than striving for a beyond that remains ever out of reach. The ultimate manifestation of observing reason is phrenology, which seems like a regression from unhappy consciousness rather than an advance. Phrenology identifies subjectivity with the shape of the skull, thus spiritualizing the materiality of the body. Though Hegel knows that phrenology is quackery (which is why he groups it with physiognomy and palmistry), he nevertheless recognizes that phrenology has a key insight into the unconscious that unhappy consciousness lacks. Phrenology surmounts the denigration of the body perpetuated by unhappy consciousness.

To put it in Freud's terms, with the onset of phrenology, the subject ceases to merely suffer its bodily symptom and begins to recognize itself in this symptom. From the perspective of the phrenologist, Hegel claims, "the *being of Spirit is a bone*."[21] Phrenology reduces spirit to the inert material being in which it exists—the skull bone. Though this reduction misses how spirit exceeds its material basis, it does correctly apprehend the necessity of the subject's bodily manifestation in a way that unhappy consciousness does not. Phrenology gives up the struggle against the body that defines unhappy consciousness. Phrenology ceases to recoil from the body's finitude by recognizing it as an expression of the subject's infinitude. We can regard the shape of the skull as the subject's bodily symptom, and this symptom expresses subjectivity rather than simply obscuring it as it does for unhappy consciousness. The psychoanalytic conceptual apparatus enables us to see the logic of the transition as a change in the position that the subject takes relative to its symptom.

All of Hegel's transitions do not fit so neatly into Freud's conceptual apparatus. But they all chronicle the moment at which some previously repressed material manifests itself. We could say that the *Phenomenology* is an account of the subject's encounter with repression. Hegel interprets symptoms that manifest this repression not with the aim of eliminating symptoms altogether but rather with finding one irreducible symptom that defines subjectivity. In this process, Hegel proceeds like the psychoanalyst.[22] The conclusion—absolute knowing—does not entail the lifting of all repression but the identification with the subject's foundational symptom. There remains what Freud calls primary repression, the unconscious stumbling block that constitutes the subject as a subject. Absolute knowing involves the recognition of the constitutive necessity of this stumbling block. It has the same structure that Freud gives to the end of analysis.

AIMS AND OBJECTS

The difficulty of Hegel's philosophy derives from his attempt to reconceptualize what drives our subjectivity. In effect, he breaks the traditional link between desire and self-identity. Thinkers from the pre-Socratics through

Kant in the Western tradition have assumed that subjects strive for the elimination of contradictions, both in thought and in being. From Zeno of Elea deducing the oneness of all being on the basis of the contradictions implied by movement to Kant discovering the limits on knowledge through the contradictions occasioned by the use of reason, philosophers have posited contradiction as what subjects avoid. From this perspective, we think and act in order to arrive at a condition of perfect harmony. Even if they believe that we never achieve this aim, philosophers have nonetheless remained united in their belief that self-identity is the aim and that contradiction can only function as a barrier we try to overcome. To imagine that the aim of thought is sustaining contradiction is untenable in the philosophical language Hegel inherits.

But Freud operates on a different terrain. When he theorizes the subject's drives, he unwittingly provides the most important clue for making sense of Hegel's philosophy. Freud's terminology and the distinctions that the terms imply offer a matrix for interpreting the role that contradiction plays for Hegel. The terms that Freud uses to discuss the drives in "Instincts and Their Vicissitudes" would have served Hegel well had he had access to them. While dissecting the structure of the drives, Freud identifies four components proper to the drive—the pressure (*Drang*), the source (*Quelle*), the aim (*Ziel*), and the object (*Objekt*). He immediately disqualifies two of these components from further elaboration. The pressure is simply a constant force, and the source lies unknowable outside the bounds of psychoanalytic inquiry. The pressure and the source play no significant role in Freud's discussion of the drives. The components that attract Freud's attention are the aim and the object, which seem as if they might overlap. One could imagine that a drive simply aims at acquiring its object. This is how our common sense (and the history of philosophy) conceives of the relationship between aim and object: the subject's aim is the object, even if it never arrives at it.[23] But Freud differentiates them completely.

According to Freud, drives aim at satisfying themselves without regard for their object. Satisfaction is the aim of every drive. What is variable is the object that the drive uses to obtain its aim of satisfaction. The drive is indifferent toward the object. It is just a vehicle through which the drive achieves its aim, even though the subject of the drive consciously believes that the object and not satisfaction constitutes its aim.[24] Despite what the subject consciously believes, the aim and the object cannot coincide. We obtain satisfaction through the object but not by obtaining the object. Obtaining an object inevitably leads to the search for another object rather than any sustained satisfaction. It is the process of confronting the absence of the appealing object that provides satisfaction rather than the moment of finally having it.

On this basis, one can see how Freud would explain why those who have the resources constantly buy new cars every year. These rabid consumers are not simply the dupes of clever advertising campaigns or exemplars of capitalist decadence (though they may also be both of these). They are unwittingly stuck in the dynamic of the drive, which just so happens to involve driving. The consumers identify satisfaction with the new model of the car, but, after driving it for a few months, they recognize that their satisfaction doesn't reside in this particular object. Thus, they return to the car dealer the next year for the newest model, hoping to discover a more genuinely satisfying object but encountering instead the same disappointment. There is satisfaction in the repetition of the purchases, but not in the cars purchased, which is where the consumer believes it is located. This dynamic, which can be infinitely repeated, reveals not only how contradiction informs thought but how it dominates our actions. The consumer of cars cannot recognize that the object is not really the aim because doing so would eliminate the repeated acts of consumption. Contradiction doesn't destroy this activity but sustains it.

There is, for Freud, a fundamental contradiction between aim and object at the core of the drive. Repression facilitates this contradiction, but it isn't entirely clear what is repressed and what is conscious. When he writes "Instincts and Their Vicissitudes" in 1915, Freud remains within his first model of the psyche dominated by the pleasure principle. According to this way of thinking, the subject strives for pleasure but finds the obstacle of repression as a barrier to its fulfillment. When Freud considers the relationship between repression and the drive, he associates repression with the object of the drive. The object is too close to the incestuous object, which is why we repress it, substituting a psychically less disturbing object for the real one. In the classic example, instead of marrying a parent, we marry someone modeled on the parent. But for the early Freud, repression does not necessarily have the final word over the drive.

At this point in his intellectual trajectory, Freud imagines a path for the satisfaction of the drive by embracing the object for what it is. To get free of the damage of repression, one must come to terms with the incestuous nature of one's sexual object. This position leads Freud to claim in 1912 that "anyone who is to be really free and happy in love must have surmounted his respect for women and have come to terms with the idea of incest with his mother or sister."[25] Here, Freud remains within his early conception of repression, in which he associates it with the object. The satisfaction of the drive can be conscious, while the object must be unconscious. The drive involves the subject in contradiction, but Freud sees psychoanalysis as the path to solving the contradiction, at least to some extent. This is the implication of Freud's thought at this point in time. While things seem dire for the subject, one can nonetheless imagine achieving equanimity with the idea of incest and thereby becoming "free and happy in love."[26]

Such an outcome is utterly at odds with Hegel's theory of contradiction. Freud appears to offer terminological aid to Hegel only to betray him conceptually. We could translate Freud's early theory into Hegel's philosophy in this way: The impetus driving the subject is an appealing but as yet unthought object, like perfect self-identity or systematic completion—the objects most associated with the aims of thought. But such a schema would transform Hegel back into the philosopher of synthesis. For Hegel, the object cannot be the site of satisfaction. Satisfaction must be provided by the contradiction itself. Though this picture doesn't jibe with Freud's early theory, everything changes in 1920.

THE JOYS OF OVERSLEEPING

After Freud's theorization of the death drive in *Beyond the Pleasure Principle* in 1920 and the fundamental shift that this occasions in his thought, the site of repression undergoes a dramatic shift. He no longer believes that the repression of the object is decisive. It is much more the way that the subject satisfies itself—the aim of the drive—that the subject must repress. The object ceases to be inherently traumatic while the satisfaction that the subject experiences in pursuit of the object becomes the site of trauma. Why is this? How could satisfaction possibly be traumatic? The problem, as Freud comes to see it, is that the subject satisfies itself through the failure to attain its object rather than in successfully attaining it. Trauma is no longer the proximity of the incestuous object but the impossibility of any complete satisfaction.[27] In this sense, for the later Freud, the idea of a completely satisfying incestuous object would actually provide respite from the trauma of an impossible total satisfaction.

The fact that the subject not only desires to fail but constantly engineers its own failure becomes the trauma that the subject must repress. The point is no longer that the subject cannot attain the truly satisfying object because this object is too traumatic for it but that there is no such thing as a truly satisfying object. Because the drive satisfies itself through the repetition of failure, the status of the object, incestuous or not, ceases to matter, as the conception of how the subject satisfies itself undergoes a revolutionary change. At the same time, the aim becomes utterly traumatic insofar as it confronts the subject with the impossibility of ever obtaining complete satisfaction. As a result, the location of the unconscious switches: the aim is unconscious, while the object becomes consciously thinkable.[28]

To return to the serial consumer of new cars, Freud after the discovery of the death drive would analyze this consumer differently than the early Freud would. For the later Freud, the customer's satisfaction lies in the repetition of the failure to find a new car that would provide satisfaction. The absence of the perfect object, not its repression or traumatic import, paradoxically becomes the avenue for the subject to satisfy itself in the drive, which is why it must be unconscious. The subject cannot know what it's doing because it is constantly thwarting its own good and finding satisfaction in this self-derailing. If one consciously thwarts oneself, one is no longer actually thwarting oneself.

We can translate this back into Hegel's idiom. We spend most of our conscious lives trying to overcome contradictions. Confronted, for instance, by the contradiction between our goal of living in a luxurious house and our lack of money to afford such a house, we endeavor to work additional hours for years in order to eliminate this contradiction and accomplish the goal. Consciously, we simply want to obtain the object. Things seem straightforward. But the unconscious throws a wrench in the plan. Rather than wanting to overcome this or any other contradiction, the unconscious revels in it and creates the conditions for sustaining it. The unconscious subverts the conscious plan to overcome this contradiction by leading us to oversleep, directing us to spike the punch at a company holiday party, or prompting us to have an affair with the spouse of our boss (or do all three at once). The unconscious corresponds in Freud's thought to the aim of the drive. It provides a satisfaction that remains barred to consciousness.

But the effect of the unconscious is even more straightforwardly at work within our conscious goals. It doesn't just subvert them; it also uses them as its means for satisfaction, just as the drive uses the object to satisfy itself. When we consciously plan to live in future luxury, we commit ourselves to years of unpleasant toil to reach this end. When we conceive of how our satisfaction will be distributed, we imagine enduring present dissatisfaction for the sake of future satisfaction. Oftentimes, the future satisfaction for which we work is not even our own. Many people spend their entire lives working so that "their children will have a better life." Though the better life of the children is the conscious goal, the struggle to attain this life functions as the unconscious aim. We should imagine that the parents who sacrifice themselves for their children are actually more satisfied than the children for whom they sacrifice.

We think that we suffer for years in order to end up in a satisfying conclusion, but we really use this image of the pleasant conclusion to satisfy ourselves through years of suffering. The unconscious satisfies itself through the toil. The payoff at the end is simply a bribe offered to consciousness. Our unconscious satisfaction is inextricable from the experience of contradiction. It ensures that we sustain this experience, which is why those who do attain the luxury that they fantasize about soon concoct new fantasies that lead to new contradictions.

Philosophers, even those who embrace poverty, follow the same trajectory in thought as those who want to live in luxury do in their lives. For instance, Baruch Spinoza, who shuns all luxury in his daily life, nonetheless orients his thinking around the achievement of a future satisfaction, what he calls *amor Dei intellectualis* or the intellectual love of God. According to Spinoza, desire aims at this love, which is a product of the knowledge of substance. It finds satisfaction in this state of perfect unity with everything. Once one achieves amor Dei intellectualis, one no longer desires something more. Spinoza would never accept that satisfaction might reside in the struggle to attain amor Dei intellectualis and the necessary failure of this struggle. The aim of Spinoza's philosophy is identical to its object. This is why Spinoza is not yet Hegel, who recognizes that our satisfaction resides in our inability to achieve harmony rather than the successful attainment of it.

If Hegel had access to Freud's conception of the unconscious and the drives, he would have been able to formulate the appeal of contradiction more straightforwardly to both himself and his readers. He wouldn't have used the misleading terms of *the good* and *unity* to describe the subject's actions. He wouldn't have said, near the end of the *Encyclopedic Logic*, "The good, the absolute good, brings itself to completion in the world eternally, and the result is that it is already brought to completion in and for itself, without needing first to wait for us."[29] Hegel has no conceptual apparatus to formulate how we seek out disturbances in the guise of success.[30]

In this sense, we can attribute some of the difficulties of understanding Hegel to his philosophy's premature birth. If Freud had been around to offer him the idea of unconscious satisfaction, Hegel would have been able to articulate a more palatable theory of contradiction. Or his philosophy of contradiction wouldn't have seemed so contradictory.[31] Though he likely still wouldn't have satisfied Bertrand Russell or Karl Popper, one can imagine a Hegel who would have won over Theodor Adorno or Georges Bataille.

Freud would enable Hegel to claim that no one sets out consciously to sustain contradiction. The very idea is absurd. And yet all subjects find ways to avoid eliminating contradictions in order to continue to draw satisfaction from them. It is only through contradiction that the subject satisfies itself. This is a satisfaction that we do not properly avow, and our inability to avow this satisfaction is inextricable from the misunderstanding that surrounds Hegel's thought.

MEANINGLESS VICTORIES

Once we see what Freud's thought reveals about Hegel's logic of contradiction, we can reexamine what happens at the end of Hegel's philosophy. When we reach the absolute, we recognize that what we took as our object—the resolution of contradiction—was functioning solely in service to our aim, which was the satisfaction provided by contradiction. Contradiction itself provides a satisfaction that its resolution would dissipate, a satisfaction that stems from giving us an object to desire. When we reach the absolute, we run out of future possibilities. As a result, the hope for resolving the contradiction evaporates, and we have only desiring itself stripped of its possible realization. As Jean Wahl puts it, "contradiction is the formal appearance of the absolute."[32] We find ourselves with nothing left except the intractability of contradiction itself, which forces us to conclude that contradiction is the source of our satisfaction.

In this sense, the absolute requires a complete revision of the path that we took to arrive at it. Instead of following a path from a series of failed solutions to an ultimately successful one, we have been ensuring ourselves of the intractability of contradiction. This has been the aim all along, but the idea of an ultimate solution has provided an object obscuring this aim from consciousness in order to make the traumatic aim palatable for the subject. At each step of the dialectic, the image of a possible end to contradiction seems to drive the dialectic forward toward another articulation. But the real engine of this movement is the appetite for contradiction. It is contradiction that sustains the subject as desiring, which no one can desire to eliminate.

Here again, the conceptual apparatus of psychoanalysis clarifies Hegel's position. Jacques Lacan's vision of the psychoanalytic cure as traversing the fantasy provides a way to theorize Hegel's sense of what happens when one reaches the absolute.[33] The subject traverses the fantasy when it recognizes that there is no object beyond the fantasy that it might obtain. Traversing the fantasy requires accepting that satisfaction derives from the fantasy itself rather than from obtaining the object or transcending the fantasy in any way.[34] This is exactly the shift that occurs with the move to the absolute in Hegel's system.

Because it cuts against common sense to such an extent, grasping the absolute as a reconciliation with the intractability of contradiction is simply unthinkable for most readers of Hegel. The misreading of Hegel's philosophy finally boils down to an inability to recognize the obstacle not just as an accident that gets in our way while trying to succeed and not just as our fate as mortal beings. This is what psychoanalysis makes clear. We suffer from an inability to recognize that finding obstacles is our aim and our only source of satisfaction. Because of his grounding in psychoanalytic theory, Žižek recognizes this structure of Hegel's thought. In *The Sublime Object of Ideology*, Žižek interprets the end of Hegel's philosophy as the moment when contradiction becomes fully installed. He writes, "'absolute knowledge' denotes a subjective position which finally accepts contradiction as an internal condition of every identity."[35] Hegel is the first thinker to show the extent of our investment in the obstacles that we believe we are trying to overcome. This reformulation of how we think about subjectivity produces a philosophy that took the discovery of psychoanalysis to become decipherable.

The greatest cinematic depiction of the logic of Hegel's philosophy occurs in David Lean's *Bridge on the River Kwai* (1957). The film shows British lieutenant colonel Nicholson (Alec Guinness) overseeing the construction of a massive bridge for the Japanese in Burma while he and his men are prisoners of war. Despite building the bridge for the enemy, Nicholson takes immense pride in the construction and drives his men hard to finish the job. His own army, however, sends commandos to destroy the bridge.

Initially, Nicholson struggles against the British commandos when they kill the Japanese commander overseeing the bridge and try to detonate their explosives. But finally, after recognizing an escaped prisoner among the commandos, he sees that his enthusiastic construction of the bridge was a betrayal of the British war effort. After being shot by a Japanese soldier, Nicholson falls on the detonator and destroys the bridge himself as he dies. The final act finds Nicholson at the point of Hegel's absolute, where he must destroy his own creation in order to remain true to his desire, which depends on the contradiction between building the bridge and the war effort. At the point of the absolute, we recognize that there is nothing outside contradiction.

This emphasis on the central role that contradiction plays as the driving force of thought separates Hegel from all philosophers before him and from most after him. Though Freud supplies a way for understanding Hegel's philosophy, there are limits that constrain even him. Freud discovers contradiction through the subject's unconscious. He recognizes it in specific phenomena, like dreams, slips, and jokes. According to Freud, philosophical thinking, because it hews too closely to the demands of reason, cannot grasp the contradictions of the psyche (such as that within the drive between aim and object). Recognizing contradiction requires not just the attentiveness of the psychoanalyst but (at the very least) the presence of an interlocutor to the manifestation of the subject's unconscious. Thinking by oneself, one is guaranteed to miss it.

In contrast to Freud, Hegel has faith in the philosopher and the philosopher's use of reason. Rather than causing us to miss the contradictions of our subjectivity, Hegel's theorizes reason (*Vernunft*) as the only way to recognize them. Freud clarifies Hegel, but, when it comes to the power of reason, Hegel takes a step beyond Freud and psychoanalysis through a revaluation of reason that grasps its impasses as the positive thinking of contradiction. He shows that philosophers alone in their rooms have as much access to contradiction as the psychoanalyst listening to a patient.

Chapter Three

WHAT HEGEL MEANS WHEN HE SAYS *VERNUNFT*

A CONTRADICTORY ACTUALITY

When it comes to ranking the worst thing that Hegel ever said, there are many competitors. But when we consider what statement had the most deleterious effect on the propagation of his philosophy, there is little room for debate. Hegel's statement in the preface to the *Philosophy of Right* undoubtedly takes the prize. There, he famously proclaims, "What is rational is actual; and what is actual is rational" ("Was vernünftig ist, das ist wirklich; und was wirklich ist, das ist vernünftig").[1] From the moment that Hegel makes this formulation, interpreters suspect that it functions as a justification for the status quo, as a clear case of philosophy serving as an apology for power.[2]

Hegel certainly sets himself up for this type of response. He knows how it sounds to the casual reader or the philosophical antagonist eager to score political points, but he courts misinterpretation in order to boil his entire speculative system down to a simple statement that would encapsulate the whole. Hegel's philosophy is rarely aphoristic, though at this moment he gestures in the direction of aphorism, which has a danger associated with it. The gesture risks having his system characterized as what he most opposes. Hegel runs the risk because he believes that the readily apparent absurdity of the statement will lead those who encounter it to consider the statement in speculative terms, as an articulation of the contradictory structure of both reason (*Vernunft*) and actuality (*Wirklichkeit*).

The directness and concision of this statement from the *Philosophy of Right* contrast with the rest of Hegel's philosophical output. In his writings and lectures, Hegel demands that the reader follow a tortuous path to grasp the idea. One must, for instance, read the entire *Phenomenology of Spirit* to gain a sense of what he means by absolute knowing. Skipping right to absolute knowing means completely missing it. Absolute knowing includes the series of failures that lead up to it, but one loses these if one goes directly to the ultimate point. Hegel penalizes the reader for the short cut. But at this one moment in his final published book when he identifies the rational (*vernünftig*) and the actual (*wirklich*), Hegel attempts to sum up his philosophy in a single sentence. He produces at once his most important statement and his most misunderstood one. The sentence articulates the relationship that exists between thought and being, which is the relationship that animates his entire philosophy. Where other thinkers see an absolute difference between thought and being, Hegel sees a speculative identity, an identity that includes difference in it.

In order to grasp Hegel's statement as a speculative claim, one must examine how Hegel uses the two principal terms from the statement in the rest of his work.[3] When Hegel employs the terms *rational* and *actual,* they always have a specific signification that Hegel makes clear through repeatedly invoking it. *Rational* does not mean our ability to calculate or deduce abstractly. *Actual* does not mean bare external reality that exists in opposition to the subject. To give these terms a precise meaning, Hegel establishes an opposition between reason (*Vernunft*) and understanding (*Verstand*) on the one hand, and between actuality (*Wirklichkeit*) and reality (*Realität*) or existence (*Existenz*) on the other.[4]

Actuality is not the reality that appears as completely external and untouched by thought. It is that reality insofar as it has been conceptualized. Reality becomes actual only when the mediation of thought determines it and causes it to lose the guise of externality. Actuality is what thought determines as significant in external reality. Given how he deploys these terms, when Hegel says that actuality is rational, he verges on making a tautological claim. To say that actuality is rational is just to say that what we have conceptualized in reality is identical with the concept, which doesn't say much at all.[5]

What invests the claim with significance and avoids tautology is not Hegel's use of the term *actual* but that of *rational*. Though defenders of Hegel have focused all their attention on what he means by "actual" (*wirklich*) and attempted to redeem the statement on this side, Hegel's radicality as a thinker resides in his way of thinking about the "rational" (*vernünftig*). Reason, for Hegel, is not disinterested analytical thinking. It is not what Sherlock Holmes uses to solve crimes or what Jürgen Habermas sees as the basis of communication. It is rather the ability to think and internalize contradiction. Reason is the highest form of thought, the point at which thought accomplishes what mere being cannot.

Reason does not collapse in the face of contradiction but has the ability to think it. It recognizes that ultimately contradiction is irreducible and cannot be eliminated. Hegel opposes this power to that of the understanding, which limits itself to avoid contradiction. Thinking from the perspective of the understanding refuses the existence of contradiction as an impossibility within the field of possible experience. For the understanding, reality cannot be contradictory, but thought can be when it tries to go beyond its proper limits. In order to maintain contradiction in reality as impossible, the understanding must enact a sleight of hand. The understanding avoids contradiction by confining itself to the field of possible experience. Any attempt to think about ultimate questions of existence—like whether or not the world has a beginning in space and time—is simply off the table. In this way, the understanding cuts off the road to contradiction before it can be built.

The thinker who does the most to block this road is Hegel's forerunner, Immanuel Kant. Hegel's distinction between reason (*Vernunft*) and understanding (*Verstand*) follows directly from Kant's. This distinction plays a crucial role in Kant's philosophy, enabling him to preserve the consistency of the understanding while still acknowledging that thought does run into contradictions. Reason tries to think beyond the limits of possible experience and thereby falls into contradiction as a result of overstepping the proper domain of knowledge. Kant makes the distinction between the understanding and reason in order to disparage reason at the expense of the understanding. Reason becomes Kant's fall guy for thought's encounter with contradiction. He wagers that confining contradiction to reason and then circumscribing the use of reason would function akin to putting a dangerous criminal behind bars. The understanding profits from the imprisonment of reason as it becomes the central faculty for thinking.

For Hegel, the situation is exactly reversed. Far from attacking Kant's characterization of reason's encounter with contradiction, Hegel gives Kant the credit of pointing out that reason always leads to contradiction. Rather than attacking Kant, Hegel's philosophical project is more one of actualizing the insights that were already latent in Kant's thought. In the *Science of Logic*, he notes that the Kantian antinomies are "contradictions, against which reason must necessarily (according to the Kantian expression) *collide*."[6] We use reason to try to resolve the intractable questions of existence: Does the world have a beginning in space and time? Is there a simple substance? Does freedom or spontaneity exist? Is there a necessary being or God? In the *Critique of Pure Reason*, Kant shows that the attempt to answer these questions with reason leads to contradiction. Hegel in no way objects but rather fervently embraces the relationship between reason and contradiction.[7]

For the first two (mathematical) antinomies, we find that both solutions are false, that the world neither has a beginning or end in space and time nor is it without beginning or end, and that there is neither a simple substance nor only complexity. We cannot successfully theorize either a starting point or an infinite progression of the world, just as we cannot successfully theorize whether or not the world is ultimately composed of isolatable simple entities. For the last two (dynamic) antinomies, we discover that both solutions are true, that we are both free and determined and that there is a necessary being and the world exists without one. In contrast to the mathematical antinomies, our theorizing succeeds too well and proves two contrary hypotheses. The four antinomies lead Kant to throw up his hands and abandon the project of resolving these fundamental questions of existence. But there is, from his perspective, a salutary result coming from the failure of this undertaking.

For Kant, the fact that reason leads to contradiction indicates that the uses of reason are severely constrained, and taking stock of reason's limits marks a genuine advance for thought. Kant believes that the *Critique of Pure Reason* places all metaphysical questions beyond the domain of our knowledge. They become questions of morality and faith rather than questions of knowledge.[8] Reason tries to deal with them but inevitably fails, which indicates that the solution to metaphysical questions exists beyond the capacities of thought.[9] The problem with reason, as Kant sees it, lies in its absence of any intuited content. Unlike the understanding, reason does not have sensible intuition to provide a content for which it can offer a form.

Because it lacks any intuited content—because there is no intellectual intuition—reason inevitably runs into contradiction. Reason becomes ensnared in traps that it has laid for itself in the absence of any intuited content to ground it. Kant takes the inevitable contradictions that reason produces as warning signs against the use of reason except as a vehicle for grasping the limits of the understanding. According to Kant, contradiction is the mark of reason's failure, and we must avoid it in order to avoid this failure of thought.

In contrast to Kant, Hegel is an apostle of reason. One might think that in order to embrace reason he would have to redefine it in terms opposed to Kant's. This is the position that many followers of Hegel tend to adopt. We can see it in the case of Craig Matarrese, a representative figure who articulates this position as if it were (as it is) common sense. He writes, "Hegel, of course, has a radically different conception of reason than Kant."[10] According to this widely held position, Hegel breaks from Kant's formalist and timeless view of reason in order to conceive it in more dynamic terms.[11] In order to explain Hegel's revaluation of reason, so the thinking goes, reason itself must have undergone a change.

While it is the case that Hegel defines reason differently than Aristotle or Leibniz, he does closely adhere to Kant's definition of it. Though Hegel does champion reason in the wake of Kant's critique of it, he does not resort to redefining it in order to embrace it. Hegel's reason is Kant's reason. The point is not to redefine reason after Kant but to reevaluate it. Hegel treats the contradictions that reason encounters when it attempts to tackle the fundamental ontological questions much differently than Kant does. For him, the contradictions are indicative not of reason's failure but of its success. When reason discovers an irreducible contradiction (as it does in the case of the question of the beginning of the world), Hegel concludes that this discovery has positive rather than only negative implications. An irreducible contradiction is not a way of not knowing but a way of knowing, the way of knowing that Hegel associates with reason. The failure to answer the question of whether or not the world has a beginning is the answer.

The answer is that there can be no pure beginning, no beginning free from the negation that implies becoming. By the same token, there can be no pure unending continuity without any discreteness. Our ability to think at all testifies to the existence of a rupture in the continuity of being. Kant's negative conclusion fails to grasp the positive insights that Hegel discovers in the Transcendental Dialectic. Arriving at irreducible contradictions is a failure to answer the question that contains an ontological revelation.

Obviously, there are times when contradictory answers to a question don't indicate anything. Suppose my spouse comes home late from work. I ask her where she has been, and she says that she went for a drink with a friend. But when I ask again the next morning, she gives a contradictory answer, telling me that she had to work late. Confronted with this contradiction, I might conclude that she just had a memory lapse that has no significance at all. But most often when we experience contradictory responses, we usually treat the situation more like Hegel than like Kant. In my situation, for instance, I interpret her contradictory responses as indicative of a hidden truth—her affair.

This becomes evident in Rob Reiner's film *A Few Good Men* (1992), in which Guantanamo base commander Nathan Jessup (Jack Nicholson) orders the use of the illicit disciplinary procedure known as a "code red" that results in the death of a soldier named Santiago (Michael DeLorenzo). At the trial of the soldiers who actually performed the code red on Jessup's orders, their attorney Daniel Kaffee (Tom Cruise) prompts Jessup to confess after pointing out the revelatory contradiction in his statements. Jessup contends that he had ordered that no disciplinary action be taken against Santiago despite poor performance. He also is adamant that his orders are always followed to the letter. At the same time, Jessup says that he decided to transfer Santiago for his own safety from other soldiers that might discipline him on their own initiative. Kaffee pounces on the contradiction in Jessup's statement as a revelation that Jessup did actually order the code red and that the soldiers were just following orders. If Jessup ordered that Santiago not be disciplined and if his orders were always obeyed, then Santiago would have not needed to be transferred for his own safety. Confronted with his own contradiction, Jessup becomes enraged and blurts out the truth—that he ordered the code red. Here, contradiction doesn't lead to a dead end but to an answer through its failure to answer definitively. In the case of questions that don't concern specific empirical events but rather fundamental ontological problems, the revelatory power of the contradiction doesn't rely on a supposition (as in the example from

A Few Good Men) but necessarily indicates a truth that appears in the form of its failure.

This is what Kant cannot see. He runs into a contradiction in thought that causes him to flee in the opposite direction. But his flight is a necessary precursor to the revaluation of reason. By showing how reason fails to eliminate contradiction, Kant inadvertently illustrates its success. In contrast to the understanding, reason reveals the secrets of being because it tries to think beyond the secure confines of possible experience. Kant's slander of reason makes visible its relationship to contradiction that would otherwise have remained hidden. In this sense, Kant's *Critique of Pure Reason* prepares the ground on which Hegel's logic would arise. Kant shows the understanding's success and reason's failure, judgments that Hegel will subsequently reverse. The success of the understanding is hollow, while the failure of reason successfully illuminates the most intractable metaphysical questions. Rather than retreating from metaphysical questions like Kant, Hegel sees the answer to them lying in Kant's retreat.

Hegel returns to metaphysics through the apparatus of the Kantian critique. Kant gives Hegel the tool of reason to address the same metaphysical questions that Kant himself finds out of bounds for thought. Hegel's revaluation of reason is not a case of him always looking on the bright side or of him transforming every loss into a gain. This is a constant critique directed toward Hegel.[12] When Hegel sees the failure of reason as a success, he forces us to look at success differently. Success is not the elimination or the overcoming of contradiction. It is not akin to winning a football game by defeating the opponent. Instead, success involves embracing the contradiction as what animates our existence—no longer seeing victory in the conclusion of the game but in the confrontation that it makes possible.

Hegel can accept Aristotle's claim that reason separates the subject from animality even though this claim appears premodern in its assumptions about human difference. This separation of the subject from the rest of the organic world derives directly from the subject's ability to think contradiction. But reason doesn't lift the subject above contradiction, as Aristotle would have it. It lowers the subject into the mire of contradiction, permitting the subject to identify with what undermines it. Reason is the key to the subject's emancipation, but this emancipation occurs only when the subject recognizes that it is what negates it.

BIRCH TREES AND SUBJECTS

Hegel distinguishes between the finitude of material things in the world and the infinitude of the subject that has the capacity to reason through the way that each relates to contradiction. Finite things are contradictory insofar as they both are identical to themselves and are not. Their identity includes otherness. Though the subject endures this same contradiction, it relates to the contradiction differently, which produces a disjunction between the finite material world and the infinite world of spirit.

There is no pure self-identity in the finite world, and this absence of self-identity is not just a result of our epistemological constraints, as we might expect. When we identify a birch tree, we differentiate it from an elm and an oak in order to understand it as a birch tree. Epistemologically, the identity of the birch tree depends on its difference. If this difference were to disappear—if all other trees vanished—the identity of the birch tree for us would change. We might cease to think of it as a birch tree at all and just think of it as a generic tree. In this sense, the identity of the birch tree is contradictory. What the birch tree is not—other types of trees—plays an integral role in establishing what the birch tree is. If we take away the otherness of these trees, the birch tree loses its identity as a birch tree. But this is simply an epistemological contradiction and not what Hegel has in mind when claims that finite things are contradictory.

The birch tree lacks pure self-identity because it is always in the process of becoming something else. It never simply is what it is. The birch tree is never the same entity from one moment to the next. There is no one moment that identifies the birch tree apart from the other moments that constitute it. The birch tree becomes what it is not and ceases to be what it is. This is what it means to exist as a finite being. What constitutes the birch tree is not simply that it remains the same over time but that it goes through a process of changes. The birch tree's identity is contradictory because it is nothing other than the changes that it goes through. And yet we can distinguish the birch tree from the environment in which it exists. It is not just lost in a flood of material that has no identity whatsoever but rather has a consistency during its development that enables us to identify it as an entity. The birch tree has an identity even though this identity is constantly undermined. In fact, the identity depends on the process that undermines it.

Natural entities like the birch tree confront contradiction in the external form of temporality, whereas the subject, through its use of reason, is able to defy temporality. Time brings the birch tree into existence and later annihilates it. Through temporality, the birch tree has contradiction imposed on it. It is the victim of time. Because reason is able to think contradiction through its own logic, the subject doesn't have to experience it merely as an external force that devours the subject. In the *Philosophy of Nature*, Hegel states, "Time . . . has no power over the concept, nor is the concept in time or temporal; on the contrary, it *is* the power over time, which is this negativity only *qua* externality. Only the natural, therefore, is subject to time in so far as it is finite; the true, on the other hand, the idea, spirit, is *eternal*."[13] As a purely finite being locked in its temporality, the birch tree experiences contradiction only in the external form of time passing. Contradiction is not internal to its identity.

The limitation of the birch tree's contradictory existence is at the same time the limitation of time as a form through which contradiction occurs. Time reveals what is constantly becoming what is not as it passes, but in time this negation is inevitably external to the entity undergoing it. The negation comes as an external future that appears to the entity as an alien force. Even the entity's own future appears as an otherness in the contradiction of temporality.

For the subject, negation is not merely external. Subjects encounter contradiction through reason rather than existence. This is the source of the subject's fundamental difference from the natural world. Nature exists in contradiction while the subject has the capacity to think it. By thinking it through reason, the subject discovers contradiction within itself and ceases to confront negation as an externality. For Hegel, contradiction is a logical occurrence deriving from the way that identity functions within logic. When one articulates any identity whatsoever, one necessarily undermines the identity. The moment that an entity appears as identical to itself—we could formulate it as $A = A$—the identity introduces otherness into itself. The repetition that occurs with the assertion of identity indicates that self-identity is, at the same time, self-difference. No identity can simply remain what it is when we consider it through reason.

But the merely finite being does not recognize the role that nonidentity or difference plays in its identity. No birch tree has ever understood that its identity depends on a fundamental negation that undermines that identity. No birch tree has ever understood that what it is not determines what it is. Instead, it dies from contradiction at the moment when difference or what the birch tree is not obliterates its identity completely, which is why Hegel insists that finite beings are really nothing other than their end or death.[14] The subject, in contrast, is a subject by recognizing itself in contradiction.

The subject, as Hegel sees it, has the capacity to grasp contradiction through reason. By doing so, the subject sees that contradiction is the source of its own being, that it cannot separate itself from what negates it. Hegel stresses the importance of the negative so often because he sees that the subject's engagement with what negates it removes the subject from the realm of pure finitude. Though the subject doesn't miraculously transcend time, the external contradiction of temporality is not how the subject relates to contradiction.

Hegel shares with the early Martin Heidegger the conviction that the encounter with its annihilation plays a formative role in differentiating the subject (or what Heidegger calls Dasein) from the rest of the finite world. Death, for Heidegger, is the source of Dasein's existential singularity. But Hegel and Heidegger quickly diverge. This encounter with annihilation forces Heidegger's Dasein to grasp its finitude, while it makes Hegel's subject aware of its infinitude, its irreducibility to the rest of the finite world. When Hegel's subject grasps its own infinitude, it finds itself even more alienated from the world than Heidegger's Dasein, which remains a being in the world rather than a subject removed from it.

Grasping the internal status of contradiction does not eliminate it but instead ensconces it as the essence of subjectivity. The subject relates to itself as a non-natural entity, an entity no longer bound by the limits of finitude. The subject is infinite because it fully takes up contradiction as the form of subjectivity itself. As a result, contradiction no longer undermines the subject from the outside as it does finite entities like the birch tree. In a way that the birch tree cannot, the subject grasps that it itself is contradictory, that it undermines itself and recognizes that what negates it is actually the product of its own desire.

Of course, most subjects don't straightforwardly embrace negation in obvious ways. Though many people kill themselves, most do not. Most subjects don't bring about their own negation in the form of death. But they do desire what disrupts their own interest, which is what Hegel identifies as the contradiction of subjectivity. The negation of subjectivity is always internal to subjectivity. The subject desires this negation even though it portends the subject's own destruction. Though a subject reconciled with contradiction can meet with a contingent end that destroys it from outside—like a lightning strike or a car crash—this contingent end is nonetheless part of the subject's world and is thus not simply an external event for the subject.[15] In the *Philosophy of Nature*, Hegel makes a remarkable statement about the subject's death that serves as a point of contrast between the subject and the natural world. He states, "A man can be killed; but this external circumstance is contingent; the truth is that man dies through his own nature."[16] The circumstances of the subject's death can be contingent and external, but the death itself is not. The subject is a self-annihilating being.

The contrast between the subject and the birch tree is clear. The lumberjack who chops down the birch tree is like the power of time—always an external figure. The death of the birch tree is a contingent fact that necessarily arrives from the outside. For Hegel, the birch tree plays no part in its own annihilation because it cannot reason. It dies from contradiction rather than being able to recognize itself as contradictory, which is the subject's great leap forward.

The privilege of subjectivity consists in its ability to annihilate itself. The recognition of the subject's constant self-annihilation is the end point of reason. Reason permits the subject to view negation as essential to its entity and thus to grasp itself as a self-negating entity. Through reason, the subject ceases to limit itself to the contradictions of the finite world. Though thinking subjects obviously remain finite beings that will ultimately succumb to the contradiction that constitutes them—they will die—they are also infinite beings that do not simply exist in pure temporality. In the act of grasping the contradictory structure of being, the subject recognizes its own being as contradictory and in this way ceases to be simply the victim of contradiction's power. Reason delivers the subject from its status as a victim of the world, but it does so by seeing the subject as the victim of itself.

BEYOND UNDERSTANDING

The ultimate problem with the understanding, in contrast to reason, lies in its surreptitious investment in the beyond. Reason does not allow itself a beyond but thinks the totality with the metaphysical questions that the totality entails. In order to avoid contradiction, the understanding brackets all metaphysical questions as irresolvable. According to the logic of the understanding, the subject simply cannot broach questions about the beginning of space and time or about the existence of a simple entity. By placing these questions outside its purview, the understanding enables the subject to think about the field of experience as a stable field. But the stability of this field depends on what lies beyond it.

In the act of making metaphysical questions off limits, the understanding tacitly indicates an investment in the beyond where the possible solution to these questions resides. Though they are unresolvable from the perspective of the understanding, they are not unresolvable as such. This burdens the understanding with an implicit beyond that it cannot think but nonetheless requires. When Kant announces not only that we cannot resolve metaphysical questions but that we cannot even raise them within the domain of understanding, he constructs a realm external to the understanding that it has no knowledge of and yet depends on. Limiting the field of the understanding implies a beyond, which Kant acknowledges when he admits that limits of knowledge create room for faith.[17]

The dependence of the understanding on the questions that it cannot address shapes its answer to the questions that it can address. The stability of the field of possible experience conceived by the understanding bears the mark of the metaphysical questions that it brackets. Even though Kant doesn't recognize it, his vision of the understanding reveals that he has not effectively bracketed the metaphysical questions from its domain. In exactly the same way as Freud envisions the return of the repressed upsetting the supposed coherence of the ego, metaphysical questions distort the conclusions that the understanding would draw about its own stable field.[18]

This distortion appears in the table of categories that provide the rules for how the understanding conceptualizes experience. Kant establishes this table of four classes of three categories each in the *Critique of Pure Reason*. Hegel (following a critique articulated by Fichte) famously takes Kant to task for simply assuming the categories from traditional logic, going so far as to call Kant's way of concocting the categories a "disgrace to science."[19] The disgrace, as Hegel sees it, lies in Kant's decision not to deduce the categories of the understanding as necessary on the basis of the structure of the understanding itself. Hegel takes this failure as a slander against the understanding, but beyond labeling Kant's decision a "disgrace to science,"

Hegel does not explore the structure of the Kantian categories. From Hegel's perspective, the absence of their deduction as necessary gives them an arbitrary status that forestalls the need for further analysis.

But the categories themselves are highly revelatory in terms of Kant's refusal of metaphysical speculation. The categories betray no overt influence of metaphysical questions but rather proclaim their absence. Even though Kant takes over most of them from Aristotle, he sees them, in contrast to Aristotle, as valid only for objects of possible experience, not for what exists beyond our representations.[20] And yet this absence manifests itself through lacunae and through the form that certain categories take. Kant's categories show that one cannot carve out a field of experience free from the stain of unanswerable metaphysical questions. We are always answering metaphysical questions even—or especially—when we are certain that we are avoiding them.[21]

The repression of the metaphysical question creates a gap within the field of the understanding. This becomes especially pronounced when we come to modality, the final class of categories. Kant draws three absolute distinctions, between possibility and impossibility, between existence and nonbeing, and between necessity and contingency. Here the consequence of the repression of the metaphysical question concerning the beginning of the world in time and space manifests itself. Kant fails to see how these oppositions might break down through their mutual dependence, how existence might include nonbeing within it, as is the case with every finite being. This involvement of nonbeing in existence is exactly what Hegel discovers when he sees the inability to answer the metaphysical questions as its own form of answer.

In the same vein, the Kantian categories cannot account for necessity using a contingent event to advance itself, which Hegel sees as inevitable. By separating necessity and contingency, Kant obscures how each makes use of the other. Kant's categories of modality transform dialectical contradictions—the relationship between freedom and necessity, for instance—into dichotomous oppositions. This is where the repression of reason returns. It creates a distortion in the form of the categories, an inability to think a modality in which the oppositions are both at work. By avoiding the confrontation with the contradictory solution to the metaphysical questions, Kant tries to purify the understanding so that it functions smoothly. But this purification fails, and the table of categories betrays him.

Rather than dismiss Kant's table of categories as a "disgrace" and be done with it, we should take stock of what this disgrace reveals about the failure of the understanding to limit itself. Though the understanding attempts to confine itself to the field of possible experience, it actually exposes the surreptitious influence of the beyond.[22] The problem with giving the beyond an influence on the understanding is that this influence remains untheorized, affecting the understanding without being taken into account. This, for Hegel, is the problem with any invocation of a beyond. The beyond always returns, and it does so in ways that escape our grasp as long as we begin by positing it as beyond. Any recourse to the beyond is untenable for thought.

THE POWER OF UNDERSTANDING

Hegel's celebration of reason (*Vernunft*) for its ability to think contradiction entails a critique of the understanding (*Verstand*) for its failure to do so. Whereas reason discovers its truth when it encounters contradiction, the understanding never even approaches it. The understanding is reason's foil. In the introduction to the *Science of Logic*, Hegel lays this out clearly. He says, "the contradiction is in fact the elevation of reason above the restrictions of the understanding and the dissolution of them."[23] The understanding avoids contradiction by restricting itself to the field of possible experience. The superiority of reason stems solely from its ability to think contradiction rather than avoiding it.

But a few hundred pages later, in the same work, Hegel modifies his apparently damning verdict on the understanding. During the first chapter of the first section of the "Doctrine of the Concept" (the final part of the *Science of Logic*), Hegel abruptly launches into an encomium to the understanding just after repeating his attack from the introduction. Not only that, but he also rejects in no uncertain terms the distinction between the understanding and reason that would allow a thinker to privilege one over the other. He states straightforwardly, "the common practice of separating understanding and reason is to be rejected on all counts."[24] When he writes this critique of separating understanding and reason, it is as if Hegel forgets for a moment that he also wrote the introduction to the *Science of Logic*, which relies on exactly this "common practice" in order to elevate reason at the expense of the understanding. But rather than view this as a strange case of a philosopher deciding to attack what he just wrote, we should see how Hegel's description of the understanding leads to this divided verdict on it—both as the failure to think contradiction in the way that reason can and as indissociably linked to reason.

Though the understanding fails to grasp contradiction, it also makes contradiction evident. If not for the act of understanding that abstracts from the mass of data—what Kant calls the manifold of intuition—in order to create fixed identities, contradiction would remain impossible to recognize. The understanding's act of creating abstract oppositions divides the world, and this division produces identities that appear independent of each other but actually require otherness. This division makes reason's apprehension of contradiction possible, which is why Hegel contends that understanding and reason must be seen in their unity.

The step of the understanding, even though it creates divisions that ultimately prove false, at the same time makes true connections graspable. Hegel does not assume that the world is naturally divided into different entities (nor does he assume that all is one). Instead, he identifies the understanding as a faculty for producing multiplicity. He writes, "we must pay due respect to the infinite force of the understanding in splitting the concrete into abstract determinacies and plumbing the depth of the difference—this force which alone is at the same time the mighty power causing the transition of the determinacies."[25] Through the activity of the understanding, we separate the entities of the world. We divide the tree from the stone and regard them as distinct entities.

Prior to this act of ripping the world apart, it is not a harmonious whole but just a mass of data. The mass of data unthought by the understanding has neither natural difference nor unity. It is nothing at all prior to the violent act of the understanding carving it up. In this sense, Hegel absolutely rejects mysticism: there is no hidden oneness uniting the whole prior to the separateness that the understanding introduces. The violence of the understanding creates the illusion of an original wholeness that it disrupts with abstract opposition, but this illusion is just the retrospective result of the understanding's act of separation. It separates what is undifferentiated, not what is whole or already different.

The succession of Southern states that triggered the American Civil War functions in the way that the understanding does. The conflict separates the South from the North, the Confederacy from the Union. It violently distinguishes the states loyal to the United States from those that want to form their own distinct nation. But there was no coherent whole prior to this break, just a loose conglomeration of states with a limited investment in the totality. The Confederacy's act of tearing itself away enables the opposition between South and North to become clear. The undifferentiated mass of states becomes explicitly the site of a profound division. The South's act of understanding that divides the mass of states into two paves the way for Lincoln's rational act of creating a contradictory whole through the war itself.

The praise of the understanding that occurs in the third part of the *Science of Logic* represents the continuation of a line of thought Hegel begins in the *Phenomenology of Spirit*, where it also sounds strange to hear Hegel praise the understanding rather than reason. Despite the fact that the *Phenomenology*, like the *Science of Logic*, points out the false limitations of the understanding, it begins with full-throated praise of this agency. In the preface, Hegel celebrates the power of the understanding to create separate entities out of the world. He says, "the activity of separating is the force and labor of the *Understanding*, the most astonishing and greatest of all the powers, or rather, the absolute power."[26] Without the dividing power of the understanding, we would have no ability to thematize distinctiveness at all. We would instead confront a mass of data in which differences would not be able to make a difference for us. The understanding's act of separation is the fundamental basis for all thought, as Hegel sees it, and lays the groundwork for reason to grasp contradiction.[27] The understanding's division of being is thus part of reason's recognition that this division involves identity in difference.

The division of being that the understanding accomplishes introduces the awareness of a total devastation to the subject, which is what Hegel stresses in the *Phenomenology*. Hegel identifies the understanding's power of division with what he calls being "absolutely torn asunder," but it is only through the encounter with this total devastation that the subject can truly find itself. Hegel states that spirit "wins to its truth only when it finds itself absolutely torn asunder [*in der absoluten Zerissenheit*]."[28] When the subject's understanding separates entities from each other, it also separates the subject not only from everything else but also from itself. The act of the understanding leaves the subject isolated from the world and alone, without even the respite of its own self-identity. The understanding enables the subject to recognize its own self-division, a self-division the subject cannot heal since it functions as the condition of the subject's own possibility. Though the subject cannot heal its self-division, it can recognize this self-division as emancipatory, which is what occurs with the move from the understanding to reason.

Being absolutely torn asunder is the only path to truth. Without this act, the subject would remain trapped within the illusion of self-identity. It would be content to be what it is—and thus to be like a table or a stone. Through the act of being absolutely torn asunder, the subject discovers that it is not what it is, even though it requires the turn to reason for it to recognize itself in this contradictory condition. The initial gesture of the understanding that defines entities as distinct and the subject as divided from itself provides the basis for the emancipatory recognition that being is contradictory.

In this sense, the subject must come to regard the being absolutely torn asunder that the understanding produces as the source of freedom. Through being absolutely torn asunder, the subject finds itself isolated and alone, but, paradoxically, it is only through isolation and aloneness that the subject can recognize its indissociable link to otherness through reason. Reason doesn't heal the subject from being absolutely torn asunder, but it does enable the subject to see this act as the basis for its freedom and for its connection to others. It is only through being torn asunder that the subject can recognize its identity with what it isn't and reconcile itself with the contradiction of its own identity.

The understanding performs an act of violence toward all the entities that it encounters. By abstractly separating entities from each other, it creates distinctions that do not emanate from the entities themselves. It forces entities into an abstract identity that they have not chosen for themselves and that separates them from the rest of the world they inhabit. The understanding is the vehicle of epistemic violence. But without this violent separation, there can be no connection, since connection occurs through the contradiction of an isolated identity. Only when we recognize that the isolated subject is dependent on otherness can connection become possible. One must submit to total isolation in order to achieve connection.

Reason does not eliminate the violence of the understanding. It does not smooth over the oppositions and conflicts that the understanding's division of the world produces. Instead, it enables us to see oppositions and conflicts as expressions of identity. Through reason, we recognize the position that the other occupies as a negation is actually essential to our identity. Reason enables us to see contradiction where the understanding has created difference.

THE IMPURITY OF HEGEL'S REASON

Defenders of reason have historically taken up this position as a rampart against the torrents of desire. Desire leads subjects to act in destructive ways, while reason operates as a check on this destructiveness. When we see someone angered without provocation in a bar, we counsel, "Be reasonable." We hope that reason will function as a brake on the desire to smash a beer bottle over a fellow patron's head. Reasonable people fight less because they see both (or many) sides of the issue. Reason offers a balance that offsets the one-sidedness of desire.

Philosophers turn to reason in the same way. It doesn't help them avoid fisticuffs, but it does help them to allow disparate phenomena and disparate positions to coincide. In the *Theodicy*, Leibniz defines reason as "the inviolable linking together of truths."[29] Reason connects series of truths so that we can draw conclusions about the world and ourselves. In the case of Leibniz, reason's unifying power enables him to solve the most intractable problem of his day, to reconcile the existence of evil in the world with the beneficence of an omnipotent God. The fact that this seems unreasonable today (and did even to many of his contemporaries) testifies even further to the power of reason to continually extend the connections that it makes in order to arrive at increasingly secure insights—and to criticize its earlier missteps.

But reason does not just reconcile adversarial phenomena. It also mitigates violence by permitting reasonable disagreement based on a more fundamental agreement about the rules of reason. This is why Jürgen Habermas champions communicative rationality. According to Habermas, the rationality that inheres in the act of speaking indicates an ultimate level of agreement that occurs whenever people speak to each other. When we argue, we affirm a shared acceptance of rationality that we will accede to during the course of the argument. Though desires can stain the pact of reason that underlies speech, they cannot eviscerate it. The rationality that inheres in discourse propels us beyond our particular desires and creates the basis for an ethical relation with others.[30]

For its champions, the appeal of reason lies in its transcendence of the subject's desire. It provides a common ground that mitigates the potential conflict between individuals because it doesn't bear the inflection of their specific desire. The image of the rational person as cold and distant stems from this conception that reason has nothing to do with the subject's desire. Reason provides respite, but the cost is an aloof and barren existence.[31]

But to return to the example of the intoxicated bar patron itching for a fight, it quickly becomes apparent how often our pleas on behalf of reason fall on deaf ears. When one feels wronged in a bar quarrel, the call for reasonable behavior is the last thing that one wants to hear. Drunken would-be quarrelers at times even turn their anger toward the one calling for reason. This suggests that reason, while desirable for stopping fights (either verbal or physical), has a rather circumscribed effectiveness. Or does it? Perhaps fights themselves, even bar fights, have their origins in reason and not in our sensibility or understanding.

When one arrives at the section on reason (*Vernunft*) in Hegel's *Phenomenology of Spirit*, one experiences a bit of a shock at the direction in which he takes the discussion. Though Hegel doesn't begin by linking reason to bar fights, he offers a picture of reason that challenges common sense almost as much as such a linkage. Hegel does allow that reason mediates our relation to others, but reason for him bears little resemblance to the pacifying rationality championed by Leibniz and Habermas. Rather than marking the subject's dispassionate turning away from the world, the turn to reason indicates the presence of a distortion in the subject's understanding of the world occasioned by the inclusion of its desire in this understanding.

Whereas consciousness and self-consciousness (the first two major divisions of the *Phenomenology of Spirit*) emphasize the subject's separateness from its world, the reason section begins with the subject losing its separateness. In the second paragraph of the discussion of reason, Hegel explains how at this point the subject grasps that "all actuality is nothing but itself."[32] Rather than distancing the subject from the world of objects and giving it a neutral perspective on this world, reason has the opposite effect: it makes evident the extent to which the subject's desire shapes the world that it apprehends. It is only with the move beyond self-consciousness to reason that the subject ceases to believe in a pure world beyond its own experience. The turn to reason brings the subject proximate to its world rather than creating a safe distance. It involves the subject in what it perceives.

After Hegel begins his discussion of reason, he soon lights on a surprising set of topics—physiognomy and phrenology. Though he has no intellectual investment in these pseudosciences, he nonetheless brings them up as examples of "observing reason." At this point, the reader can be forgiven for wondering if Hegel has lost his mind. But both practices show how the subject's desire would manifest itself in a distortion of the subject's material being. Even though both physiognomy and phrenology are mistaken about the way that desire manifests itself—the size of one's skull bone is not, for Hegel, a measure of one's intelligence—they do illustrate the necessity of desire's material embodiment. But reason doesn't conclude with this contradiction.

The development Hegel traces in the reason section of the *Phenomenology* moves through various attempts to theorize reason as the manifestation of the subject's desire in shaping the world. In the middle of this section, Hegel contrasts two positions that he calls "virtue" and "the way of the world" in order to reveal that reason involves the impurity of desire rather than the elimination of this impurity. The subject of virtue wants to sacrifice individuality for the sake of the general good, which seems like a rational position. But the problem is that this call for sacrifice doesn't really desire the good that it proclaims to want. Any realization of virtue suffers from the taint of the way of the world, which privileges individuality at the expense of the general good, which is why virtue rejects it. Virtue wants the general good without the necessary detour through the individual act. No matter how much I sacrifice as an individual, I remain guilty because I do so as an individual. I am like the self-flagellating monk who finds the sin of individual pleasure in every purportedly virtuous act. Thus virtue finds itself in a perpetual struggle that it cannot win without simultaneously destroying itself as virtue. Virtue cannot enact virtue while remaining virtuous.

The way of the world, in contrast, marks a genuine advance for reason. Whereas virtue is not as virtuous as it imagines itself to be, the way of the world is not as self-interested as it believes itself to be. The way of the world involves the individual acting for itself without concern for the universal, but it is impossible for the individual to act simply in its self-interest. The individual's act realizes the universal unbeknownst to the individual. The private self-interested acts of the way of the world are not really private acts. The subject ensconced in the way of the world believes itself to be acting as an individual just when it acts on behalf of the universal.[33]

This dynamic defines the capitalist economy. I believe myself to be pursuing my private interest when I open a doughnut shop. In doing so, I hope to take advantage of people's appetite for food that will expedite their self-destruction and make a fortune so that I can retire early. But what results is that I have to work long hours every day over vats of steaming oil, while the doughnut shop turns into a site for universality. People come not just to eat doughnuts but to interact with each other and thereby recognize the universal. My attempt to satisfy my private desire fails because the desiring subject cannot simply be a private being. The subject's desire divides the subject from itself, producing an entity unconsciously attached to the public.

Reason in the *Phenomenology of Spirit* indicates how the subject's desire forms the world that the subject experiences. But it does so because reason is the subject's faculty capable of grasping and enduring contradiction. This connection between contradiction and desire is one of the foundations of Hegel's thought, and the connection manifests itself in reason. Hegel's insight into the contradictory nature of desire indicates his position within the orbit of what would become psychoanalysis.

Desire emerges out of the subject's failure to coincide with itself, its lack of self-identity. The desiring subject is a contradictory being that wants to be other than it is. For example, I have a secure heterosexual relationship, but I secretly desire a same-sex romantic partner. As I contemplate this desire, I imagine it as the true or authentic vision of myself in contrast to the vision of my actual self. What the subject desires—whether it is a new sexual partner or a new commodity—provides an alternative vision of the subject's identity that competes with the identity that the subject actually has. As long as I desire (and desire is inescapable for the subject), my subjectivity contains within it contradictory visions of myself: one in which I am a heterosexual and another in which I am gay, or one in which I am living on a subsistence wage and another in which I have won the lottery. Even when not taken to such extreme oppositions, desire always confronts the subject with what it is not and demands that it see itself in the negation of itself. In this sense, desire is the form that contradiction assumes in the subject, while reason is the apprehension of this contradiction.

THE POLITICS OF *VERNUNFT*

The danger that critics of Hegel see in his identification of the actual as rational stems from the apparent depoliticization that it produces. There is no need to take political action if we know a priori that the structure of the world articulates that of our rationality. As Bertrand Russell points out, "the identification of the real and the rational leads unavoidably to some of the complacency inseparable from the belief that 'whatever is, is right.'"[34] If ever a philosopher formulated a politics of quietism, Hegel's identification of reason with actuality must be it. But when we examine Hegel's claim in light of his revaluation of reason (*Vernunft*), the political calculus of the statement changes 180 degrees.

We can find a clue about the practical political consequences of the statement from the *Philosophy of Right* in a work that Hegel writes four years earlier. At this time, he intervenes in a political dispute concerning the king's introduction of a new constitution in the Kingdom of Württemberg.[35] This is one of the few works that Hegel devotes to a practical political situation. When first glancing at Hegel's review essay on this debate, things don't look good. The essay seems to confirm the most conservative reading of the famous statement from the *Philosophy of Right*. In the conflict between the king and the Estates Assembly, Hegel takes the side of the king and argues against the people's representatives. He associates the king's position with modern universality while criticizing opposition to it as mired in a bygone particularity. What's worse, when he does criticize the king's constitution, Hegel attacks it for an excess of liberality—the version of suffrage that it proposes—rather than for the power it grants to the king. If this work puts into practice what Hegel would a few years later call identifying the rationality of the actual, then the judgment that that practice is fundamentally conservative seems assured.

But when one looks closer at Hegel's critique of the Estates Assembly, this quick judgment becomes increasingly dubious. Hegel appreciates the king's constitution for its break from the system of privileges that controlled Württemberg in the past. In the guise of defending the people against the monarch, the Estates Assembly, for its part, is simply defending the privileges that it enjoyed under the old constitution. This reactionary resistance to the king's constitution earns Hegel's enmity. It is the king, despite the fact that he is a figure of authority, who is on the side of modern freedom.

The Estates Assembly uses its position to defend private right against the king's attempt to render the universal explicit through the new constitution. Hegel contends that "all that Estates deputies bring with them is the sense of private interest and . . . thus come into the Assembly with the will *to give and do as little as possible* for the universal."[36] By intervening on the side of the king's constitution, Hegel intervenes on the side of the universal against the private interest of the deputies that these deputies support with an appeal to tradition and history. Private interest has the effect of hiding contradiction, while the universal makes it apparent. By making contradiction apparent, the universal provides the ground for subjects to grasp their freedom. There is no freedom outside the universal.

Though Hegel privileges freedom above all other values, he recognizes that freedom does not come naturally. Not only are we not free as natural beings, we do not even desire a constitution that would grant us freedom. The subject's freedom derives from the people's lack of identity with itself. This means that the free state forms through a contradictory process in which the people cannot freely decide on a free constitution.

Hegel defends the king's constitution for the freedom that it acknowledges for the people. But he sees that the state of freedom must be imposed on the people. He writes, "if historical experience be our guide, we must admit that oftentimes even peoples who loved their freedom above all else have confessed their incompetence to frame a constitution on their own and entrusted a *Solon* or a *Lycurgus* with the task—men who moreover resorted to deception to get around the so-called will of the people and the necessity of submitting their constitution to it for approval."[37] A free state cannot arise on its own but comes through a violent and even deceptive imposition. Universal freedom emerges out of an individual act.

In his rational analysis of the debate in the Estates Assembly, Hegel identifies the central contradiction of the actual: the king, not the deputies, is on the side of the people. Though the king is the sovereign of Württemberg, he is actually closer to the people than their representatives in the Estates Assembly. He is on the side of the people's freedom even as the people themselves resist this imposition of freedom through the new constitution.

Because they remain attached to the traditions of the past, the people require a monarch to free them. This is how the rational asserts its actuality. In this way, Hegel puts into practice the famous statement from the *Philosophy of Right* in the decade before he writes it.

But in fact the statement is even more radical than Hegel himself understands and has implications far beyond Hegel's analysis of the Württemberg constitutional debate. The call for theorizing the rationality of the actual places Hegel in the company of the greatest political revolutionaries rather than that of apologists for power. The discovery that contradiction is actual and knowable through reason makes possible the theoretical dismantling of inequality. The structure of inegalitarian, hierarchical relations in the world has its basis in the conviction that contradiction doesn't actually exist and that, as a result, a privileged identity can separate itself definitively from what negates it. Every inegalitarian relation depends on this separation, which serves as its justification.

In the modern epoch, this is clear, and it manifests itself in the accumulation of capital. Subjects view capital as purely self-identical. It simply is what it is. This failure to recognize that capital also is what it is not—that it becomes capital through labor time rather being a self-identical substance—is the lifeblood of the functioning of the socioeconomic system. Once subjects recognize capital as contradictory, capitalism can no longer function.

The divorce of capital from labor time enables capitalist subjects to view the wealthy as either hardworking or lucky, according to their ideological bent, rather than as the beneficiaries of class warfare. Because we don't recognize the contradiction within capital itself, it becomes inoculated to a revolutionary critique. The apparent self-identity of capital separates it from its accumulation. This transformation of contradiction into difference is how inegalitarian relations of all stripes, like those of capitalism, operate.

When Hegel claims that reason is actual, he contests the possibility of such a separation. Capital's identity must include that which negates it. The labor time that brings capital into existence is inseparable from it. Capital is not only itself but also the labor time that it leaves in its wake. Though Hegel himself never performs this analysis of capital, his grasp of the rationality of the actual makes it possible. As a result, it is not at all surprising that when Marx writes *Capital* he returns to Hegel's logic.[38] The contradiction of actuality is what we discover when we recognize that reason is actual.

The emancipatory quality of the statement from the *Philosophy of Right* goes beyond Marx's critique of capital. We can see it at work in a variety of political movements. Though Hegel was himself not a feminist, the use to which second-wave feminism put the idea of the rationality of the actual indicates that, if he had followed his own thinking, he should have been. Second-wave feminism in the 1970s made the rationality of the actual a central part of its political program. Feminist thinkers constantly pointed out the contradictory status of women in the patriarchal world. By drawing attention to the actual situation of women, they revealed that their existence itself was contradictory and that they were able to think this contradiction.

During their diagnoses of the contemporary situation of women, the major feminist theorists of the 1970s show that contradiction invades all aspects of a woman's existence. According to Germaine Greer in *The Female Eunuch*, the most blatant contradiction that the woman embodies concerns menstruation. It is at once divinely ordained and so repulsive that it cannot even be mentioned.[39] It is a sign of a great privilege and a bloody curse. Patriarchal ideology tries to separate these judgments, but Greer insists on recognizing the contradiction and its actuality. Menstruation must be both at the same time.

But contradiction is not just confined to the female body. In *The Dialectic of Sex*, Shulamith Firestone points out that patriarchal society forces women to place their economic and social hopes in winning the love of a man and at the same time condemns women for adopting a calculating attitude toward love.[40] Women must truly love and must be calculating. They must be innocent and coquettish. Despite the fact that these two positions contradict each other, women take up both. On these counts, women are contradictory beings, and yet they are actual. As long as we remain within the patriarchal standpoint, the loving woman and the calculating woman have to be distinct subjects. But feminist theory reveals that what patriarchal ideology passes off as difference is actually contradiction—the identity of opposites within the same subject.

Perhaps the best example of the contradiction of female actuality occurs in the competing ideals that govern femininity: the caring maternal figure and the alluring sexual object. Of course, in order to become a mother, a woman must at some point act as a sexual object, but this contradiction remains unthinkable within the patriarchal universe. The mother and the sexual object are opposed rather than contradictory. They are simply different women. The real feminist achievement occurs when we can see the identity in difference of these two figures. Reason enables us to see that the mother is a sexual object and vice versa. In this way, reason—the ability to grasp the contradiction of the actual—is the path to feminist emancipation from the differences imposed by patriarchy.

As the great feminists theorists of the 1970s understand, feminist victory cannot consist in the elimination of these contradictions. Not only is this impossible—there is no noncontradictory woman, just as there is no noncontradictory man—but such a project has the effect of substantializing different female particularities. This plays directly into the hands of patriarchal ideology and gives birth to the resignation of postfeminism. Rather than overcoming the contradictions of femininity, we must reconcile ourselves with them as absolute. This is what only reason can accomplish.

To say that rationality is actual is to say that actuality is contradictory—and thus not just inherently changeable but already subverting itself. If one pays attention to Hegel's use of the terms *rational (vernünftig)* and *actual (wirklich)*, one comes to the conclusion that his statement from the *Philosophy of Right*, far from bowing to the ruling powers, represents perhaps the most significant philosophical challenge to the dominance of the ruling class that anyone has ever uttered. Inequality has its basis in the reduction of contradiction to difference. The authority of those who propagate inegalitarian relations depends on their ability to sustain the illusion that their identity does not suffer from contradiction, and this is precisely what Hegel's famous statement deprives them of. If the claim that "the rational is actual" has led to the condemnation of Hegel's political philosophy in some quarters, perhaps this is because Hegel's opponents have sensed its radicality and recoiled from it. To say that the rational is actual is to insist on an unremitting universal equality.

Chapter Four

THE INSUBSTANTIALITY OF SUBSTANCE

Restoring Hegel's Lost Limbs

A ROUNDABOUT ONTOLOGY

The limits that Kant imposes on reason restrict our capacity for ontological speculation. When it attempts to think about ontological realities, reason encounters contradiction, which is why, according to Kant, we cannot freely indulge in speculative philosophy. Just as Hegel counters Kant's critique with an embrace of reason (*Vernunft*), he also recognizes how our insights into epistemological constraints entail an implicit ontology. For Hegel, ontological speculation is not an embarrassing residue of traditional metaphysics that we should leave behind but an inevitability: we cannot escape ontological speculation. By confining ourselves to phenomena as Kant does, we allow our ontology to remain obscure but in no way manage to avoid it. Hegel, in contrast, insists on the necessity of ontology.

For more than a century and a half after his death, considering Hegel as an ontologist meant seeing him as a pre-Critical philosopher, as someone who tried to bypass Kant's critique of traditional metaphysics.[1] In recent years, however, it has become possible for the first time to take Hegel seriously as an ontological thinker. Thanks to interpretations promulgated by Slavoj Žižek and others, Hegel's ontology has ceased to be a site of embarrassment those invested in his philosophy and has become instead the most contemporary moment within his thought. As ontological claims have begun to proliferate in today's world, Hegel's renewed importance as a thinker has become inseparable from his insistence on ontology, an insistence that separates him from Kant. During the twentieth century, those who saw Hegel as an ontologist were seeking only to discredit his philosophy for its overreach, for its refusal to accept the fundamental division between thought and being.[2] But now the proponents of an ontological Hegel are his defenders, not his detractors.

Hegel's ontology begins by accepting, not rejecting, the division between thought and being. This is the division that Kant establishes in order to refute the most cherished claims of metaphysics like the proofs for the existence of God or the deduction of the soul. For Kant, there is no necessary connection between our thought of God and the actual existence of God, just as there is no necessary connection between the idea of a hundred thalers and having a hundred thalers in hand.[3] Nor can we establish the existence of the soul on the basis of a thinking subject as rational psychology would like to do.

Though Hegel accepts the division between thought and being, he doesn't believe that thought cannot reveal anything about being. The challenge that Hegel poses to the absolute status of this division in Kant's philosophy becomes evident in the preface to the *Phenomenology of Spirit* when Hegel describes the subject. Here, Hegel claims that "what seems to happen outside of it, to be an activity directed against it, is really its own doing, and substance shows itself to be essentially subject."[4] Historically, Hegel's critics have read this statement as the reduction of substantial reality to being nothing but the manifestation of the thinking subject. According to this view, the subject can know the world because the world is the product of the subject's own activity. Hegel not only seems to toss aside Kant's caution about our capacity to know, he also grants the subject an extraordinary power to create the world in its own image. Even worse, the entire history of the universe becomes the manifestation of spirit, an all-encompassing force that necessarily determines everything.

This interpretation of Hegel's project dominates throughout the nineteenth and early twentieth century in the works of Hegelian philosophers such as John McTaggart.[5] McTaggart views Hegel as an exponent of the purposive rationality of the world. For him, the contingencies of history and nature exist within the necessity of spirit's self-expression and self-externalization. There is no fundamental barrier to the subject's knowledge of the world because the subject participates in spirit's production of the world. When the subject attempts to understand what appears external to itself, it is engaged, even if unknowingly, in an act of self-understanding.

Even though this interpretation of Hegel is completely untenable today, we must nonetheless not abandon the possibility of an ontological Hegel. While Hegel does accept the Kantian critique of traditional metaphysics, he nonetheless finds a way to assert ontological claims: not bypassing the Kantian critique but going through it. This is what Žižek is getting at in *Less Than Nothing*, his groundbreaking volume devoted to laying out Hegel's relevance, when he says, "in Hegel, an epistemological obstacle becomes an ontological feature of the Thing itself (contradiction is not only an index of the imperfection of our knowledge, the limitation of our knowledge brings us in contact with the [limitation of the] Thing itself)."[6] Hegel is not just an epistemological or political thinker but a thinker who generates compelling ontological claims, claims that have nothing to do with the standard image of Hegel who champions reason guiding the development of history. Hegel is an ontological thinker who comes to his ontological claims through the exploration of the epistemological quandaries bequeathed to him by his immediate philosophical predecessors.

Kant's discovery of the antinomies of pure reason in which our thought contradicts itself in the attempt to answer the ultimate questions about existence leads Hegel to his fundamental ontological claim: it is not just thought that contradicts itself, but being itself is contradictory. For Hegel, nothing simply is. Everything is also what it is not and has its identity in what negates it. This is Hegel's great ontological insight, which he discovers through the problems of epistemology. If we don't acknowledge this ontological insight, we lose much of Hegel's contemporary relevance for a world that has rediscovered ontology. An ontological Hegel is a contemporary Hegel. But it is only today that Hegel's ontology and the political position that follows from it have become visible. We are now able to rediscover Hegel for the first time after a long obscurity.

This obscurity did not end with the abandonment of the view that Hegel sees the universe as the expression of the subject. The untenable status of this version of Hegel doomed his thought to a marginal position within the larger philosophical universe. In order to restore Hegel's influence, emergency surgery became necessary, and this surgery involved a radical amputation: to save Hegel as a viable philosopher in a universe dominated by neo-Kantianism and positivism, twentieth-century followers of Hegel had to remove the ontological claims of his thought. Hegel thus underwent a dramatic transformation in the early part of the twentieth century, from being a thinker immodestly announcing the structure of the universe to one humbly confining himself to the structure of subjectivity.

THE DANGERS OF AMPUTATION

Hegel has a vast influence on thought in the twentieth century, but this influence comes at a cost. His philosophy helps to produce the Marxism of György Lukács, the existentialism of Jean-Paul Sartre, the feminism of Simone de Beauvoir, the critical theory of the Frankfurt School, and the anticolonial theory of Frantz Fanon. But in each case the influence comes through an avoidance of any of Hegel's ontology. It is Hegel's insistence of subjectivity and its difference from the rest of being that influenced Lukács, Sartre, Beauvoir, the Frankfurt School, and Fanon. In order to make Hegel's philosophy significant for the twentieth century, it requires amputation. We can judge this amputation as successful because it does relegitimize his philosophy. If one took the ontological pretensions out of Hegel's philosophical body, one could both save the patient and enable him to prosper in unanticipated ways. He could become the ally of Heidegger and the friend of Marxism. This amputated and reformed Hegel finds its most profound expression in the thought of Alexandre Kojève.[7]

In his lectures on Hegel given in Paris during the 1930s, Kojève rescues Hegel from the naive ontological interpretation of his philosophy that dominated in the nineteenth century.[8] Kojève centers Hegel's philosophy on its thoroughgoing commitment to the fact of human reality as the sole province of thought and as the sole source for thought. Far from being an ontologist, Hegel shows us that thought never escapes the subject itself. It has nothing at all to say about the universe beyond the subject. As Kojève puts it, "Hegel rejects all species of 'revelation' in philosophy. Nothing can come from God: nothing can come from any extra-worldly non-temporal reality whatever. It is the temporal creative action of humanity or *History* that created the reality that Philosophy reveals."[9] For Kojève, Hegel has value for what he says about the struggle of the human being in the history that humanity itself creates and not for what he has to say about the nature of being. As a result, Kojève dismisses the entirety of the *Philosophy of Nature* as a fantasy that anyone who takes Hegel seriously must abandon as a worthless relic.[10] Confining Hegel to what he says about the situation of the finite subject enables Kojève to redeem Hegel as a viable thinker for the twentieth century. In Kojève's interpretation, Hegel's philosophical project comes to resemble that of the early Marx as well as that of Heidegger in *Being and Time*.[11]

Though Kojève's version of Hegel does not go unchallenged throughout the middle of the twentieth century, it does nonetheless shape the ways that thinkers both mobilize Hegel and fight against his influence. In the former case, it informs Maurice Merleau-Ponty's discussion of time in the *Phenomenology of Perception* and Jean-Paul Sartre's theorization of concrete relations with others in *Being and Nothingness*. In the latter case, it influences Georges Bataille's insistence on an excess that surpasses every system and Michel Foucault's critique of dialectics as an approach to history. Kojève's removal of any ontological claims from the Hegelian edifice has the effect of recreating Hegel as a force to be reckoned with in the philosophical universe. Those who simply dismiss Hegel as spouting nonsense have to stick to an image of him prevalent before Kojève's reinterpretation. Kojève shifts the terrain and transforms Hegel from a caricature into a philosophical titan against which subsequent philosophers have to define their thought—and most continental philosophers after Kojève do so.

Even the followers of Hegel in the later part of the twentieth century who explicitly reject Kojève's influence do not depart from his de-emphasis on Hegel's ontological claims. The movement away from Kojève's anthropological interpretation in the late twentieth century occurs through a resituating of Hegel within German Idealism. Robert Pippin in the United States, Béatrice Longuenesse in France, and Dieter Henrich in Germany lead the way in this effort. All three insist on Hegel's position within the Kantian critical heritage. As they clearly show, Hegel is no apostate.[12]

This new turn aims at minimizing the break between Kant and Hegel by viewing Hegel in terms of the Kantian tradition that prioritized epistemological questions. For Pippin and Longuenesse (though not for Henrich), Hegel is primarily an epistemologist, and that is why his philosophy retains its importance for us. He is simply pushing Kant's epistemological project further than Kant himself did but in no sense departing from it. Though

Kojève errs in moving Hegel in the direction of anthropology, he is not wrong to dismiss Hegel's ontology.

Pippin's justification for Hegel's continued importance depends on situating Hegel in the direct lineage of Kant and the transcendental break that brackets ontological questions in favor of epistemological ones. Hegel is not only not a pre-Critical philosopher, he is working on precisely the same philosophical question with which Kant struggles. Here, Pippin deserves great acclaim for putting the interpretation of Hegel back on its proper course. But his corrective overstates Hegel's proximity to Kant. According to Pippin, Hegel's breakthrough consists in going further than Kant by rejecting any recourse within thought to what lies outside thought. Though Pippin explicitly criticizes Kojève's interpretation of Kant in his *Hegel's Idealism*, he too takes the emphasis off ontology in Hegel's system and highlights Hegel's contribution to a revolution within epistemology.[13] Despite its insight, this approach unduly limits the purview of Hegel's philosophy.

For thinkers such as Pippin, Longuenesse, and Robert Brandom, Hegel's philosophical system indicates the constraints that exist on the possibilities for rational argumentation. The difference between Kant and Hegel is that Hegel extends our thinking about the constraints of language further than Kant.[14] Kant errs not by confining himself to the realm of possible experience but by failing to see how language involves us in an unavoidable dialectical process. But, in formulating his critique of Kant, Hegel's speculation never extends to the nature of reality or being.

The fact that important interpreters of Hegel in the late twentieth and early twenty-first century sustain the rejection of Hegel as an ontological thinker bespeaks the lingering shadow that the time of the naive ontological interpretation casts over this period. Hegel's ontology seems so much a caricature at this time that no one can hazard a reassertion of this crucial dimension of Hegel's thought. But the act of saving Hegel by amputating limbs ends up effectively killing the patient. The amputation is simply too extensive. It is as if Hegel goes in for surgery to have a toe removed and comes out missing both legs. Restoring his importance for contemporary thought requires taking up the question of his ontology, which is what Slavoj Žižek, Catherine Malabou, Adrian Johnston, and others have done.[15]

Rather than relying on empirical research into the natural world, Hegel approaches being through analysis of the structure of thought. His refusal of empirical data reaches its apex with the legendary claim that Hegel makes at his thesis defense when confronted with the existence of a possible eighth planet, Ceres—Neptune is not discovered until 1846, after Hegel's death—between Mars and Jupiter. According to the myth surrounding this event (which almost certainly did not occur), Hegel refuses to admit that Ceres might exist because it contradicts his theory of interplanetary distances. In the face of this discrepancy, he sides with his theory against empirical reality, supposedly claiming, "When the theory doesn't agree with the facts, so much the worse for the facts."[16] Despite the falsity of this legend, it continues to resonate because it accurately speaks to Hegel's attitude: he does care more for the theory than for the facts, in contrast to Kant, who tries to construct a theory that would fit the facts.[17] As Hegel sees it, facts without theory are not even facts. We would have no idea how to register them without the concept. In this sense, Hegel is much more a transcendental thinker than Kant, but he takes his transcendentalism so far that he finds himself on the terrain of ontology. Hegel's ontology is not naive but distinctly post-Critical and post-Kantian.

The return to Hegelian ontology does not require abandoning the Kantian critique but rather insisting on it more completely than Kant himself did. One comes to ontological insights, Hegel believes, not bypassing epistemological quandaries but going through them, recognizing that how we think must have its condition of possibility in what is. Epistemology has an ontological significance. On this basis, Hegel becomes a viable ontological thinker for today.

CARTESIAN SUBJECTS

Ironically, Hegel's ontology is located at exactly the same point where the naive ontological interpretation finds it. This is Hegel's statement in the preface of the *Phenomenology of Spirit* that "everything hangs on grasping and expressing the true not just as *Substance* but just as much as *Subject*. At the same time, it is to be noted that substantiality comprises within itself the universal, or it comprises not only the *immediacy of knowledge* itself but also the immediacy of *being*, or, immediacy *for* knowing."[18] This statement appears to ask us simply to rethink substance as the effect of the subject and thus to justify the naive ontological interpretation of Hegel. According to this interpretation, we should read the term *subject* as the name for the creative unfolding of spirit and *substance* as merely the receptacle for this unfolding. But this involves a basic misunderstanding of Hegel's use of the term *subject*.

From Descartes on, the concept of the subject has two distinct meanings. On the one hand, it is the act of thinking that doubts all its representations and has certainty only about its capacity for doubt. It is divided against itself, thereby distinct from the self-identity of substance. But on the other hand, *subject* names the entity at the center of the Cartesian world that has a secure knowledge of its clear and distinct ideas, ideas underwritten by a God who doesn't deceive.[19] The former subject is unable to know itself fully or attain self-identity. The latter acts like the master and possessor of the world it surveys. One of the chief reasons for the misreading of Hegel is an emphasis on this second conception of subjectivity at the expense of the first. But Hegel holds unfailingly to the first—to the subject as split from itself. When we examine Hegel's thought with this conception of subjectivity in mind, everything changes.

When Hegel asks us to consider substance as subject, his conception of subjectivity is not that of a subject that produces all that appears external to itself. Instead, Hegel uses the term *subject* as a contrast with substance. Whereas substance is self-identical, subject is inherently divided against itself.[20] By insisting that we view substance as subject, Hegel provides a radical rethinking of the category of substance. There is, for Hegel, no such thing as a substance that is a purely self-identical being. There is no being that is entirely independent and self-sustaining. We know this because our very act of speaking testifies to a contradiction both in ourselves and in what we are speaking about. Hegel's ontology begins with this rejection of pure substance and affirmation of the inherent self-division of being. Where the naive ontological interpretation of Hegel finds the megalomania of the subject, we should see an impoverishment of substance.

On the question of substance, Hegel takes one step further than Spinoza. Spinoza recognizes that there cannot be multiple substances because their very interaction would testify to their interdependence. Multiple substances would implicitly avow their insubstantiality or lack of independence. He concludes that there can only be one substance: it is only the whole that can be truly independent and not suffer from self-division. But Spinoza's philosophy fails to account for the inability of the whole to be perfectly self-identical while at the same time opening up the space for Spinoza himself to analyze its distinct modes. In order to arrive at *amor Dei intellectualis*, which overcomes the illusory divide between Spinoza and the substantiality of God, this divide must first exist. Even if the divide is the result of our misperception, there must be the space for this misperception itself. This is a space that Spinoza's philosophy of a self-identical substance does not allow for. In the act of articulating his system, Spinoza disproves it.

For Hegel, Spinoza's attempt to think a unique substance has profound implications. His inability to avoid subjectivizing this substance is a necessary failure. Spinoza's philosophy ends up showing the opposite of what he intends and thereby paves the way for Hegel's own ontological claims. Hegel takes Spinoza's self-contradiction as an affirmation of the subjectivity of all substances, even the whole itself. Whenever we think we can identify an independent and self-identical substance, a divided subject is lurking.

In the *Philosophy of Religion*, Hegel theorizes the division of substance that becomes apparent through the subject's own activity. The contradictory status of the natural world is evident, Hegel believes, even in our quotidian actions, like eating an apple. He states, "my eating an apple means that I destroy its organic self-identity and assimilate it to myself. That I can do this entails that the apple in itself (already in advance, before I take hold of it) has in its nature the character of being subject to destruction, and at the same time it is something that has in itself a homogeneity with my digestive organs such that I can make it homogeneous with myself."[21] The subject's ability to eat an apple and thereby tear apart its wholeness, to make it no longer an apple, indicates, for Hegel, that the apple cannot have the perfect self-identity of a substance. The apple must be vulnerable to being eaten. Its identity must involve contradiction. or else the subject couldn't eat it.

Substances themselves are already subjectivized. This is not to say that we might have a conversation with apples prior to eating them. They don't have the capacity for language, but their being attests to the same division that ultimately constitutes the speaking subject. That is, they must be able to be eaten, even if they don't necessarily desire it in the way a speaking subject might. Being is self-contradictory or divided in the way that necessarily prefigures and enables the subject's self-division. Being must be such that it was possible for the subject to emerge. The speaking subject can appear because being suffers from a failure to be self-identical. If being were one or whole, it could never provide the opening for the emergence of speech. One must examine the natural world retrospectively with the lens of its distortion through signification in order to see this. The speaking being renders the self-division of the natural world explicit for itself in a way that the natural world cannot, which is why Hegel privileges spirit above nature. An examination of the constraints on subjectivity—namely, the necessary self-division that renders speaking possible—illuminates substance itself. The structure of subjectivity has ontological implications.

The philosophical revolution that comes from reinterpreting the significance of "not only as *Substance,* but equally as *Subject*" is akin to that which occurs in the key moment of Francis Ford Coppola's *The Conversation* (1974). Electronic surveillance expert Harry Caul (Gene Hackman) records a conversation in a park between lovers Mark (Frederic Forrest) and Ann (Cindy Williams) in which Mark says, "He'd kill us if he got the chance." When Harry and the spectator first hear this line, the emphasis seems to be on the word *kill,* which suggests that the two lovers are in danger from Ann's husband, known in the film only as the Director (Robert Duvall). Harry spends much of the film's running time convinced the Director is a potential murderer. He assumes that he was working for the Director and is thus complicit with the planned murder, which triggers feelings of guilt.

After Harry clears all the static from the recording, however, the emphasis—and thus the significance—undergoes a radical shift to the word *he.* The shift in emphasis from the word *kill* to the word *he* indicates that it is not Mark and Ann who are in danger but rather the Director himself. Mark is not expressing fear but rather justifying their involvement in the Director's murder by saying that he would have killed them if they hadn't killed him. The transformation of the sentence "He'd kill us if he got the chance" completely transforms Harry and furthers his sense of guilt. When he makes this discovery, he realizes that he has completely misunderstood the situation and inadvertently assisted in a murder (though not in the way he had foreseen).

The consequences are equally grave for the misreading of Hegel's statement that the panlogical interpretation produces. We require the act of Harry Caul—clearing away the static so that a new reading of the statement becomes self-evident. This is the part that Žižek plays with his assertion of an ontological and yet thoroughly post-Critical Hegel. When we understand subject as Hegel's name for self-division rather than mastery, his statement ceases to be the emblem of his philosophical arrogance and becomes his great ontological insight.

The redemption of Hegel as an ontological thinker does not require a return to the naivete that sustained the panlogical interpretation. Hegel's ontological claims are not the result of a rejection of the Kantian critique and a return to what Kant calls dogmatic metaphysics. Instead, Hegel radicalizes Kant's epistemology and through this process discovers an ontological claim inhering within it. The point is not that the constraints on our knowledge must imply similar constraints on being, which is what a cursory reading of Hegel's critique of Kant would suggest. This reading would entail a retreat to pre-Kantian metaphysics, in which the philosopher attains direct insight into the nature of being through reason. Instead, Hegel's claim is that the contradictions within our knowledge must be ontologically possible—there must be some disruption within the realm of being that gives rise to the disruption in language—which suggests that being itself cannot be self-identical.

In the face of this ontological claim, it seems commonsensical to retort that what we find true of subjectivity has no necessary connection to the natural world. The emergence of subjectivity changes the deal entirely, leaving us with an absolute chasm between it and nature. We should, according to this line of thought, confine ourselves to the realm of subjectivity and leave questions about the natural world to scientists better equipped to address them. Despite the appeal of this apparently modest proposal, like all attempts to limit the province of knowledge, it is far more grandiose than it lets on. Its absence of any ontological claim implies that we can know precisely what it insists that we cannot know.

The status of being as not self-identical is the basis of Hegel's ontology, but it is not a premise or a presupposition. Hegel founds his philosophy on the absence of any foundation, on the rejection of every philosophical premise or first principle. This is why he attacks Fichte's philosophy so viciously: Fichte begins with subjectivity itself as his starting point, and he offers no ground for the assumption of the subject. We cannot assume anything, not even the original act of the subject positing itself, as Fichte does. The case is altogether different with Hegel's ontology of the self-division of being.

We know that being is not self-identical because of our existence as alienated speaking beings. The speaking being's division from itself—its inability to realize its desires or achieve wholeness—must have a condition of possibility within being itself. Thus, we can work our way backward from the self-division of the subject to the self-division of being. Our ability to pose the question of our subjectivity testifies to the subject's noncoincidence with itself, and this noncoincidence appears to separate speaking beings from rocks. This leads Kojève to confine Hegel's philosophical purview to the speaking subject and its history. But there is a clear error in positing this artificial limit to Hegel's reach. Even beings that cannot demonstrate their self-division through speech nonetheless participate in an ontological self-division. We know about this ontological self-division because of beings who exhibit it explicitly.

RECONCILED WITH KANT

Kant correctly discovers a gap in subjectivity separating appearances that we can know from things in themselves that we can't. But one must not denigrate appearances as a pale copy of the actually existing external world. For Kant, truth is on the side of the appearances.[22] We can consider things as appearances or as things in themselves, and it is only when we consider them as appearances that we avoid the contradictions that befall the project of knowledge when it concerns itself with things in themselves. The domain of appearances is a limited domain. This enables it to remain free of the contradictions that knowledge encounters when it tries to conceive of a totality. As Kant sees it, any ontological claims depart from the limited domain of appearances, which triggers the fall into contradiction.

Kant's error, for Hegel, does not lie in confining his inquiry to knowledge but in failing to see that the contradictions our knowing encounters when it tries to think the absolute must have their basis in the nature of being. According to Kant's antinomies of reason, the world neither has a beginning in space and time nor doesn't; there are neither simple substances nor is everything infinitely divisible; we are both free and determined; there is a necessary being or God, and there isn't. These contradictions occur when we transcend the realm of appearances, which is why Kant is chary about doing so.

But, for Hegel, if thought necessarily contradicts itself, even when it is not erring logically, this indicts not just the realm of thought but also that of being. Thought's necessary contradictions point back to a world out of which thought emerges. In the *Science of Logic*, Hegel makes this clear. Discussing Kant's solution to the problem of the antinomies, he writes, "It is excessive tenderness for the world to keep contradiction away from it, to transfer it to spirit instead, to reason and to leave it there unresolved. In fact, it is spirit that is strong enough that it can endure contradiction." Then he adds, crucially, that what we call the objective world itself cannot escape contradiction. It is worse off than spirit because "it is not capable of enduring it and for that reason it is abandoned to coming and ceasing to be."[23] The antinomies mark a point at which thought reaches outside itself and reveals a fundamental truth about the nature of being. The existence of necessary or irreducible contradictions in thought, contradictions that are not simply the result of ignorance, must have their condition of possibility in being, or else they could never arise.

An irreducible contradiction is not like the many contradictions that we discover throughout Hegel's philosophy. In the opening section of the *Science of Logic*, for instance, Hegel sees the contradiction in the attempt to determine an entity as something. The quality that defines a something derives from the border that separates this something from the rest of being. As a result, the finite something depends on what marks its end, and it is itself only through its disappearance (which is why it is finite). For Hegel, this is why we cannot approach the world as a collection of discrete somethings. This position is contradictory and leads Hegel to a being for itself that posits its own negation in the other. Though the way out of the contradiction causes another contradictory position to emerge, there is nonetheless a way out, which distinguishes the contradiction of quality from that of the beginning of the world.

The contradiction that thought encounters when it tries to solve the problem of the beginning of the world in time and space is an ontological contradiction, not an epistemological failure. At first blush, the transformation of an epistemological contradiction into an ontological one seems unwarranted. It is why so many subsequent philosophers disagree about taking Hegel seriously while agreeing about Kant's significance. Though he makes an ontological claim, Hegel has no special access to the beginning of the world, no more than Kant does, who contents himself with an epistemological claim. But Hegel does recognize that our inability to cognize the beginning must itself be possible. The impossibility of thinking a beginning without contradiction must have its condition of possibility within being itself. If it weren't possible, obviously, we couldn't even think it. The epistemological deadlock has an ontological origin.

As a result, being must be organized in such a way that it allows for the emergence of this impossibility within thought. The discovery of an irreducible contradiction is not, for Hegel, simply a negative discovery. The negative epistemological discovery is at once a positive ontological one. We know that being cannot involve a pure beginning, just as we know that being cannot be purely continuous.

If there were a pure beginning to being, thought would be unable to pose the problem of the beginning or any question at all. A pure beginning would not have its own negation within it, and thus what would follow from it would be a constant iteration of itself. The very purity of the pure beginning would preclude it from beginning anything different. Difference depends on impurity—or what Hegel calls negation. In this sense, positing a pure beginning to being leads to exactly the same result as positing being as continuous. Though Hegel never spells this out explicitly, it is the clear implication of his position.

If being were purely continuous, if it existed without any breaks, we would never be able to think discreteness and difference, which result from ruptures within being. The idea of discreteness cannot be a mere idea. Though it is obviously possible for the subject to fantasize objects or events that don't exist in reality (like unicorns or reality television stars becoming president), the subject cannot think what being does not make it possible for the subject to think. Fantasy bears the mark of an ontological constraint, and this constraint bespeaks an implicit ontology.

Revelatory contradictions appear only when we push thought to its end point, when we go to the absolute, which is why Hegel finds so much of value in the Kantian antinomies. Attempts to address the ultimate questions of existence lay bare the point at which contradiction ceases to be an error of thought—like the square circle—and becomes a necessity. This is also why Hegel insists on attaining the absolute in his own thought. Only at such moments do we encounter the inevitability of contradiction that permits us to draw out the ontological implications of the epistemological deadlock. We know that this deadlock must be ontologically possible and thus that being must be fundamentally at odds with itself.

Hegel is not so naive as to believe that thought and being are directly identical, but he also grasps that thought could not become contradictory if being itself were not also capable of contradiction. Self-identical being would never open up the space in which one could think about it at all, because it would entail no gaps. If contradiction is necessary in thought, then being must be structured in a way that gives rise to it. Kant's limited speculation—his decision to limit speculation to the subject—results in a system that cannot explain the emergence of the subject on which it speculates. Only an objective idealism or a speculation on the object could hope to transcend this limitation.

Hegel contends that contradiction in being is even more intractable than contradiction in thought. Most philosophers view thought as inferior to being: thought, which has less or no reality, aspires to the status of being, which has concrete reality. But Hegel reverses this relationship. Though being has a chronological priority—obviously being is a necessary condition for the emergence of thought—thought has a logical priority because it has a capacity for enduring and reconciling itself with contradiction that being lacks. Being simply succumbs to contradiction without gaining any purchase on it, whereas thought has the ability to reconcile itself to contradiction.

Reconciliation (*Versöhnung*) is the great achievement of thought. Through the act of reconciliation, thought adopts a relationship to contradiction that being cannot attain. It doesn't overcome contradiction but grasps its necessity. Even though contradiction acts as a limit or obstacle to thought, thought nonetheless has the ability to grasp this limit as what defines it rather than as what it must surmount in order to realize itself. Spirit is, for Hegel, thought's capacity to recognize contradiction not simply as an obstacle to overcome but as is own innermost condition of possibility. Reconciliation embraces the necessity of contradiction.[24]

Chapter Five

LOVE AND LOGIC

CONCEIVED IN THE BREAK

When does Hegel become Hegel? From the publication of his first book, *The Difference Between Fichte's and Schelling's System of Philosophy,* in 1801 to his final lectures in 1831 on logic, Hegel displays a remarkable philosophical consistency. Though some Marxists contrast the radicality of the early *Phenomenology of Spirit* (1807) with the conformism of the late *Philosophy of Right* (1821), the two texts exhibit an almost complete continuity.[1] Throughout his philosophical career, Hegel sticks with the dialectical system he develops early on, which always concludes with some form of the absolute (absolute knowledge, the absolute idea, the absolute work of art, and so on). To locate the origins of this system, we must look prior to Hegel's published books and examine his earliest writings. The break that defines Hegel as a thinker occurs during the late 1790s prior to the publication of his first book. This break defines him as a thinker by separating him from Immanuel Kant.

Hegel begins his intellectual life, like many from his generation, as a Kantian. Kant's conception of freedom through the moral law shapes the young Hegel. But Hegel emerges as Hegel at the moment when love enters his philosophy. Though Hegel is a thinker that we associate with an absolute commitment to logic rather than with love, it is love that enables Hegel to break from the spell of Immanuel Kant and to begin to forge his own philosophy, in which logic would predominate. Hegel's logic is not the logic of Aristotle or the rationalist tradition; his logic develops out of love. When logic comes to assume the role that love plays in Hegel's early thought, it retains the same structure that Hegel sees at work in love.[2] Hegel is the first modern secular philosopher to make love the point of departure for his entire philosophical project.[3]

Love fascinates the young Hegel because it represents the identification of contraries and the sustaining of contradiction as a positive force. When one is in love, one unites one's own identity with that of the other. The lover and the beloved become one in their way of finding satisfaction. Lovers do not just privilege the other's satisfaction over their own but adopt the other's satisfaction as their own. And yet love would not be love if a distinction between subject and beloved other did not remain. The act of love requires at once the elimination of difference and its perpetuation. It is the identity of identity and difference, a contradictory identity that enables Hegel to navigate a way out of the one-sidedness of Kant's and Fichte's philosophy that he inherits.

In the act of love, the lover allows the beloved to have more value than the lover herself or himself while, at the same time, the lover remains the source of this valuing. The value of the other outweighs that of the subject but only because the subject grants the other this value. Through the subject's own act, the subject affirms its own secondary status. Love thus enables the subject to translate difference—the difference between the lover and the beloved—into contradiction.[4] As his thought matures, Hegel identifies this structure of identity in difference as the basic form not only of all thought but of being itself. The first insight into this structure comes to him in the formulation of Christian love. Love provides the avenue for granting contradiction a privileged ontological position.

After it appears in Hegel's early writing, love never vanishes from Hegel's thought. That said, love plays a role in the beginning of his philosophy that it would not play in the fully developed system. Though references to love abound in the system, love takes up a position within the system rather than remaining the animating principle of the system. For instance, in his later writing on politics and right, Hegel identifies love as the bond that unites the family, which is the beginning of ethical life.[5] Here, love is essential for the establishment of an ethical order. But the concept (*Begriff*) has taken over the central place in Hegel's system. As it has done so, the concept has assumed the structure of love. This becomes clear in Hegel's account of the universal concept in the *Science of Logic*. He states that the universal concept "is itself while reaching out to its other and embracing it, but without *doing violence* to it." As a result, it is "*free love* and *boundless blessedness*."[6] The concept in Hegel's thought is not cold calculation but free love. It belongs on a commune in the 1960s rather than in a typical philosophy classroom. Hegel discovers his version of the concept through exploration of love, even though he never articulates this relationship between love and the concept or announces the turn from one to the other.

In Hegel's thought, the concept does not exist in isolation but relies on a negation that undermines it while simultaneously sustaining it. In order to be what it is, the concept must involve itself in what it isn't, which parallels the structure of love. If we try to keep a concept pure from its negation, we lose the concept itself, just as trying to have love without the other deprives us of love. The concept without its negation becomes nonsensical, which is why the concept of nature, for example, must include the unnatural. When we try to define nature as a concept, not only do we have to have recourse to the unnatural in order to define it but we inevitably demonstrate that there is a point at which the distinction between the natural and the unnatural breaks down.

If we look at the case of cloning, this becomes clear. Cloning represents a human intervention into the cycle of natural reproduction. The natural world itself reproduces through asexual or sexual reproduction, not through cloning. And yet humans developed the process of cloning through their investigation and mimicking of natural reproduction. The break from nature that occurs with cloning also exhibits characteristics of a natural phenomenon. Cloning is both natural and unnatural, which reveals that nature is not simply identical to itself but involves what negates it. This in no way means that the concept of nature has no sense or that we must abandon it. Instead, we must think of every concept as a certain form of contradiction on the model of love.

Throughout the *Science of Logic*, Hegel describes the concept in these terms. What Kant dismisses as an antinomy of reason, Hegel takes as the definition of the concept. Contradiction doesn't undermine the concept but rather animates it. Along these lines, Hegel claims, "if a contradiction can be pointed out in something, by itself this is still not, as it were, a blemish, not a defect or failure. On the contrary, every determination, anything concrete, every concept, is essentially a unity of distinguished and distinguishable elements which, by virtue of the *determinate, essential difference*, pass over into elements which are contradictory."[7] The concept becomes the enactment of contradiction. This conception of the concept gives Hegel his radicality as a thinker, which stems directly from the concept's origin in Hegel's discovery of love.

Hegel contrasts conceptual thinking with analytical thinking. Unlike the former, the latter does not share the structure of love. Conceptual thinking reveals the relationship of identity that exists within what appear to be simply external differences. It never remains content with difference that doesn't involve relation. To put it another way: conceptual thinking grasps the internal contradiction lurking within external difference. As a result, it makes evident the mutual dependence of every entity. External differences hide internal contradictions because nothing can be thought or even can exist in isolation. For analytical thinking, the case is entirely different. Differences are simply external and have nothing to do with each other. One can treat each entity as independently existing and analyze its interactions with other entities as entirely contingent relations. According to analytical thinking, every apparent contradiction masks the play of pure difference.

The model for analytical thinking comes from arithmetic. Hegel calls arithmetic "the very opposite of the concept" because of the way that it deals with difference, "because of the indifference of the combined to the combining."[8] One adds $5 + 7$, but there is no internal connection that occurs in the act of addition. The number 5 has no necessary relation with the number 7. One could substitute a different number for 7 without changing the operation. The operation is not conceptual, as Hegel sees it, insofar as it holds the entities in an external relationship with each other. This type of thinking blinds the subject to the inability of identity to exist without difference and the inability of the concept to exist without contradiction. When taken as the only model for thought, analytical thinking misleads because it does not take the structure of love as its starting point. The idea is not that we should avoid working math problems but that we cannot take arithmetic as paradigmatic.

The contrast between arithmetic and love is instructive. Arithmetic allows for the free substitution of one number for another, while love insists that no possible substitute for the beloved exists. The moment anyone suggests the adequacy of a substitute, we know that this person is not in love. Similarly, love rejects counting. Those who add up the number of partners that they have had are not talking about love. When we start doing arithmetic, we stop loving. Mathematicians may be great lovers, but they aren't great lovers as mathematicians.[9]

Like love, conceptual thinking refuses a merely external relation between identity and difference. To put it in the language of love, conceptual thinking in Hegel's sense refuses to use the other but rather identifies itself with the other insofar as the other remains recalcitrantly different. In this sense, every act of love is a failure to integrate the difference of the other into the identity of the subject, while every conceptualization is a failure to integrate the difference of the other into the concept. This failure defines love and the concept. Love and the concept are the names for the way that otherness disturbs identity. Hegel is the first to see that the failure of the concept to integrate difference is actually its success, that there is no success beyond this contradictory identity. He arrives at this insight as a result of seeing love, rather than mathematics, as the model for the concept. There is no identity outside this disturbance, no pure identity. Each love relation and each concept fails in a specific way that gives it its identity.

Neither love nor the concept promises a mystical connection to the other. The unity they provide does not erase the contradictory status of the relationship. The other's difference remains difference that disturbs both love and the concept. This disturbance is crucial to Hegel's understanding of love and the concept, and it gives both their revolutionary status. Everyone knows the dangers of falling in love. Not only can one endure trauma when the other abandons the relationship, but even a successful love relationship leaves the subject's satisfaction in the hands of the other.

Though no conceptual thinker has suffered a lifetime of anguish after being spurned by an object, the structure of the risk in love and the concept is actually the same. Rather than marking a point of thought's mastery over being, the concept is the moment at which thought faces the test of being. Concepts, for Hegel, are not just thoughts. Concepts of pure thought would be akin to a imagined love affair and equally unsatisfying. Just as the lover must work up the courage to talk to the beloved, the concept must prove itself in being. The drama of the concept's actualization is integral to the functioning of the concept. In order to be a genuine concept, the concept must be actual.

FROM CRITIQUE TO EMBRACE

Hegel never directly links love and the concept but moves from one to the other as the animating principle of his philosophy. One can locate the moment when love enters into Hegel's thinking through the contrast between two early works. Only a few years separate "The Positivity of the Christian Religion" (1795–1796) and "The Spirit of Christianity and Its Fate" (1798–1800). Yet the divide between the two unpublished works is greater than the divide between any other works that Hegel wrote. In the first text, Hegel presents himself as an unabashed disciple of Kant who insists on the moral law as the foundation for all religions. At this point in his philosophical development, the only difference between religions concerns their particular ways of articulating the moral law. In the second, Christianity becomes a revolutionary religion due to its substitution of love for the law.

The first essay, "The Positivity of the Christian Religion," argues that the truth of religion has nothing to do with the doctrines or practices that a particular religion advances. What counts is the moral law. At this point, Hegel is a completely ecumenical thinker. As he puts it, "the aim and essence of all true religion, our religion included, is human morality."[10] He is careful to link Christianity horizontally with other religions, not singling it out for special approbation or censure.

Just as every religion has the promulgation of morality as its aim, each also betrays the freedom that the moral law inaugurates by turning from morality to positivity. A positive religion establishes doctrines through authoritative decrees and encourages belief in miracles, dogmas, and religious figures rather than facilitating the creation of subjects committed to their free moral being. In the positivity essay, Hegel contends that positivity—in the form of a morass of arcane rules—overtakes Judaism during Christ's epoch. As Hegel sees it, Christ emerges as a response to this stifling positivity. Christ did not intend to start a new religion but to free the existing one from its retreat from the moral law into a legalistic morass of rules. In the context of the first essay, Christ is simply a Jewish reformer rather than the herald of an entirely new religion. Christianity introduces no new distinctive principle.

Though he chronicles Christ's critique of Judaism, Hegel's primary target in the positivity essay is not Judaism but Christianity itself. While it begins as a critique of Jewish positivity, Christianity itself falls into the same trap with its fetishization of ritual, its partitioning of the Kingdom of God into the afterlife, and its ecclesiastical usurpation of civil authority. The positivity essay is a thoroughgoing critique of what Christianity becomes. It betrays the revolutionary possibility of its origin, a situation that requires another revolutionary upheaval to rectify.[11]

Christianity begins with an assertion of freedom through a return to morality. But it ends up propagating unfreedom, as if the driving idea behind it were that the sacrifice of freedom offers the keys to the kingdom. Hegel writes, "The church has taught men to despise civil and political freedom as dung in comparison with heavenly blessings and the enjoyment of eternal life. Just as lack of the means to satisfy physical needs robs us, as animals, of life, so too, if we are robbed of the power to enjoy freedom of mind, our reason dies, and once we are in that position we no more feel the lack of it or a longing for it than the dead body longs for food and drink."[12] The Christian church becomes the enemy of freedom and true religion when it places its emphasis on eternal life rather than morality, which is the terrain of the subject's freedom.

At this point in his intellectual history, Hegel remains nominally devoted to Christianity, but he is not at all a genuine partisan. He takes the side of Kantian morality even further than Kant himself did—to a position where religion is nothing but a vehicle for the development of our freedom through morality. Christianity has no specific appeal that renders it superior or even different from other religions. This is the most ecumenical moment in Hegel's entire philosophical trajectory, but it is also a moment before he became Hegel.

Though Hegel is at his most open to other religions at this point, he is also at his most elitist. He believes that the task of the philosopher is one of bringing enlightenment down to the unenlightened people intent on remaining ensconced in the ignorance perpetuated by their religion. Hegel's critique of Christianity is also a critique of hoi polloi. Christianity serves to manipulate the masses, who in turn slavishly allow themselves to be manipulated. The acquiescence of the people to the pieties of religion stems directly from what Hegel calls (in a letter to Schelling) their fear of illumination.[13] All religions are equal in their manipulation of their people, but the people share in this culpability for their readiness to be manipulated.

This entire diagnosis undergoes a revolutionary change in a very short period of time. By the time that Hegel moved from Bern to Frankfurt in

1797, his attitude toward religion and to the people transformed.[14] This transformation coincides with Hegel's discovery of love, which begins to have a privileged position in his writings. As morality cedes its place to love in Hegel's philosophical universe, everything changes.

Between the two early essays, "The Positivity of the Christian Religion" and "The Spirit of Christianity," Hegel writes several short texts soon after his move to Frankfurt. The texts are not published in Hegel's lifetime and survive only in a rough and sometimes fragmentary form. In these brief essays, we can see the first evidence of Hegel's turn to love.[15] The most famous of the essays is a fragment known simply as "Love," in which Hegel describes the relationship of the two beings in love. Love, for Hegel in this fragment, has the effect of uniting while not eliminating what initially exists as separate. The result is separateness without separation.

The more significant texts, "Religion, Founding a Religion" and "Love and Religion," link love to religion. Here, Hegel formulates very clearly his changed attitude toward Christianity. Instead of facilitating our morality, he states, "Religion is one with love."[16] In these short essays, Hegel discovers the philosophical importance of love, which overcomes the one-sided subjectivity of Kantian morality and the objectivity of Spinoza's system. He had sought a magic bullet to reconcile the subjective philosophies of Kant and Fichte with the objective ones of Spinoza and Schelling, a way of conceiving subject and object interacting without presupposing their perfect alignment. Love provides the solution.

Love for Hegel has nothing to do with narcissistic self-affirmation through the other. It is rather a profound disturbance for the subject's identity. Hegel's definition of love has a radicality that he would sustain in his love-inspired definition of the concept. He writes, "Love can only occur against the same, against the mirror, against the echo of our essence."[17] When the subject loves, it doesn't just seize the other but encounters the other as a disturbance of the self. In this way, love defies the mirror relation to which critics would want to confine it.

The turn to love inaugurates a complete revaluation of Christianity that coincides with a decision to give up the position of trying to enlighten the duped masses. In a letter to Nanette Endel in early 1797, Hegel proclaims, "upon mature reflection I have decided not to try to improve anything in these people, but on the contrary to howl with the wolves."[18] Though this sounds like a cynical retreat following a failure to change the world, the statement actually results from the decisive philosophical transformation in Hegel's life that serves as the engine for all of his later political insights. At the moment he seems to give up, he makes his most important advance.

We must look at the letter to Nanette Endel through the lens of the writings on love from 1797 and 1798. Hegel comes to see that Christianity, as the religion of love, already signals a move beyond the limitations of religion centered around the moral law. Thus, there is no longer any need for the philosopher to bestow the light of morality on the Christian masses. Acceptance of Christian love is actually an advance on the enlightenment that Kantian morality offers. Christian love has a dialectical connection with otherness that the religion of morality lacks. The philosopher need only reveal the structure of love already in place, not teach the people the moral law. Hegel can "howl with the wolves" because the wolves are simultaneously Christian lambs.

It is significant that Hegel's interlocutor at this moment is Nanette Endel, who is one of the leading candidates for being Hegel's first lover. If she was indeed Hegel's first lover, we might hazard the wild hypothesis that his philosophical turn from morality to love made the affair with her possible. As long as Hegel remained Kantian, he might have remained trapped within Kant's own insistence on chastity. Perhaps the embrace of the religion of love made the act of love imaginable for Hegel.[19]

The shift in attitude toward Christianity manifests itself in "The Spirit of Christianity and Its Fate." For someone who has read "The Positivity of the Christian Religion," which dates just a few years earlier, it is difficult to believe that the same thinker wrote both works. Though he continues to assess the philosophical significance of the religion, the critique transforms into appreciation. The interpretation seeks to uncover Christianity's insights into our relations rather than lambasting it for obscuring the moral law with positivity.

The aspects of Christianity that the earlier essay had singled out for disparagement become indications of its theoretical acumen. The focus on the person of Christ, which was a sign of Christian positivity just a couple of years earlier, is now central to the message of love. Furthermore, Hegel celebrates not just the Crucifixion as an act of love but even proclaims the necessity of the Resurrection. In a remarkable passage from "The Spirit of Christianity," he writes, "in the risen Jesus, lifted up heavenward, the image found life again, and love found the objectification of its oneness. In this remarriage of spirit and body the opposition between the living and the dead Jesus has vanished, and the two are united in a God. Love's longing has found itself as a living being and can now enjoy itself."[20] The doctrine of the Resurrection is no longer evidence of Christianity's turn away from the truth of morality to the mystification of positivity. In this passage, Hegel contends that Christ must rise from the dead so that Christian love will not fall into the infinite longing that befuddles Kantian morality. The risen Christ and the emergence of the Holy Spirit bonding the community together represent the actualization of love. In this community, the subject is at home in absolute otherness, an achievement only possible thanks to the Christian event.

Hegel not only esteems Christian love for its philosophical insight into the identity of identity and difference. He goes so far as to credit Christianity with accomplishing what philosophy cannot. Caught up in propositional logic, philosophy cannot see its way to engage the necessity of contradiction in the way that Christian love can. Hegel no longer wants to teach the unenlightened Christians about the true religion of morality because he now believes that their religion achieves more than Kant's philosophy.

RUPTURE FROM JUDAISM

Hegel was never an anti-Semite. Even when his invective against Jewish legalism reaches its most extreme point, the critique is always doctrinal. Unlike many prominent thinkers of his time, his support for Jewish civil rights within the modern state remains unconditional throughout his life. He never shares the dream of excluding Jews, which is undoubtedly why neither Hitler nor Alfred Rosenberg nor any other Nazi theorist found Hegel's philosophy hospitable territory. That said, it is clear that his attitude toward Judaism undergoes a dramatic change between writing "The Positivity of the Christian Religion" and "The Spirit of Christianity." This change occurs when Hegel discovers the revolutionary status of Christianity and adopts its principle of love for his own philosophical project. Hegel's increased hostility to Judaism is the sign of Hegel becoming himself. The point is not that a critique of Judaism is a necessary condition for the Hegelian system but that Hegel's philosophy has an inextricable tie to the Christian revolution that manifests itself in a critique of Judaism.

The fact that Hegel becomes much more hostile to Judaism in the later essay suggests that Terry Pinkard cannot be right when he attributes Hegel's critique of Judaism to his debt to Kant. It is rather the break from Kant that occasions the increased invective. In his biography of Hegel, Pinkard argues that Hegel's "clearly negative attitude toward Judaism at this period in his development—an attitude that changed dramatically in his later life—was clearly linked to Kant's own discussions of Judaism in his religious writings."[21] The problem with this conclusion is that it leaves unexplained the difference in the attitude evinced toward Judaism between the two early essays on Christianity. It is Hegel's turn away from Kant that leads him away from Judaism and its commitment to the law. Kant's own hostility to Judaism has nothing to do with Hegel's.

In the earlier essay, Hegel views Judaism as a religion that goes awry at the time of Christ and that consequently needs Christ's corrective. Here, Christ's intervention occurs strictly within Judaism itself. It does not confront Judaism with a new principle foreign to its essence but merely pushes it back toward its origin in morality that has now become obscured. Hegel notes that "Jesus recalled to the memory of his people the moral principles in their sacred books."[22] The project of Christ, as Hegel conceives it here, is to return Judaism from its misstep into legalistic positivity with a reassertion of the moral law as the foundation of the religion. The primary object of the essay is not the critique of Judaism but an attack on Christianity for precisely the same transgression.

At this point, Christianity has become worse than Judaism on the path toward positivity. The positivity essay judges Christianity more harshly than it does Judaism. Whereas Judaism confines its dogmatic imperatives to outward rituals, Christianity demands that believers have the proper feelings as well. Judaism concerns itself only with actions, not with feelings. As a result, according to Hegel, Judaism at least allows its adherents some inner freedom beyond the province of its injunctions. Christianity intrudes even on this domain. When it comes to the betrayal of the freedom that derives from the moral law (and that religion should facilitate), both religions come up short, but Christianity infringes on the subject's freedom in a way that no prior religion does.

One cannot find what Yirmiyahu Yovel colorfully calls "his venomous youthful bias" against Judaism in the positivity essay, which is Hegel's earliest significant work.[23] Ironically, what might pass for venom comes only with Hegel's turn to love, which is simultaneously an embrace of Christianity as a revolutionary break from Judaism. This suggests that Hegel's critique of Judaism is not a bias at all but a theoretical move. Though Hegel remains far removed from anti-Semitism, he clearly changes his tune about Judaism in "The Spirit of Christianity," the second of the early essays. This essay no longer lumps Judaism and Christianity in the same basket. Though modern Christianity remains beset by problems of positivity, the religion as such nonetheless occasions a fundamental rupture in human history.

Christ is no longer fine-tuning Judaism. Instead, he breaks with all religion of the law and introduces a religion of love. In the earlier positivity essay, love plays no part at all in Hegel's analysis of Christianity. The word *love* never appears. The sole value of religion in this essay derives from its connection to the moral law. But in "The Spirit of Christianity" love gives Christianity its worth, and love creates a clear contrast with Judaism.

Whereas in the earlier essay Judaism's foundation in the law signaled its forgotten link to freedom, now the law indicates the undoing of the free subject within Judaism. Judaism becomes the religion of obedience that Hegel juxtaposes with Christianity, which is the only religion of freedom. In "The Spirit of Christianity," he writes, "In contrast with Jewish reversion to obedience, reconciliation in love is a liberation."[24] Though the law uproots the subject from its natural determinations and endows it with a subjective freedom, this freedom remains always opposed to objectivity. Only the religion of love leads to freedom that isn't determined negatively by the objectivity that it opposes. Love does not require the external other that the moral law does.

Hegel sustains the association of Judaism with Kant's moral law that he develops in the positivity essay. But he divorces Christianity from this law. Judaism is still Kantian, which is why Hegel becomes more critical of it. Christianity ceases to be one religion among many and becomes the religion that completely refigures the subject's relationship to the other. To the extent that this requires a more pejorative account of Judaism, we might lament it. But, on the other hand, it is the embrace of Christianity as the religion of love that enables Hegel to find a way beyond duty and beyond Kant.

THE LIMITATIONS OF DUTY

The discovery of Kantian morality is an epochal moment for Hegel, as it is for Fichte before him. The moral law is not just part of the Kantian system but the key to its radical break from the past, far outstripping the theoretical formulation of a priori synthetic judgments or inherent limitations on our use of reason that Kant lays out in the *Critique of Pure Reason*. Kant's formulation of the moral law in the *Critique of Practical Reason* represents the revolutionary breakthrough for Hegel. When Kant deduces "can" from "must," he shows that the bare existence of the moral law—in whatever form we articulate it—testifies to our freedom. Up to this point, the freedom of the subject was just an assumption. All of a sudden it becomes a proven fact of reason.[25] Our ability to formulate the moral law proves that we are free.[26] The young Hegel finds Kant's link between the law and freedom appealing, but ultimately he recognizes how Kant's understanding requires the subject to presuppose the foreignness of the external world and the impossibility of ever fully doing one's duty.

Kant grants the subject freedom, but on condition that the subject never actualize this freedom in the external world. In order to do this, Kant must play fast and loose with the status of externality. The subject occupies itself with the moral law without regard for the external world. The subject cannot calculate the impact that doing its duty will have on the world without betraying its duty in the name of what Kant calls pathological concerns. If I worry that my truth telling to the National Security Agency might put my innocent neighbor in danger, I abandon the ground of morality for that of calculation. Such external factors cannot factor in moral deliberations.[27]

But, on the other hand, Kantian morality presupposes a certain vision of the external world, even though this world is not supposed to enter into morality. Kant assumes that the world is itself not already morally structured but instead completely indifferent to the moral law. What if, rather than acting as an indifferent (or even resistant) field for my moral acts, the structure of the world facilitated my morality? What if the laws of my country made it possible for me to tell the truth about my neighbor's religious beliefs without any negative ramifications? Kant's theory has no place for this reconciliation between the moral subject and the external world, the possibility that the world is not external to my morality but internal to it. The theory depends on a specific image of the external world as completely indifferent to the subject's morality. And yet the moral law is supposed to be indifferent to the external world, to operate without presuppositions about it. Kant relies on a presupposition of externality that he must disavow, leading him to fail to see the role that externality or otherness plays in the accomplishment of morality. Recognition of this blind spot soon leads Hegel to break from Kant.

Hegel moves from a Kantian conception of duty to a Christian conception of love. Though he continues to appreciate the inroads on freedom made possible by Kantian morality, the limits of this conception of freedom become impossible to ignore. It is only love, for Hegel, that points beyond the strictures of the moral law. Love enacts the subject's reconciliation with the other. Through love, the world ceases to be an externality on which the subject acts.

For the loving subject, objectivity no longer confronts the subject as an opacity that the subject can never penetrate, as it does for Kant. Instead, love identifies with the most obscure objectivity and reconciles the subject with it. According to Hegel, "Only through love is the might of objectivity broken, for love upsets its whole sphere. The virtues, because of their limits, always put something objective above them, and the variety of virtues an all the greater and insurmountable multiplicity of objectivity. Love alone has no limits."[28] Love has no limits because, in contrast to duty, it has the ability to identify with the difference of the other without eliminating that difference.

In other words, love enacts and sustains contradiction. The contradiction of love is the identity of identity and difference, a contradiction that animates love rather than destroying it. In the case of duty, the situation is reversed. The opposition between duty and the external world becomes a contradiction that leaves duty always unaccomplished. The contradiction of duty renders duty, for Hegel, a position that constantly undermines itself since it cannot integrate this contradiction into its structure. Love is able to succeed at exactly the point where duty fails. Love's success consists in its ability to endure contradiction and even to find its essence in it.

We can see a revelatory example of contradiction animating love in Michael Curtiz's classic love story *Casablanca* (1942). The film depicts Ilsa (Ingrid Bergman) coming into the café owned by Rick (Humphrey Bogart) in search of means to escape for her and her husband Victor (Paul Henreid) from Vichy-controlled Morocco to the United States. The Nazis are pursuing Victor for his activities as an outspoken opponent of fascism and freedom fighter. Prior to the arrival of Ilsa, Rick has a comfortable existence with a stable income, casual sexual affairs, and pleasant interactions with the local authorities. His life runs smoothly, but Ilsa's arrival disturbs the equilibrium that Rick creates for himself.

Ilsa represents the great love of Rick's life, though this love ended abruptly on the day the Germans occupied Paris. Rick and Ilsa had planned to leave Paris together by train, but Ilsa left him standing in the rain at the train station with nothing but a note explaining that she could not come with him. When she arrives in Casablanca, her presence reminds Rick of their time together in Paris and of her betrayal. Eventually, Rick learns that Ilsa did not betray him at all but rather heard, on the day of their planned departure, that her husband Victor was alive when she thought him dead. Rick also finds out that Ilsa still loves him, just as he continues to love her. But the effect of this love completely uproots Rick's existence and doesn't even enable him to spend any additional time with Ilsa.

In order to love Ilsa, Rick must abandon his café in Casablanca, accept being hunted by the Vichy authorities, and send Ilsa away to the United States with Victor. Love deprives Rick of everything, yet it provides him with a satisfaction that completely outweighs what he has lost. At the end of the film, he is on the run without anything, including Ilsa. Nonetheless, his satisfaction at the ending contrasts with the tedium of his life before Ilsa's arrival.

Rick falls in love without regard for his own interest. The contradiction of love destroys the stability of Rick's life. But this contradiction also animates Rick's subjectivity by giving his life a value it otherwise wouldn't have. The disruption that love causes derives directly from its contradictory status. Love forces the subject to recognize that it is not a self-identical being but a being whose identity is out there in the other.[29]

In love, the subject identifies itself with the other's difference, but this identification does not eliminate the difference. It creates a disturbance in the subject's identity that transforms that identity, revealing that identity is never isolated. Love is possible because the relation to difference is already part of identity even before the subject falls in love. But love makes this difference explicit.[30] In doing so, the contradiction of identity becomes evident.

THE CHRISTIAN COMMANDMENT

When Hegel turns from his critique of Christianity for its positivity to his embrace of it, he singles out the Christian commitment to love as the religion's defining feature. Whereas all religions propagate the moral law (albeit often in a distorted or positive fashion), only Christianity introduces love as the source of a bond that goes beyond that produced by the moral law. From this moment on, Hegel can no longer treat religions in a relativistic fashion, but this turn also creates a significantly more radical thinker. The embrace of Christianity radicalizes Hegel as a thinker and enables him to theorize the radicality of Christianity.

In Hegel's hands, Christianity becomes the most revolutionary religion ever conceived. It embraces love as the actualization of the law, an actualization that makes possible a new way of communal living. Rather than relying purely on the restrictiveness of law to bind us together, we recognize the bond that occurs through love. Love reveals that our relation to the other is never an external relation but always an internal one that shapes our own identity. Love announces the subject as divided in itself and thereby invaded by the other. The Christian commandment of universal love becomes in Hegel's eyes the enactment of contradiction. I am both myself and other. It enables subjects to engage with the disturbance of the other as constitutive of their own identity.

Despite his newfound appreciation for the Christian revolution, Hegel does not accept everything that Christ has to say. He even questions the way that Christ formulates his most important statement. Following Kant (but for different reasons), Hegel cannot wholeheartedly accept Christ's injunction to love one's neighbor as oneself.[31] The problem is not that Hegel cannot imagine individuals capable of loving others with the same intensity that they love themselves, which is the typical cynical response to this injunction. Instead, he rejects out of hand the possibility of self-love, which reveals exactly the role that he gives to love in his philosophy. He writes, "'Love thy neighbor as thyself' does not mean to love him as much as yourself, for self-love is a word without meaning."[32] Christ's commandment doesn't make sense to Hegel because he conceives love as necessarily involving the other.

As a result, Hegel's interprets Christ's commandment as signifying that one must love the other as a being akin to oneself, not as a superior or an inferior. The other must be an equal in order to enable the subject's identity in difference. Hegel's rewriting of the Christian injunction indicates that his investment in love stems from its introduction of a radical difference into the subject's identity. For Hegel, it is impossible to love oneself: love always involves an investment in an otherness that would negate the subject. Through its call for love, Christianity makes clear that identity is constantly involved with what would negate it. Love is the experience of this involvement.

At the time of "The Spirit of Christianity," Hegel cannot imagine that propositional thinking (with its separation of subject and predicate) could accomplish the identity of identity and difference as love does. Propositional thinking, he believes, is necessarily constrained to figure the relationship between subject and predicate as an external one. When I say "Walt is a poet," it seems that this proposition adds a predicate of difference to the subject without changing either element of the proposition. "Poet" helps to define "Walt" without implying identity between the two. The universal "poet" cannot achieve identity with the particular "Walt." Because love is not a concept and not a universal, it can achieve this identity in difference. At this early point in his intellectual development, this is how Hegel differentiates conceptual thinking from love.

Philosophy describes what love can do, but it can't do this itself. The propositional form so distinctly divides subject from object that exposing their identity in difference would prove an impossible task. But something happens to Hegel between the conclusion of "The Spirit of Christianity" in 1800 and the publication of the *Phenomenology of Spirit* in 1807. He redefines the concept in a way that reaches its culmination in the *Science of Logic* in 1812. Now, the concept itself does what Hegel thought only love was capable of. The separation of subject and predicate in the concept is also an expression of identity. The concept is not, as Hegel once believed, a pure vehicle for external relations. It introduces precisely the same contradiction that love does. It is the discovery of the impurity of the concept that allows Hegel to invest himself in it. This is Hegel's second revolution. Initially, Hegel replaces the moral law with love, and then he sees that the concept works like an act of love.

In 1800, Hegel accepts Kant's conclusion in the Transcendental Dialectic of the *Critique of Pure Reason* that concepts transcending sense experience necessarily entail contradiction. He even takes Kant's thinking one step further and contends that all concepts—even those tied to sense experience—end up in contradiction. At this point, Hegel can't imagine that theoretical reason could ever move beyond antinomies. If he held to this position, he would have been unable to write the *Phenomenology*.

But soon Hegel brings the lesson of love to bear on the concept. He begins to think about the contradiction of the propositional form as not just a negative result (in the way that Kant does) but as a positive conclusion. The concept becomes the positive bearer of contradiction.[33] It enables us to access the contradictions that define our subjectivity and the world the subject inhabits. As Hegel sees it, reason is our ability to think the identity of identity and difference. We think contradiction through reason. Reason takes the place of love when we see that reason models itself on love.

_____

Chapter Six

HOW TO AVOID EXPERIENCE

SPATIOTEMPORAL DECEPTION

The most obvious manifestation of contradiction is also the most misleading. It occurs in our sensibility, the faculty to which Kant attributes our capacity for representing the intuitions that we receive from our senses. The sensibility is not just receptive but always receives sense data in certain forms—the forms of space and time. According to Kant, we cannot perceive phenomena in the world except insofar as they are spatial and temporal, even if things in themselves do not obey these constraints. As the forms that our sensible intuitions assume, space and time rule the sensibility completely and provide the basis through which the subject receives its representation. Space and time are the ground floor for the structure of how the subject experiences the world.

Kant's proof for this is very simple. We know that space and time organize our sense experiences because we can't even imagine a sense experience outside the context of either space or time.[1] Our attempt to think of a spaceless void necessarily gives it spatial coordinates, and any effort to imagine eternal life figures it as an infinite extension of time (which is why the idea of eternity is more horrifying for us than that of death). We can't help but think spatially and temporally. The necessity that governs how we register our sense experience seems to indicate that Kant's argument is sound.

Hegel does not attempt to refute this argument, but nonetheless he sees space and time in a dramatically different way. Like Kant, Hegel accepts that all our representations occur in space and time, that representation is impossible without these restrictions that are simultaneously conditions of possibility. But they are not simply the basis of the field of representation. For Hegel, they express the contradiction of being itself in a disguised and potentially misleading form. When we experience spatial and temporal difference, we are actually experiencing entities as contradictory, but the form of space and time permits us to see difference in the place of contradiction.

In this precise sense, one might say that space and time are the primal forms of ideology. If the task of ideology is to enable us to see contradiction not as contradiction but as difference, space and time perform this function on the level of the form of representation. Regardless of the content we experience, the fact of experiencing in space and time leads us to mistake the contradiction that we are experiencing for difference. Of course, one cannot miraculously avoid spatiotemporal representation, which makes a compelling case for the impossibility of ridding ourselves of ideology.[2]

The turn that modern physics makes in the twentieth century appears as if it has taken heed of Hegel's warning about spatiotemporality. The concerns of physics come to defy our capacity for experience. Our experience proves to be a barrier to understanding wave-particle duality, the elasticity of time, dark energy, or additional spatial dimensions. As Brian Greene points out in his summary of the developments in physics, "*The* overarching lesson that has emerged from scientific inquiry over the last century is that human experience is often a misleading guide to the true nature of reality."[3] In order to make sense of physical reality, scientists must disregard what appears in our experience if they are to avoid missing reality altogether.

Of course, no physicists base their insights into the nature of reality on their interpretation of Hegel. But this shared turn away from experience as the site for authoritative revelations indicates that there is nothing preposterous in Hegel's philosophy. Both modern physics and Hegel recognize that spatiotemporal experience cannot serve as our guide if we want to confront the ultimate questions of existence. Hegel comes to this conclusion through the concept, while modern physics arrives at it, ironically enough, through the failures of experimentation and calculation. Relativity and quantum theory emerge when empirical research demonstrates its inability to provide an accurate picture of reality. In the end, however, Hegel and modern physicists come to a similar viewpoint about why spatiotemporal experience deceives us. For both, its propensity for producing clear differences is the source of the problem.

In a key passage from the final chapter of the *Science of Logic* devoted to the absolute idea, Hegel clarifies the relationship between contradiction and spatiotemporal representation. He claims that the danger of representation is that it depicts contradiction "in space and time, wherein the contradictory is held *external to itself*, next to and after itself."[4] Rather than seeing an entity as both itself and what it is not, rather than seeing identity as established through contradiction, we separate identities through space and time. Once we perform this operation, we quickly mistake internal contradiction for external difference. Experience induces this error because it represents contradiction in the externality of spatiotemporal terms.

As a result, the difference between who I was as a young boy and who I am now, for instance, becomes attributable to the external factor of time. This enables me to believe that as a young boy I had a certain positive identity and that now I have a different one. But this belief is utterly false: I never had an identity separable from its failure or was an entity distinct from what it was not. What I would become informs what I was and what I was informs what I have become. I had an identity as a young boy on the basis of the fantasy of my future self becoming a professional football player, and my present self exists on the basis of my fantasy of my prior self as an adequate college football player. At all moments, what I am not remains integral to what I am.

Acorns don't fantasize about becoming oak trees, and kittens, as far as we know, don't fantasize about becoming cats. But contradiction inhabits these entities even more than it does the fantasizing subject. While the subject has the ability to include its otherness in how it conceives itself, the acorn and kitten cannot. As a result, contradiction completely dominates them. It entails their absolute demise. The subject, in contrast, can reconcile itself with contradiction, finding itself in its own destruction. But when the subject considers itself and other entities as simply existing in space and time, it misrecognizes contradiction as difference.

The danger of thinking of contradiction as difference is that it obscures how every entity is at odds with itself before it is at odds with others. Difference creates the illusion of the possibility of harmonious coexistence, which is why it is such an attractive position. Contradiction, in contrast, reveals that no entity can even harmoniously coexist with itself. But this failure of self-harmony is at once the source of all vitality. The substitution of difference for contradiction not only masks the inevitable internal strife within everything but also the fecundity that this strife bespeaks.

At the extreme limit, the sensibility's transformation of contradiction into difference leads to David Hume's error, in which he conceives entities as distinct in each discrete moment of time and space that they occupy.[5] As Hume sees it, habit leads us to think of ourselves as the same entity existing over an extended period of time and moving through a spatial distance. But this enduring self that habit posits is merely an illusion, one that an empirical approach to existence will enable us to treat as a custom. The self is nothing apart from the series of perceptions that it experiences. Nothing authorizes us to connect one experience to another except the force of habit. Hume does not suggest that we abandon this habitual reference to the self, only that we recognize its habitual rather than ontological status.

Hegel is perfectly prepared to accept Hume's claim that there is no substantial self that subtends all its experiences. But he rejects the conclusion that Hume draws. Whereas Hume confines himself to experience and sees only differences, Hegel opens himself to the operation of the concept and recognizes that what appears as difference is actually contradiction. But Hegel is not so naive as to believe that the concept comes chronologically prior to sensible experience. We aren't first pure spirits subsequently thrust into a material world. We are able to conceptualize only insofar as we have had sensible experiences. When Hegel talks about contradictions in the mind of God prior to creation, he does not believe that we have direct access to necessary ontological structures without going through the detour of sense experience. Our thinking always relies on a material base.[6] But nonetheless the concept has a logical priority insofar as it enables us to recognize the constitutive status of contradiction.

Contra Kant, Hegel does not believe that the forms of space and time simply provide the framework through which we can represent the world to ourselves. These forms also lead us down the garden path. Because he grasps the error that spatiotemporal representation creates in even the greatest philosophers, Hegel claims that thought has a truth that experience lacks. He makes the astounding claim that sense experiences have priority over the concept "only in that the concept emerges *out of their dialectic* and *nothingness* as their *ground*, but not in that it would be conditioned by them." That is, sense experiences have a chronological priority equal to their utter logical inferiority or nothingness. Thus, Hegel adds contemptuously of sense experience, "Abstract thinking is therefore not to be considered as the setting aside of sensuous material, which does not suffer any harm in its reality, but rather is the sublation and reduction of that material as bare *appearance* to the *essential*, which is manifested only in the *concept*."[7] Relative to the concept, sense experiences have little philosophical worth. They obscure what the concept reveals. Hegel here praises "abstract thinking" for its ability to marginalize and denigrate the very sensuous material that makes up all of our experiences. This contempt for sense experience stems from Hegel's insight into its misleading structure relative to that of the concept.

That said, sense experiences provide much of the richness of our existence: the touch of a lover, the look of a Bierstadt painting, the smell of a coming rain storm, the taste of a Twinkie, or the sound of a late Beethoven piano sonata. In each case, how the experience feels plays an essential role in its value for us. To subtract sense experience from our consideration and hew only to the concept seems like a betrayal of what makes life worth living. If spatiotemporality is the base level form of ideology, perhaps one should simply choose to live in ideology and abandon its critique. It would be tempting to follow the model of Cypher (Joe Pantoliano) in the Wachowskis' *The Matrix* (1999), who gives up the fight against the control exerted by the matrix in order to regain the deceptiveness of ordinary sense experience. He concludes that living outside the ideological illusion of the matrix deprives one of what makes life most worth living—intense sense experiences. This is not the choice that Hegel would make, but it is nonetheless easy to understand its appeal.

The problem is that the moments during which sense experience seems decisive are not at all unambiguous. Sense experience alone is never the source of the enjoyment that we derive from such moments. For instance, the touch of the lover has great value for us—one such caress might be the most memorable moment of one's life—because of the sublime value that the subject attaches to the lover. This is even clearer in the case of the painting by Albert Bierstadt or the piano sonata by Ludwig van Beethoven. Sense experience doesn't determine this value, even when it involves a Twinkie. The value derives instead from how our desire shapes this experience, which is why the same touch from a different person could be offensive or humiliating rather than enjoyable. Sense experience never has any significance on its own. Though it is a necessary condition for certain significant moments of our lives, it is not a sufficient one. When we look to sense experience itself for theoretical guidance, we are sure to be misled.[8]

But this doesn't mean that we have to marginalize sense experience. Instead, we must consider it in terms of the concept. Once we begin to think in terms of the concept, we can interpret space and time through contradiction rather than difference. This is the revolution that Hegel can bring to our understanding of experience. After this revolution, spatiotemporal differences will appear to us as contradictions. Like Neo (Keanu Reeves), the hero of *The Matrix*, we will be able to see through the ideological distortion and recognize the contradiction that it obscures.

For instance, space and time separate the mineral mines in the Congo and factories in China from my enjoyment of the latest iPhone. I experience the labor that goes into producing the phone and my enjoyment of it as different, not as contradictory. Once I take the Hegelian red pill, however, I can recognize the contradiction that this difference hides. Difference ceases to blind me to the horrors of capitalist production that make my enjoyment possible. The contradiction of the commodity—its simultaneous embodiment of exploited labor and enjoyment—becomes constantly evident. One must see the labor in the enjoyment. One must see what is there within what isn't and what isn't within what is.

THE NECESSITY OF EXPERIENCE

In his first major philosophical work, Hegel offers a radical revision of experience in terms of the concept. Rather than adopting the standard understanding of experience as the arena of contingent occurrences, the *Phenomenology of Spirit* indicates how one might interpret it as the terrain on which contradictions play themselves out. Hegel's aim is not to strip away all contingency from existence and reduce it to pure necessity but to highlight the presence of contradiction obscured by spatial and temporal difference. This requires a redefinition of experience. Whereas prior and subsequent philosophers define experience broadly as whatever occurs in space and time, Hegel provides a restricted definition. Contingent occurrences can take place, but these do not count as experience as Hegel defines it in the *Phenomenology*. Focusing on the contingency of experience—the path that empiricists and those who privilege experience opt for—causes us to miss the determinative role that contradiction plays in our existence. Thinkers conceive of experience as the arena where anything might happen in order to avoid recognizing that contradiction must happen.[9]

According to Hegel's redefinition of experience, we must relate what emerges in experience to what has come before. We cannot isolate one moment from another. To do so is to fail to experience. For instance, in order to experience my spouse leaving me, I must recognize the link between this act and our most enjoyable times together as a couple. The moments of seemingly absolute joy must have had the germs of the departure within them, while the departure reveals the prior moments of joy as not absolute. Without the previous joy, the departure wouldn't be a traumatic event. Without the future end of the relationship, the moments of joy would not have been joyful. Linking the moments of joy and the departure makes clear the contradiction that defines the relationship. There are not two different noncontradictory experiences but one experience of contradiction.

Hegel lays out his theory of experience in the crucial final pages of the introduction to the *Phenomenology of Spirit*. There, he insists on the role the subject plays in the objects it experiences. Hegel admits that his account of experience varies from what we usually associate with the term. The distinction centers on one specific moment. He states,

In this exposition of the course of experience there is a moment in which the exposition seems not to correspond with what is ordinarily understood by experience. The transition, namely, from the first object and the knowing of it to the other object *about which* one says that experience would have been made, was specified in such a way that the knowing of the first object, or the being-*for*-consciousness of the first in-itself, is itself supposed to become the second object.[10]

The distinction between Hegel's understanding of experience and the traditional understanding involves the rejection of contingency's role. For Hegel, we genuinely experience only when the differences in space and time indicate not just the emergence of a contingency but an underlying contradiction of the object that we encounter.[11] It is only by subtracting contingency from experience that it becomes revelatory.

Hegel's elimination of contingency from what he theorizes as experience seems like a complete betrayal of experience. If experience becomes nothing but an iteration of what is necessary, what's the point of having an experience at all? He has taken all the fun out of it. We believe that experience can have a pedagogical effect—we can learn from experience—because we don't know what to expect. Stripped of contingency, however, experience loses its ability to teach us what we don't already know. This is what makes Hegel's insistence on the role that necessity plays in experience so unpopular.

The total openness of contingency appears very attractive. If anything can happen, then perhaps we will find a way out of our most intractable political or even existential problems. A solution to the planetary dominance of self-destructive capitalism might present itself, or we could even find a way to eliminate human death. Hegel accepts that the impossible is always possible, but he insists that there is no possible solution to contradiction itself. This is the one genuine impossibility that no contingent occurrence could ever make possible. Contingency misleads us because it suggests that anything could happen, even the final elimination of contradiction, which is why Hegel refuses to grant that experience is just contingent.

In the main text of the *Phenomenology of Spirit*, experience becomes the site of contradiction rather than contingent difference. Each position that the subject takes up must be submitted to the travails of experience in which its contradiction becomes evident. We can see this dynamic present in the "Perception" chapter from the opening section on "Consciousness." In this chapter, Hegel explores how we divide the world into independent things that are distinct from the various properties that constitute them. But the attempt to distinguish the thing from its properties falters. We cannot say what constitutes the thing outside its properties unless we have recourse to its relationship with other things. The problem with this solution is that this transforms the thing into a relational entity rather than an independent one, moving us beyond the restrictions of bare perception, which concerns only independent things.[12]

The chronicle of perception's failure to grasp the independent thing is what Hegel sees as the experience of perception. We don't experience one unrelated object after another but the contradictory relation of one object with itself that provides the opening for the emergence of another. One only experiences perception when one grasps that the conception of the thing as independent entails its dependence on other things, which marks the failure of perception. To consider the engagement with the thing in isolation as the experience of perception is to see experience in terms that are too broad and abstract. The experience of perception is the experience of a necessary contradiction.

For Hegel, the contingent aspects of experience—say, whether I am struck by lightning or not—do not count as experience unless I recognize the contradiction that the contingency hides. My own nonchalance in golfing during an electrical storm has a direct link to the lightning that subsequently strikes me. These are not two distinct experiences but part of the same one, one that exhibits the contradictory structure of experience. This is not to say that we cause all our experiences to occur. But it is the contradiction of our subjectivity that does make them possible. Unless we interpret experience in this way as the expression of our own contradiction, it will remain fundamentally misleading. It will seem like a terrain in which we can escape the contradiction of the concept and interact with the possibilities of difference. But difference is always an ideological trap.

A DIFFERENT WAY OF THINKING

Hegel's interpretation of temporal and spatial difference as contradiction earns him the special ire of Gilles Deleuze. For Deleuze, the great error in the history of philosophy is its proclivity for thinking about difference in terms of identity, as if differences had their status as differences only in relation to an original and hierarchically elevated identity. This way of thinking grants existential and political priority to the original and denigrates what is different. When one thinks of difference in these distorted terms, according to Deleuze, it appears not as difference but as contradiction. Contradiction results from mistakenly conceiving difference in terms of identity. In the history of Western philosophy, according to Deleuze, no one falls for this error more than Hegel.[13]

Hegelian philosophy clings to contradiction because of its inability to think pure difference, which Deleuze locates in the power of sensation.[14] This is Hegel's great failure, which emanates from his supposed prioritizing of identity.[15] Deleuze puts this opposition very straightforwardly: "Our claim is not only that difference in itself is not 'already' contradiction, but that it cannot be reduced or traced back to contradiction, since the latter is not more but less profound than difference."[16] We initially experience (through sensation) a plethora of differences, but we submit these differences to the law of identity and end up with contradictions that dimly echo the more "profound" differences. Contra Hegel, sensation doesn't mask contradiction. It is rather the law of identity that masks difference.

As Deleuze frames the question, one must simply choose between contradiction and difference. Hegel chooses contradiction, and he chooses difference. The argument for this choice is axiomatic: there are only differences, and thus contradiction creates a representation of identity that obscures this fundamental ontological fact. Deleuze never deduces the existence of differences but instead presents his emphasis on them as a counterattack to the dominance of sameness and identity that begins with Plato and reaches its apogee with Hegel. One recognizes difference by simply paying attention to our experience, in which differences manifest themselves. One need not deduce difference because difference is self-evident. I am different from you; Deleuze is different from Hegel; each particular oak tree is different from the other; even every clone is different from every other one. Difference is natural within what Deleuze calls the univocity of being, whereas sameness arrives only through the philosophical abstraction from this difference.

When one thinks inductively about it, the case seems open and shut. But the problem with it lies in its reliance on induction.[17] Difference appears ubiquitous, though Deleuze never asks what enables him to perceive this ubiquity of difference nor what authorizes the inference from the perception of difference to the universal claim that there are only differences. The universe of pure difference that Deleuze posits assumes a univocity of being in which differences coexist. Univocal being is not like a genus that groups together the species of difference. Instead, the univocity of being just ensures that all differences can peacefully coexist on the same ontological plane.[18]

It is the image of peaceful coexistence that marks the key difference between Deleuze's philosophy of difference and Hegel's philosophy of contradiction. For Hegel, not only are entities unable to coexist peacefully with each other, but they cannot coexist peacefully with themselves. This failure, however, animates them at the same time as it ultimately destroys them. Deleuze, in contrast, envisions all entities existing in their difference moved by a presupposed natural vitality. Conflicts in Deleuze's universe are always only the result of bad external encounters rather than internal strife. Even suicide is the result of an external force acting on the individual. In this way, Deleuze fails to see the ubiquity of conflict. Taking his lead from the logic of sensation, Deleuze experiences a world of differences existing without any apparent relation to each other, which leaves him unable to explain convincingly why they do interact through conflict. Unless all entities are just collectively unlucky, they must have some drive that leads them to seek out conflict. This shows just how misleading experience can be.

Our experience constantly bombards us with contradictions assuming the form of differences, which is why, in the last instance, Hegel refuses to put his faith in the power of experience. His investment in the concept rather than experience threatens to transform him into a nineteenth-century relic. Even those who take up the mantle of Hegel's philosophy in the twentieth century do so through a dramatic turn toward experience, which they feel is necessary to sustain its viability. It becomes evident that concepts cannot survive the rough and tumble world of experience and that we must submit them to the rigors of this world.

But in the face of this seemingly damning critique, Hegel would hold out for the superiority of the concept relative to our experience. We reach truth through thought rather than experience. Even though this sounds like heresy to contemporary ears, it is the only authentically Hegelian position. It is solely through the concept that contradiction becomes accessible in its irreducible form. But it is precisely the concept that twentieth-century thought takes aim at.

THE EDMUND HUSSERL EXPERIENCE

Though the prioritizing of experience over the concept occurs among a wide variety of thinkers in the wake of Hegel, it is with phenomenology that this prioritizing becomes the foundation for the entire philosophical project. Phenomenology doesn't jettison the concept but focuses its attention on the experience through which the concept comes into being.[19] The name *phenomenology* signals a link with Hegel, but the central concerns of phenomenology represent a decisive turn away from his philosophy. Phenomenology is far removed from the *Phenomenology of Spirit*. As phenomenology sees it, the problem with Hegel and other metaphysical thinkers is that they assume objects are given for the subject without ever questioning how they arise.

Phenomenology examines how knowledge arises through experience. It has its basis in the recognition that no knowledge arrives all at once but comes through a temporal sequence. The major phenomenologists— Edmund Husserl, Martin Heidegger, Jean-Paul Sartre, Simone de Beauvoir, Maurice Merleau-Ponty, Emmanuel Levinas—take experience as the point of departure to understand being rather than beginning with the concept in order to understand what occurs in experience. Phenomenology is the examination of what is more primary than concepts—the experiential building blocks out of which concepts form.

Hegel's error, from the perspective of phenomenology, is that he fails to account for how the concept arises. Hegel simply elides the question of the emergence of the concept and assumes that it's there. In order to remedy this deficiency, the phenomenologist must introduce temporality into the concept. Our knowledge of the concept doesn't come all at once but emerges through a temporal unfolding of the experience that precedes it. Hegel's denigration of time and space leaves him little to offer, once we grasp that everything must come into being, which seems like a commonsensical claim.[20]

Phenomenology aims at constructing a philosophical approach adequate to our experience. This project begins in earnest with Edmund Husserl's *Logical Investigations* in 1900. In the second volume of this work, Husserl offers a canonical definition. He writes, "*Phenomenology* is accordingly the theory of experiences in general, inclusive of all matters, whether real (*reellen*) or intentional, given in experiences, and evidently discoverable in them."[21] Though this early foundational work highlights the logical structure of our experience, experience nonetheless has primacy. But after the *Logical Investigations* Husserl turns even further in the direction of experience and away from the concept.

Husserl's phenomenology tries to extricate experience from the concept that deforms it. To this end, Husserl becomes convinced that logical structure, rather than constituting our experience, separates us from it. He recognizes that experience occurs prior to the mediation of logical structure, that is, prior to where he locates it in the *Logical Investigations*. It is, first and foremost, immediate, though we use our conceptual knowledge to make sense of it. I have an original experience of a mountain lake, and then my thinking brings the concept of a mountain lake, with all its romantic resonances, to bear on this experience. The result is a loss of access to the original experience of the lake in its temporal emergence for me. I end up with a "mountain lake" instead of experiencing a mountain lake. The premise of phenomenology is that we initially interact with objects through a preconceptual relation in which they come to be objects for us.[22]

In his later works, Husserl develops a method to reverse the conceptual baggage that obtrudes on our original experience. He calls this the "phenomenological reduction." This is a process in which thought brackets the concept in order to provide access to our unmediated experience. In the *Cartesian Meditations*, Husserl states, "phenomenological explication does nothing but *explicate the sense this world has for us, prior to any philosophizing*, and obviously gets solely from our experience."[23] The phenomenological reduction promises to return us to a sense of experience prior to the sedimentation of the concept that has blurred its true nature.[24] In other words, phenomenology moves in the opposite direction as Hegel's philosophy.

But if one finally arrives at pure preconceptual experience to which phenomenology aspires, one discovers nothing at all. Without the concept, Hegel recognizes, there is no such thing as experience. Instead, we experience through the concept, which is why all attempts to move prior to it inevitably fail. Without the deformation enacted by the concept, we would have no experience. Rather than seeking an escape from this deformation to understand our experience, we must plug ourselves fully into it. Rather than striving for an impossible original immediacy, we can affirm that our conceptual distance from the world is actually our mode of access to it.

ABSTRACTING TOWARD CONCRETION

The first gesture of thought is abstraction. The subject doesn't confront a world of particulars and subsequently derive its concepts from those particular starting points.[25] Instead, it begins with abstraction and discovers particulars through this initial abstraction. Hegel reverses the usual relationship between abstract and concrete. The concrete is not given to the subject. As he puts it in the *Science of Logic*, "everywhere the abstract must constitute the starting point and the element in which and from which the particularities and rich shapes of the concrete spread out."[26] One must begin with the abstract in order to attain the concrete. But the move from the

abstract in order to attain the concrete requires taking stock of the inadequacy of abstraction.

Hegel spends a great deal of time criticizing other thinkers, especially
Kant, for remaining stuck in abstract philosophizing. They find a set of
abstract concepts and assume that this is as far as a philosopher can go. Kant
treats the categories of the understanding as formal abstractions that permit us to know the concrete content of the sensibility. What he doesn't recognize, according to Hegel, is that these abstract categories in fact fail to
abstract themselves completely from the content of the sensibility. The categories are not completely external to the sensible intuitions that make up
their content.[27] But the failure of abstract categories is not an end point.
This failure creates the path to the concrete.

As Hegel unfolds his philosophy, he moves from the abstract (like sense
certainty or being) to the concrete (like absolute knowing or the absolute
idea). When he arrives at the absolute, he attains an absolute concreteness,
which is nothing but a recognition of how the concepts necessarily contradicts itself. Without this dialectical movement and final punctuation, we
remain caught up in the lure of abstraction. The problem with our experience is that we typically experience abstractly rather than concretely. The
length and unwieldiness of the *Phenomenology of Spirit* indicate the difficulty of experiencing concretely, since we only arrive at a concrete experience after reaching the end point of absolute knowing.

Though it seems impossible to challenge the idea that experience weighs
more than the concept, there is a way to redeem Hegel in the midst of this
critical onslaught by claiming that there is no experience that escapes the
concept. One could claim that we don't first have an experience and subsequently conceptualize it. The conceptualization of the experience occurs
within the experience itself and serves as its condition of possibility. This
is certainly Hegel's position, which is accurate as far as it goes. But Hegel
himself goes even further in his claim of the priority of the concept relative to experience.

For Hegel, the concept renders contradiction thinkable as contradiction.
Concepts do not simply make assertions but bring together oppositions
and force us to think them as a unity. Even a simple concept like "Leonard Nimoy is mortal" expresses a contradiction by its linkage of "Leonard
Nimoy" with the otherness of "mortality." The experience of living and
dying does not present contradiction in so clear a manner. Life and death

appear as different states that have nothing to do with each other. The role of contradiction in their relationship is not immediately evident. We require Hegel's interpretation of life always involving death for the contradiction to become visible. We require the concept as the key to unlocking experience as contradictory. As Hegel emphasizes, one must take the long detour through the concept to discover what one is actually experiencing. The point is not to abandon experience altogether for the life of the mind but to approach experience through the concept so that we recognize it properly as replete with contradiction.

It seems to go without saying that the turn to experience in twentieth-century thought was a moment of philosophical progress. Surely there must be something revolutionary (or at least democratic) about asserting the privilege of experience relative to the concept. Experience is the domain of everyone, while philosophers assume for themselves the prerogative of exploring the concept. But in the aftermath of the triumph of experience and its displacement of the priority of the concept, it is time to take stock of where the revolutionary power actually lies. As long as we confine ourselves to the field of experience, we remain blind to the necessity of contradiction through succumbing to the lure of difference. The verdict on the struggle between the concept and experience is unambiguous: ideology resides in the difference of experience, not the contradiction of the concept.

Involvement with negation is the speculative genius of the concept. When we think conceptually, we encounter a fundamental negation as the essence of every identity, a negation that produces identity. This contradiction runs throughout conceptual thought, but at the moment when one introduces spatiotemporal experience, it becomes possible to see contradiction as difference: the human who was once living is simply different from the one that is now dead. The distinction between this experience and the concept "humans are mortal" is the distinction between difference and contradiction. It is only contradiction that enables us to see that the possibility for a radical transformation exists within every assertion of identity.

Chapter Seven

LEARNING TO LOVE THE END OF HISTORY

Freedom Through Logic

ON NOT PRIVILEGING HISTORY

The most unfortunate development in the dissemination of Hegel's thought after his death was the central role that his lectures on the *Philosophy of History* played in this dissemination. Despite the fact that Hegel himself never published his thoughts on world history, the transcriptions of his own and student notes to his lecture course came to define the popular image of Hegel. This work—usually just the introduction, labeled "Reason in History (*Vernunft in der Geschichte*)"—became the beginning and end of the Hegel canon for nonspecialists. The *Philosophy of History* is not at all a representative work by Hegel, as even the key terms reveal. Terms such as the *world historical individual* play a pivotal role in the *Philosophy of History* and exist nowhere else in Hegel's philosophy. And yet this term, along with other clichés from this work (like Hegel's dismissal of the importance of the individual in history), are often the only references to Hegel that many people have at their disposal.

What's striking about the relative weight that the *Philosophy of History* receives in the analysis of Hegel's thought is the dramatic difference between Hegel's champions and his detractors. Adherents of Hegel's philosophy looking to elucidate this philosophy almost never take the *Philosophy of History* as their starting point. It is difficult to think of an exception, especially in the last fifty years. For those seeking to poke holes in Hegel's system or to set him up as their philosophical fall guy, however, the *Philosophy of History* is their go-to text. It provides much juicy material (apparent ethnocentrism, justification of violence, indifference to real historical events, and, most damningly, teleology) to bury the entire system. It is the work that Benedetto Croce has in mind when he says, "Before Hegel seeks the data of facts, he knows what they must be."[1] Opponents glom onto this text as a representative one, but they are able to glom onto it with such vitriol precisely because it isn't.

One of the key features of Hegel's philosophy is that it contains multiple points of entry. One can begin with the *Phenomenology of Spirit*, the *Science of Logic*, the *Encyclopedia*, or even the *History of Philosophy* without suffering any initial missteps. Each of Hegel's works has a legitimate claim to serving as an introduction to the entire system. In this sense, there is no bad choice when one begins to read Hegel for the first time—except the *Philosophy of History*, which has, not coincidentally, for a long time functioned as the standard shorthand for Hegel's entire philosophy. Because the *Philosophy of History* offers the easiest image of Hegel's thought both to apprehend and to caricature, people unfamiliar with Hegel wrongly embraced it as his key text. Whereas each of Hegel's other major works rehearses in some way his dialectical system while introducing the subject matter (logic, philosophy, religion, and so on), the *Philosophy of History* does not. It is a work in which dialectics has only a peripheral role relative to the description of various societies and their development of freedom.

If we just examine the *Philosophy of History* on its own terms, it is evident that Hegel himself is responsible for much of the misunderstanding that surrounds it. He leads the reader unfamiliar with his other work to believe that he sees history as a progressive march to a preordained goal achieved only by Christian Europe. The potential for this dramatic misreading arises because Hegel, when he gives these lectures, is talking to students already schooled in his philosophy. Properly grasping what Hegel is up to in the *Philosophy of History* requires, I claim, a background in Hegel's other works, though Hegel himself never says as much. He never states that the *Philosophy of History* can't stand on its own, but, in order to salvage it at all, this must be our conclusion today. This work misleads because it seems to present a triumphant image of progress that leads inexorably to the Europe of Hegel's time without any consideration of those sacrificed for the sake of this progress.

In this work, Hegel describes history as the progressive unfolding of freedom, but he does not fully develop the foundation of freedom. His concern is to distinguish his concept of freedom from the liberal or romantic version that associates freedom with an absence of social constraint. For Hegel, there is no natural freedom. Instead, freedom arises through subjectivity's break from the immediacy of the natural world. He claims that "the human being as spirit is not an immediate being but essentially a being that returns to itself. This movement of mediation is thus the essential element of spiritual nature; in this way human beings become independent and free."[2] Hegel argues here that mediation is not the interruption of our naturally free inclinations with the restrictiveness of law. Instead, mediation provides freedom.

But at no point in the *Philosophy of History* does Hegel offer a precise definition of freedom. He tells us clearly what his vision of freedom is not, but not what it is. Nevertheless, the *Philosophy of History* operates with a tacit definition of freedom based on his own ontology, which otherwise plays no role in it. In order to understand what Hegel means by freedom in this work, one must have recourse to the text that he wrote ten years before giving his first lectures on the subject. It is most likely because the *Philosophy of History* is Hegel's most accessible work that teachers and students seeking a short cut to his philosophical system flock to it. But the accessibility of this work is entirely misleading. The work is not valueless, but, to get at the conception of history articulated here, one must navigate a perilous path. The only way to the purported ease of the *Philosophy of History* is through the minefield of Hegel's most difficult work—the *Science of Logic*. It is impossible to understand the stakes of the *Philosophy of History* without grounding it in the *Science of Logic*.

Ironically, this is exactly the claim of Hegel's enemies. For them, the *Science of Logic* establishes a pattern of thought that the *Philosophy of History* imposes on a recalcitrant history, with the result that his version of history resembles his logic but not history as it really happened. In this picture of Hegel's philosophy, he is so arrogant—or so naive—as to assume that real history corresponds to the dialectical unfolding he discovers in the structures of thought. Obviously, such a position would be indefensible today (or, frankly, even when it was first formulated). But if we understand the *Science of Logic* as the key not to how the course of history logically develops but to the definition of freedom that animates the *Philosophy of History*, its theoretical primacy seems less ridiculous.[3]

The great insight of the *Science of Logic* is that the contradictions of thought necessarily entail contradictions in being itself. When thought tries to determine the identity of any entity, it discovers a contradiction because every entity involves what it is not and every identity depends on what negates it in order to have identity at all. Nothing simply is what it is. In the final chapter of the book, Hegel distinguishes the revelations of his logic from ordinary formal thinking. He writes, "The firm principle that formal thinking lays down for itself here is that contradiction cannot be thought. But in fact the thought of contradiction is the essential moment of the concept."[4] Whereas Kant sees the contradictions that reason discovers as an index of its overreach and its errors, Hegel views the contradictions of reason as a positive assertion of knowledge. Reason's great achievement is its ability to think the contradiction that inhabits all being, to articulate how being necessarily involves its own negation.

If there is no aspect of being that escapes contradiction, if every entity (even God) includes what negates it, then there is no consistent authority in the world. Authority depends on consistent self-identity: we attribute authority where we posit an absence of contradiction. But we do so only insofar as we leave the figure of authority unthought. Its consistency depends on our positing it as unknown, and when we try to know it, as Kant does in the Transcendental Dialectic from the *Critique of Pure Reason*, its contradictory status becomes evident. The subject finds itself enthralled to external authority only as long as it can believe in the consistent status of this authority, and the discovery of its contradiction has the effect of freeing the subject, as the subject recognizes that even the ultimate authority is in the same boat as the subject itself.

According to Hegel, we know that there is no possible higher end for the subject than its own freedom because we have discovered that there is no being without contradiction. Freedom is the result of this discovery. In a discussion of Kant's discovery of the categorical imperative in the *History of Philosophy*, Hegel provides his most thorough and compelling definition of freedom. He claims, "For the will there is no other end than the one created out of itself, the end of its freedom. It is a great advance when this principle is established that freedom is the last hinge on which humanity turns, the last summit from which humanity lets nothing impress it and accepts no authority that goes against its freedom."[5] The key point in Hegel's definition of freedom here is that it coincides with a refusal to be impressed by the Other. As he sees it, subjects are impressed by substances, by beings that appear beyond any contradiction. Being impressed by substances, however, is a barrier to recognizing one's freedom. But reason comes to the rescue and reveals that the substantial beyond does not exist. It shows that every being, even those that appear substantial, exists through contradiction.

History is the arena in which we discover the contradictions that strip the authority from figures of authority. Each discovery frees the subject from its investment in the authority, until there are no more figures of authority left. Even the subject's own natural inclinations suffer from contradiction, which disqualifies them from any authoritative status over the subject. That is, the subject is naturally inclined to act in mutually opposed ways—say, to survive and to propagate itself. This absence of any authority—either external or internal—bespeaks for Hegel the subject's freedom. The free subject relates to the figure of authority as a fellow being divided by contradiction rather than as a self-identical substance. The authority is just another subject, not a self-identical being elevated above the subject.

When one examines Hegel's conception of freedom as he articulates it here, it becomes clear just how far it is from the liberal conception. Liberalism conceives of freedom as the absence of constraint. One is free, for the liberal thinker, when no one is unjustly hindering what one can do. But liberalism misses how constraint most often operates. Direct constraint is the primary concern of liberalism. And yet, direct constraint is the easiest to defy. The most pernicious form that constraint takes occurs when the external authority presents itself as substantial and thus impresses the subject. Impressing the subject is far more threatening to its freedom than imposing on it and is usually propaedeutic to imposing on it. Authentic freedom requires an absence of impressive external substances, which is why Hegel says in the passage cited earlier that we achieve freedom only when we allow nothing to impress us. Otherwise, the subject finds itself devoted to an external authority while remaining utterly convinced of its own freedom. This is the classic liberal trap.

The great instance of this liberal trap is freedom in capitalist society. Capitalist subjects believe themselves to be free to act however they want. Yet they also believe in the perfection of the market. It functions as a substantial Other that impresses them and guides how they act. They buy what the market offers, invest in what the market proposes, and work in jobs where the market identifies a need. The belief in the market goes hand in hand with the liberal conception of freedom, but not with Hegel's, because truly free subjects cannot prostrate themselves before any self-identical idols, which is what the market is within capitalism.

In the *Philosophy of History*, Hegel constructs a narrative of the history of freedom. His concern is not with the actual freedom that people experienced but with the expansion of the idea of freedom. Hegel famously divides history into three primary epochs: the Asiatic world in which one (the ruler) is free, the Greek and Roman world in which some (those of the ruling class) are free, and the modern world in which all are free. This schematic history actually recounts how the recognition of contradiction has developed, even if Hegel's societal alignment of this recognition isn't perfectly accurate. Despotic rule involves the freedom of only one because it is only the ruler in a despotic regime that can act without reference to a substantial external authority. The despotic ruler, by virtue of the ruling position, recognizes that every Other suffers from self-division, and this is the basis for the ruler's freedom. To be a ruler is to recognize that one's followers are subjects, not pure substances. In the Greek and Roman world, the free men collectively share this position, but it is denied to women, slaves, and men without citizenship. Freedom is the refusal to endow the Other with wholeness or self-consistency. It is the refusal to treat the Other as a substantial being.

The modern world permits every subject to experience this revelation of the inconsistency of authority. Every subject can recognize that contradiction is coextensive with being itself because no subject in modernity has any necessary superiority to any other. This is why modernity is the epoch of revolutions: if there is no undivided Other, no figure of authority that avoids contradiction, then no one has a right to rule.[6] As a result, rule becomes the object of contestation, and, what's more, subjects must learn to exist without reliance on any consistent external authority whatsoever. At the end of history, they must give duties to themselves rather than receiving them from an authoritative Other.[7] Every subject must wrestle with the self-division of the Other.

The claim that history comes to an end seems odd coming from the philosopher who introduced history into philosophy.[8] It seems like a retreat from the radicality of Hegel's own recognition of our inescapable historicity. For this reason, critics often see the proclamation of an end to history as a sign of Hegel opting out of political struggle, of him taking a position above the fray. Critics have endlessly taken him to task for this move. But the proclamation that history ends with the modern world does not function as an escape hatch from politics or freedom. It assures us that we are condemned to freedom, that we cannot turn back to the assurances of a consistent authority. Hegel's assertion of an end to history is not a retreat but a refusal of retreat. Those who would reassert the claims of history today are themselves looking for respite from the traumatic and liberating implications of its end.

The proclamation of an end of history is the most radical step that Hegel takes in the *Philosophy of History*. History ends when freedom becomes accessible for all. As Hegel sees it, freedom can be the only possible end of history because being itself has given it to us. Whatever end we erect for ourselves beyond freedom will always have its basis in freedom, which derives from the absence of any substantial authorization. The ontology of contradiction assures us that we will never have any assurance and that history will never move beyond freedom. No matter how advanced humanity becomes, no matter how far we go down the road of posthumanity or metahumanity, we will remain within the ontology of contradiction. We cannot overcome contradiction because contradiction is the source of our capacity for overcoming. This leaves us on the terrain of freedom. It is in this extreme sense that freedom marks the end of history.

THE ALLURE OF MODESTY

It is tempting—and even the greatest Hegelian thinkers sometimes succumb to the temptation—to interpret the end of history in relative terms. They infer from Hegel's formulation that he is making the modest claim that one cannot but relate the narrative of history from its end point. Because the future is radically foreclosed to our thought—Hegel never wavers on this point—we cannot anticipate, so the argument goes, the direction that history will go or the future truths that it will reveal. As a result, when recounting history, we necessarily find ourselves at the end.

This is how Slavoj Žižek conceives of the end of history. For Žižek, the end of history signifies our total immersion in history, which condemns us to speak about history as if we were at its end. According to this position, Hegel theorizes an end of history in order to acknowledge that there is no exit from history, that we can never view the world *sub specie aeternitatus*.[9] Žižek believes that we cannot subtract ourselves from the historical process that we are recounting, which gives this process the appearance of an end with us. Hegel's point, Žižek claims, is not that all of human history ends with him, but that we cannot but think history from the end, which is always now. This closure is the result of the standpoint from which we speak, the result of the act of speaking history. Our position of enunciation manifests itself within our historical statements in the form of a retrospective account. Zizek puts it like this: "at every given historical moment, we speak from within a finite horizon that we perceive as absolute—every epoch experiences itself as the 'end of history.'"[10] We are, in other words, condemned to locating ourselves at the end of history.

Žižek's analysis of the end of history is correct as far as it goes. It is accurate to say that we cannot avoid speaking from the perspective of the end when we narrate history. But this interpretation of the end of history has the effect of minimizing Hegel's claim when he announces that history reaches its end with the full development of the concept of freedom. This interpretation reflects a modesty in relation to Hegel that Žižek typically avoids. My contention is that Hegel's claim here is stronger than an admission that the end of history constantly imposes itself on us as historical subjects. Instead, Hegel believes we will never move beyond the recognition that all are free, which is the recognition that occurs in modern Europe (as well as in North America and Haiti).

This does not mean that significant historical events will cease or that no new avenues for the articulation of freedom will be discovered—like some new form of communism, for instance. But, for Hegel, history as a field for the unfolding of new insights into existence reaches its conclusion with the recognition of universal freedom, which occurs with the development of modernity and the French Revolution. The assertion of freedom based on the recognition of intractable contradiction is the most important event in the history of subjectivity. It marks the end of history because no subsequent event can ever top it.

Though it has become fashionable to bash Francis Fukuyama's proclamation of liberal capitalist democracy as the end of history in 1989 as a terrible reading of history and of Hegel, his thesis is true to Hegel's thought in one crucial sense.[11] Like Fukuyama, Hegel believes that history can come to an end, that we can reach a decisive recognition that no subsequent event can dislodge. The difference is that for Hegel the end of history is not the end of political struggle because it has its origins in the recognition of a divided substance rather than in the achievement of a particular political regime.

Freedom is the key to history for Hegel because freedom is the correlate in the subject of the recognition of being as contradictory. The freedom of all that Hegel sees manifest in modern Europe has its basis in the absence of any consistent Other that might function as an authority for the subject. The subject is free because it has nothing external to it that it can rely on for guidance. Every external authority that the subject would defer to—God, nature, the monarch, the people, history itself, and so on—suffers from the same contradictory logic that besets the subject itself. The modern subject can fantasize a consistent Other, but this consistency can only be fantasmatic for it. When it posits laws of historical development or harmony in nature, the modern subject attempts to avoid the fundamental insight of modernity—the inconsistency of the Other—and thereby to escape its own freedom. But the problem with these stratagems is that they rely on the freedom they purport to escape.

THE END OF FREEDOM

While one temptation is to relativize Hegel's conception of the end of history, the other is to reject it altogether, which is the majority position. Most interpreters of Hegel refuse the image of Hegel as a philosopher of the end of history.[12] Because it seems so evidently wrong, because history clearly introduces fundamental substantive changes to existence after Hegel's death, Hegel's champions have found this thesis untenable, which has led them to attribute it to someone other than Hegel himself. That someone is Alexandre Kojève.

For much of the twentieth century, Kojève seems like the most important interpreter of Hegel's philosophy. Though his interpretation cuts against the grain and marries Hegel with Marx and Heidegger (who were, to say the least, strange bedfellows), it reignites the spark of this philosophy and creates an awareness of Hegel as a valuable thinker that otherwise would not have existed. The Hegel of the twentieth century is more or less Kojève's

Hegel. When Kojève gives his lectures on Hegel in Paris during the 1930s, there is no extant translation of the *Phenomenologie des Geistes* in French.[13] There is one soon afterward, just as there are philosophers like Jean-Paul Sartre, Jacques Lacan, and Georges Bataille seriously engaging with Hegel's thought in a way that would have been unthinkable without Kojève's epochal intervention. Kojève created a contemporary Hegel, but the price of this currency is that Hegel becomes the thinker of the end of history.

In his lectures, Kojève makes it clear in no uncertain terms that Hegel formulates an end to history. Kojève idiosyncratically bases his reading of Hegel's philosophy of history on the dialectic of the master and slave in the *Phenomenology of Spirit*.[14] Rather than read the *Philosophy of History* directly on its own, Kojève hits on the idea of a detour through the *Phenomenology*, and this detour produces stunning results. According to Kojève's interpretation of Hegel, humanity begins in the struggle for prestige or recognition. A long series of senseless fights to the death in order to gain prestige dominate prehistorical human existence. The winner of these fights gains prestige but lacks anyone to bestow it because the others are dead. No one is left to laud the winner. This war of all against all is, according to Kojève, Hegel's version of the state of nature.[15] History proper begins when the fight to the death for prestige ends not with death but with the acquiescence of one subject to another. At this point, the slave offers to work for the master in order to avoid death, but, even more importantly for Kojève, the slave also agrees to recognize the master. The slave's gesture of capitulation, rather than simply indicating cowardice and dishonor, becomes the inaugural gesture of history and the basis for all cultural achievements. Kojève's revaluation of the slave parallels Marx's revaluation of the proletariat. In each case, the apparent historical loser becomes responsible for the creation of value in history.

The contradiction within this relationship is the motor for history. It is the slave that drives history progressively forward while the master ends up cast aside. For Kojève, the master suffers from an untenable position. He claims, "the Master struggled and risked his life for recognition, but he obtained only a recognition without any value for him. This is because he can only be satisfied by the recognition from someone whom he recognized as being worthy of recognition. The attitude of the Master is thus an existential impasse."[16] The master desires recognition from someone worthy of recognition, but, at the same time, she or he cannot tolerate the existence of another master who would have this status. There is only the slave to recognize the master, and the slave's recognition is really no recognition at all. As a result, mastery leads to a historical dead end or an existential impasse. As Kojève sees it, history is the struggle for recognition, and the master has no way of achieving it.

Slaves, in contrast, have history on their side. Through the dread of death and subsequent work for the master, the slave finds another avenue for recognition that is not open to the master. When slaves successfully revolt, they establish a society of mutual recognition in which they can achieve satisfaction. This society is the end of history. In his lectures and subsequently, Kojève waffles on just when history does come to an end. He begins by accepting the verdict he attributes to Hegel—that history ends with the Napoleonic regime after the success of the French Revolution. But later Kojève sees the end in American capitalism and, ultimately, in what he calls Japanese snobbism. In each case, the end of history arrives when subjects attain mutual recognition.

Despite the enormous influence that Kojève had on French thought in the twentieth century (and on American neoconservative thought), most committed readers of Hegel view Kojève not as a commentator on Hegel but as an altogether separate thinker—the thinker who believes in the end of history.[17] Philip Grier gives this position its most compelling formulation. He painstakingly shows how Kojève's thesis of the end of history borrows liberally from Alexandre Koyré's own distortion of Hegel's philosophy of history in order to produce a distinct philosophy.[18] Grier claims straightforwardly that "Kojève's end-of-history thesis has no obvious grounding in Hegel's text."[19] By interpreting the end to history as foreign material inserted into Hegel's philosophy, Grier can simply dismiss this troubling idea and preserve Hegel as the thinker of a continually evolving history. But the price of this corrective is too high. While Kojève's conception of the end of history may have gone astray, we cannot abandon the idea altogether while remaining true to Hegel's project.

Grier simply sidesteps Hegel's own direct statements on the end of history, statements that force us to grant that Kojève is onto something. For Hegel, history has an end in both senses of the term—an aim and a terminus in which this aim has been reached. When spirit "is at home not with another but with itself, with its essence, not with something contingent but rather in absolute freedom," Hegel believes that this is "the final end of world history."[20] History achieves this end in modern Europe.[21] Here, Hegel gives Kojève enough material to justify his claims about history coming to an end, an end that he identifies with freedom.

The problem with Kojève's interpretation is not, as Grier would have it, that it lacks textual warrant. The fundamental problem is that Kojève imagines history coming to an end through the elimination of contradiction. Kojève supplements the *Philosophy of History* with the *Phenomenology of Spirit* (specifically the master/slave dialectic) when he should have supplemented it with the *Science of Logic*. He rightly sees the need for another text to make sense of Hegel's most idiosyncratic work, but he chooses injudiciously. Kojève identifies a society developed out of servitude in which mutual recognition overcomes social antagonisms. This is the point at which Kojève's debt to Marx gets the better of his allegiance to Hegel.

Contra Kojève, history doesn't come to an end when a society emerges that no longer suffers from self-division. Hegel's point, I claim, is exactly the opposite. History comes to an end when we recognize that we are all free, and we recognize that we are all free when we recognize that nothing can avoid contradiction, that there is no possible consistent authority to provide a ground for our identity. Kojève is on the right track when he identifies the end of history as a crucial pillar of Hegel's edifice. But his attempt to theorize it has the effect of knocking it down. Thinking the end of history requires seeing Kojève as symptomatic of its refusal.

A CHRISTIAN THAT REFUSES HERESY

When we grasp Hegel's conception of freedom and its relationship to contradiction, the explanation for the privileged role that Christianity plays in his thinking about history becomes clear. It is not that Hegel simply prefers his own religion and that of Europe, which is what it seems on the surface. Christianity offers a philosophical insight that no other religion does. This insight derives from the unprecedented act of divine humiliation that it enacts, and this is what Hegel finds so appealing about it. With the death of Christ on the cross, humanity is able to witness the contradiction at the heart of the divine, the revelation that the divine endures the travails of finitude. It is a moment at which the infinite shows itself as finite, an event that strips all authority from the divine.

The divine humiliation that Christianity enacts follows directly from Christ's message of love. A loving God or a God capable of love cannot be a pure substance but must be a subject. Only divided subjects can love because only divided subjects turn to the other to look for a corresponding division. The message of love initially draws Hegel to Christianity, but it is the humiliated God entailed by love that sustains Hegel as a devotee.

The advent of Christianity marks the end of history for Hegel, even though it takes over fifteen hundred years for the world to register this end. With Christianity, it becomes possible to recognize that even the highest authority imaginable, even the infinite authority of God, suffers from the same contradiction that besets the lowest subject. But Hegel does not end his account of history with the death of Christ or with the Edict of Thessalonica in 380 CE that installs Christianity as the religion of Rome.[22] The decisive blow in the development of Christianity occurs with Martin Luther, who offers subjects a direct relation to God.

As long as the Church functioned as a mediator between the subject and God, the subject could not partake in the freedom that Christianity enacts.[23] The presence of the Church sustains God's obscurity for the subject and leaves God in a position where divine contradiction does not become evident. History ends only when the God of the beyond comes down to earth for all subjects, which is what Protestantism occasions. At this point, everyone can see the divine humiliation that transpires in Christianity.[24]

But Christianity is not the only religion in which the divine manifests itself in a finite form. Both Hinduism and Buddhism have their own versions of incarnation, each different from the Christian version. Both fail, according to Hegel, to formulate the severity of the humiliation that God suffers in Christianity. The point is not that Hinduism and Buddhism lack the sophistication or elegance of Christianity but that they lack its extreme humiliation of the divine. For instance, a certain version of Buddhism posits God's reincarnation in another Dalai Lama after the death of one, whereas in Christ God dies once and for all. The Buddhism of the Dalai Lama preserves God from the depths of finitude to which Christianity subjects the divine. The profound abasement of God in Christianity is the source of the freedom that it provides. This is what leads Hegel to make the impolitic remark that "a human being who has not the truth of the Christian religion has no truth at all; for this is the one and only truth."[25] Here, Hegel not only fails to be a good multiculturalist, but he also theologizes truth, which would appear to make him a bad subject of modernity as well. Two strikes against him in a single sentence. But he doesn't strike out. His statement about the truth of Christianity is neither a failure of multiculturalism nor a retreat from modernity. Christianity is "the one and only truth" insofar as it proclaims that the subject must experience divinity through its humiliation, which any modern subject—Hindu, Buddhist, Muslim, Jew, Christian, or Taoist—can do by recognizing that the divine doesn't exist beyond contradiction. Otherwise, one condemns oneself to unfreedom.

Protestant Christianity implies freedom for all because it exposes the fundamental contradiction of God itself. It represents an advance beyond Catholicism, for Hegel, because it does away with the intercessor of the pope, a figure that has the effect of obscuring the subjectivity of the divine. The true Christian ceases to be impressed by the glory of God. This glory loses its ability to dominate the subject insofar as it comes down from the beyond and exists in a finite form (and dies). The recognition of contradiction at the heart of the divine announces the end of all slavery. Of course, slavery continues well into the era of Christianity, but for Hegel this requires a betrayal of the foundation on which Christianity is built.

History ends with Protestant Christianity and the freedom that it unleashes, but most often modern subjects take up a heretical attitude to their Christianity. Hegel stands out as a Christian because he absolutely refuses heresy. Unable to confront the humiliation of God, most Christians restore the divine to the position that it has in other religions. Every claim that "no one knows God's plan" or "I have faith in the man upstairs to guide me" or "we look to God for assistance in our crisis" indicates a thoroughgoing abandonment of the basic tenet of Christianity: God is no longer a mysterious being existing beyond the contradictions of our existence. The real heretics are those who cling to an unknown God in order to avoid confronting a divided God, a God suffering from the same humiliation that subjects themselves endure.

Hegel recognizes that his version of Christianity is not the garden-variety version. During his theorization of its link to freedom, he admits, "We need to remember that we are not to be thinking of a Christianity of the man in the street, as whatever anyone makes it out to be."[26] The problem with the "Christianity of the man in the street" is that it refuses the full weight of the divine humiliation and clings to the existence of an undivided God. For Hegel, this recalcitrance from the average Christian does not have the power to block Christianity's philosophical revelation. It is this revelation that brings history to an end, despite the rearguard efforts of most contemporary Christians.

THE ABSENCE OF IDEALISM

There are two standard readings of the *Philosophy of History*, both of which take Hegel as an idealist in the strict sense. The worst of these, favored especially by Hegel's opponents, sees history as a teleological narrative directed by a transcendent God who uses particular historical events and actors to accomplish the universal goal of freedom. According to this reading, Hegel's indifference to the suffering of particulars sacrificed in the slaughterhouse of history is the necessary by-product of his investment in the end point of the historical narrative.

The second reading posits an immanent development of freedom in history: though no transcendent force plans the development of history, it moves in the direction of freedom because of a human longing to be free. The spirit of freedom guides subjects unconsciously toward history's ultimate end point. In the most sophisticated form of this reading, the dialectical logic of historical development doesn't determine specific events but relies on a series of contingent events to achieve its aim.

The majority of the significant interpreters of Hegel writing today— Slavoj Žižek, Catherine Malabou, Rebecca Comay, Sally Sedgwick, and Susan Buck-Morss, just to name a few—avoid the *Philosophy of History* like the plague. When one sees how much fun Hegel's opponents have with this work, it's tough to blame them. Karl Popper's sarcastic quip—"it was child's play for his powerful dialectical methods to draw real physical rabbits out of purely metaphysical silk-hats"—hints at the extent of the ridicule heaped on this work.[27] Those who do discuss it, such as Robert Pippin, do so in much the same way that Kojève does—through their reading of the *Phenomenology of Spirit* and the project of mutual recognition they find in that text. The *Philosophy of History* is anathema because it seems impossible to reconcile it with the materialism that these interpreters (along with most contemporary subjects) share.

Hegel's account of history is unabashedly idealist. Hegel envisions subjects driving the movement of history through their commitment to realizing their ideas. It is not "the mode of production of material life" that triggers historical transformation but the idea of freedom, which is why this work from Hegel, more than any other, leads Marx famously to accuse Hegel of standing on his head and thinking the dialectic upside down. Marx offers a corrective in his thought: turning Hegel right side up, putting the dialectic on its feet, and advocating materialism. Marx has it right when he describes Hegel as turning thought upside down, but this is the source of his radicality that Marx pulls back from. As a thinker of contradiction, we should imagine Hegel, as Marx does, thinking while standing on his head. Perhaps thinking dialectically requires such a position, which expresses the discomfort that dialectical thought brings to our everyday life. But, in any event, Marx's materialist corrective is unnecessary. When we consider the *Philosophy of History* in light of the *Science of Logic*, its runaway idealism diminishes.

From this new perspective, freedom ceases to exist as an idea separated from any material origin and becomes the ideal correlate of the structure of being. Though subjects pursue freedom as an end, neither God nor some amorphous humanist impulse has given them this end. It is the product of God's failure, a failure shared with all being. The contradiction of being rather than the idea of freedom becomes the engine of history. The self-division of being is the material cause of the development of human history that Hegel recounts. If Hegel himself never articulates this, it nonetheless is apparent from the way that he describes freedom throughout his philosophy.

THE OBJECT OF THE CUNNING

If the *Science of Logic* enables us to understand the material basis of freedom in the *Philosophy of History*, it also provides an important corrective for one of this work's most troubling ideas—the cunning of reason. The cunning of reason appears to give the lie to the reading of history as the unfolding of freedom. According to the traditional interpretation of this idea, reason exhibits its cunning by using the activity of individuals to enact its own goals, so that individuals are nothing but the tools of reason. Hegel even seems to celebrate reason's ability to profit on the suffering and death of individuals that struggle without any personal investment in advancing reason's agenda.

Interpreters who encounter the cunning of reason while reading the *Philosophy of History* have been taken aback. With this idea, Hegel justifies the most brutal horrors of human history as the means through which reason asserts itself as the end of history. The idea of the cunning of reason seems to be that one cannot make an omelet without breaking millions of eggs. Understood this way, the cunning of reason is clearly at odds with the discovery of freedom that animates the *Philosophy of History*.

But the problems go even further. The idea of the cunning of reason also makes it seem as if history knows what it's doing. The universal has a plan that individuals enact unknowingly while pursuing their particular aims. In this way, the cunning of reason operates like Adam Smith's invisible hand of the market, which uses the selfishness of individuals to create social cohesion.[28] They don't know, but history itself does, which is why everything goes according to plan even when everything seems to be going awry from the perspective of individuals caught up in history.[29] The cunning of reason enables interpreters of history to identify the universal always at work in history.

In the *Philosophy of History*, Hegel's presentation of the cunning of reason appears unambiguous. He famously claims that "the *cunning of reason* . . . sets the passions to work for itself." As a result, "individuals are sacrificed and abandoned. The idea pays the penalty of determinate existence and of transience, not of itself, but from the passions of individuals."[30] In this passage, Hegel's investment is not with the "passions of individuals" but with the idea that profits from their sacrifice. The problems here are twofold: suffering individuals don't matter and the universal directs human history like a puppeteer. The worst stereotypes of Hegel's philosophy are compressed into a few sentences.

Just as one must read the development of freedom in the *Philosophy of History* through the discovery of contradiction in the *Science of Logic*, one must have recourse to this earlier text to make sense of the cunning of reason in the latter. Hegel addresses the cunning of reason when he comes to the discussion of teleology near the end of the *Science of Logic*. The fact that

he brings up the cunning of reason during a discussion of teleology immediately raises red flags, suggesting that Hegel will go down the path sug-
gested by the passage in the *Philosophy of History*—that the cunning of reason ruthlessly exploits means to accomplish universal ends. But then things
take a surprising turn.

In the *Science of Logic*, the cunning of reason does not involve the universal using individuals as tools for its own advancement. Instead, the situation is reversed. Individuals establish their own ends, and the cunning
of reason is nothing but the fact that individuals must use some sort of
means to accomplish these ends. This is where the universal intervenes. For
example, I must have recourse to public transportation to accomplish my
aim of going to the movies. This particular aim doesn't advance the universal, but the means that I use—public transportation—does. This is the
cunning of reason as Hegel defines it in the *Science of Logic*. Despite what
critics of Hegel proclaim, it concerns only the means, not the end. The cunning of reason is the product of the subject's own purposiveness but is not
itself teleological. Reason doesn't use individuals; they use it when they pursue the ends that they give themselves.

In the course of their activity, subjects do not accomplish their ends
directly but do so via another object. Reason depends on this mediation,
which intrudes on every action. As Hegel puts it in the *Science of Logic*, "that
the purpose posits itself in a *mediate* connection with the object, and
between itself and this object *inserts* another object, may be regarded as the
cunning of reason."[31] He goes on to celebrate the means as the manifestation of reason. Hegel insists that "the *means* is higher than the *finite purposes* of *external* purposiveness; the *plough* is more honorable than are
immediately the enjoyments which it procures and which are the purposes."[32] What passes for a mere means ends up being more significant
than any conscious ends for which we use this means. Subjects use reason
even—or especially—when they have no conscious intention of doing so.

The importance of the cunning of reason resides in its dramatic reversal of the relationship between means and ends that it enacts. What subjects consciously try to accomplish takes a back seat to how they accomplish it. Through this reversal, the cunning of reason supports rather than
undermines the role that freedom plays in the *Philosophy of History*. To
recognize the value of means at the expense of ends is to free oneself from
one's social or natural determinants. Means are the site of freedom.

The most significant instance of the cunning of reason in the modern world is the creation of public transportation. We most often use public transportation to move from one private action to another—from our life at home to our job or to some sort of entertainment. The transportation is just a means to serve our private ends. But in the act of using public transportation, we form a public world with others and create a bond that connects us with strangers. This connection is more important than our private ends, but it emerges out of the means that we use to accomplish these ends.

Freedom does not reside in the subject's ability to consciously choose its own ends—it is always just choosing among given possibilities—but in its ability to invest itself in the means without regard for the ends. When this occurs, the subject loses its dependence on the particularities of its situation that determine its ends. Rather than working to ensure my survival, I can find satisfaction in my work for its own sake. Just as a tool can become more valuable than the end it serves, my work can become more valuable for me than what it accomplishes. When this occurs, I break from the constraints of survival and reproduction. I even break from the social demand for productive labor. While occupied with the means, I am free from the prescribed ends, and it is the cunning of reason that makes this freedom evident. Though the cunning of reason seems to mark the absence of freedom within Hegel's system, there is no freedom without it.

When we take the explanation of the cunning of reason from the *Science of Logic* into account in the interpretation of Hegel's *Philosophy of History*, the indifferent brutality of the idea vanishes along with the sense that reason externally manipulates history. The point is not that reason uses unsuspecting individuals to advance its agenda but that reason itself is the means they use when advancing their own agenda. We think that we employ means in order to accomplish the ends that we set out for ourselves. But our ends are not free. We discover freedom through the means we use to accomplish our unfree ends.

WHY HISTORY DOESN'T SEEM OVER

When Hegel lectured on the philosophy of history in the 1820s and early 1830s, he could still feel the aftereffects of the American, French, and Haitian Revolutions. It seemed as if the freedom deriving from the recognition of the contradictory status of all authority would change the world irreversibly, enabling the philosopher to announce the end of history. But the two subsequent centuries did not bear out Hegel's certainty that the recognition of freedom had become ineluctable. What we have witnessed in the time since Hegel's death has been a desperate search to erect a new authority that would avoid God's humiliation, an attempt to avoid recognizing God as contradictory and confronting the freedom that this implies.

This turn toward authority is not a rebirth of history but rather a neurotic response to its end. If Hegel did not predict this reaction against contradiction, it was because he was not yet Freud and lacked a theory of neurosis. The neurotic subject confronts the absence of a substantial authority and rather than taking up the freedom that this absence grants, this subject fantasizes an authority not riven by contradiction. Hegel never spends any time in the *Philosophy of History* dealing with those who want little to do with the freedom of contradiction, but this position is far more prevalent today than the one that accepts freedom without asking for assurances from the Other.

The two basic forms that the neurotic reinstitution of authority take today are naturalism and fundamentalism. The naturalist sees the natural world as bereft of contradiction and thus capable of acting as an authority for the subject. According to this position, the subject's freedom disappears in the face of the dictates of its nature. In its most popular form, naturalism envisions the gene as the noncontradictory figure of authority. The self-identical gene knows what it wants and pursues its aim with a ruthless purpose. Though subsequent scientists have complicated the picture that Richard Dawkins lays out in *The Selfish Gene*, his classic text still provides the most compelling account of the gene as the contemporary authority figure. He writes, "The genes are master programmers, and they are programming for their lives. They are judged according to the success of their programs in coping with all the hazards that life throws at their survival machines, and the judge is the ruthless judge of the court of survival."[33] The position that Dawkins espouses here is a neurotic one because it evinces the belief that genes know what they want, that they have a purposiveness not at odds with itself.

In this sense, genes take up the position once occupied by the pre-Christian God. They are more appealing than the Christian God because they have not yet succumbed to the Crucifixion, which enables them to retain the status of an undivided authority. It would be interesting to see a gene die on the cross, which would allow the believer in the self-identical gene to discover the freedom of the Christian. But this has not occurred. Dawkins does not believe himself to be a believer, but this disavowal of belief permits it to function all the more vehemently.

We can see a similar example of belief in the noncontradiction of the gene in a discussion that took place in a film course that I recently taught. While explaining the concept of the femme fatale in film noir to a group of students, I showed the scene in which Gilda (Rita Hayworth) first appears in Charles Vidor's film *Gilda* (1946). In this famous scene, the camera cuts to Gilda with her long hair covering her face, and she flips her hair back in order to reveal her face to both the other characters in the film and to the spectator. This is a classic image of the femme fatale establishing her allure. But rather than seeing this as either a sexist image of the woman or a bold assertion of femininity (or both at the same time), the students labeled it an instance of "peacocking"—someone displaying her reproductive appeal to prospective mates interested in propagating their genetic material. As the students (to a person) proclaimed, we choose our sexual mates on the basis of an unconscious instinct that seeks out the best genes in possible sexual partners. A woman with hair like Rita Hayworth's, they reasoned, undoubtedly possesses excellent genetic material. The students might not know their desire, but at least their genes do. While applying this naturalist concept, it did not even strike them as odd that the female peacock isn't the one who does the peacocking. The important point was the authority that the naturalist explanation could provide. For them (and for Richard Dawkins), the gene is a noncontradictory authority that provides refuge in the modern abyss of freedom.

Naturalism is not, however, the only neurosis at work today, though it is the most widespread. The other neurosis, while exponentially more rare, is also much more visible. Fundamentalism of all stripes does not rediscover the substantiality of authority in the obscurity of a gene but prefers a more grandiose form. The embrace of God, nation, or ethnicity as an undivided authority amid the contradictions of modernity enables the fundamentalist to exist in this world without confronting its consequences.

But because the modern world denies the existence of any substantial authority, fundamentalists must resort to extreme acts to assure themselves of the authority's presence. By blowing up a nightclub or shooting an abortion provider or participating in ethnic cleansing, one acts in order to provide proof that the authority is an authorized authority. The fundamentalist act is an effort to substantialize the authority, but the act inevitably undermines itself. If the authority really were substantial, such acts would not be necessary.

The fundamentalist attempts to reignite history and deny the Crucifixion by sustaining the idea that God still exists in the beyond, where the divine can remain substantial and avoid the pitfalls of contradiction. The fundamentalist's version of God defies revelation, which means that fundamentalist Christians must betray the core tenet of their own religion. But the question for the fundamentalist runs deeper: if God exists beyond all revelation, and thus beyond all contradiction, how can the subject receive the divine message? The very fact that the believer hears from God indicates that God too is a subject and not just a substance.

Both the naturalist and the fundamentalist try to work around the end of history and its irreducible contradiction. They seek out an identity that can be what it is. But for the modern subject this position is only ever a neurotic fantasy that collapses when confronted with the exigencies of the modern world. Contradiction and its correlate of freedom continue to bombard the neurotic subject with revelations of nonidentity at the heart of their authority's identity. One never escapes contradiction for good through the neurotic fantasy because this fantasy nourishes itself on contradiction. It stages what it avoids.

When we recognize the radical implications of Hegel's *Philosophy of History* and the proclamation there of history's end, we can reconcile ourselves more easily to its outsized position within the popular image of Hegel. Even though the interpretation of this work depends on a reference to the *Science of Logic*, it nonetheless has something important to tell us about our contemporary condition. The *Philosophy of History* is not just a way of avoiding Hegel. It is also a path leading to the most pressing questions of contemporary politics.

The end of history is not the end of politics. In some sense, it marks the beginning of political contestation in its most authentic form. Rather than struggling for freedom, subjects must now struggle for the form of life most adequate to their freedom. The liberal capitalist answer has clearly revealed itself as wanting. Its failure stems directly from its basic misconception of freedom as the absence of overt constraint and its superstitious investment in the market as an authority without contradiction. Attempts to realize a communist society have betrayed contradiction through adherence to either the laws of history or the apotheosis of the party leader. These two failures leave the field of politics open. We have witnessed how freedom will not manifest itself. It remains to be seen how and if it will.

Chapter Eight

RESISTING RESISTANCE, OR FREEDOM IS A POSITIVE THING

AFTER TARRYING WITH THE NEGATIVE

Freedom is unimaginable without negation. The ability to negate the givens of its existence, whether they come from biology or from culture, provides the basis for the subject's freedom. Hegel, because he recognizes the central role that negation plays in the formation of subjectivity, is a philosopher of freedom. As Hegel sees it, the subject doesn't just play out the various determinations governing its actions but has the ability to determine itself, and this ability begins with the negation of what would otherwise determine the course that the subject pursues.

The role of negation in the subject's freedom shows itself clearly in the relationship of a child with its parent. The child experiences its freedom from the parent at the moment it defies the parent's commands and acts contrary to what the parent dictates. By transgressing the parent's authority, the child reveals that this authority does not have a determinative power. Parental authority appears as less than authoritative in the face of the child's disobedience. This lack of authority serves as an indication of the child's freedom.

And yet this example reveals the essential problem of the association of freedom with negation. As long as one negates an external authority, one remains on that authority's terrain rather than on one's own, which produces a very circumscribed notion of freedom. The child can disobey, but it is still the parent who establishes the rules that the child disobeys. If freedom manifests itself only as rebellion or resistance, it isn't freedom as such. The child really becomes free when it moves past rebellion, lives on its own, and determines its own life. In the same way, Hegel's conception of freedom begins with negation, but it ends with the recognition that this negation must manifest itself in some positive form if the subject is to free itself completely from the external authority that it negates.

Hegel's subject discovers its freedom not just through a single negation but through a series of negations. In the "Self-Consciousness" section of the *Phenomenology of Spirit*, this dynamic unfolds in its most straightforward fashion, which is why so many discussions of Hegel and freedom focus on it. In the dialectic of the master and the servant, Hegel famously locates freedom on the side of the servant. Even though servants must act according to the masters' whims and have limited control over the direction of their own lives, servants have negativity on their side: they experience their own nothingness through the confrontation with the fear of death, and they experience the nothingness of the external world as they negate this world through work.

The fear that keeps a servant a servant and impedes servants from risking their lives in revolt is actually an emancipatory fear that reveals the insubstantiality of the servants' own identity. Hegel notes that the servant "felt the fear of death, the absolute master. In that feeling, it had inwardly dissolved, has trembled thoroughly in itself, and all that was fixed in it was shaken. However, this pure universal movement, the way in which all stable existence becomes absolutely fluid of everything permanent, is the simple essence of self-consciousness, the absolute negativity, *the pure for-itself*."[1] The negativity of an absolute fear emancipates servants from their attachment to themselves as substantial beings. They grasp that everything about themselves that they assume to be fixed and stable can simply melt away, and this frees servants from a belief in their own identity as something determinative and authoritative.

According to Hegel, the same process occurs with the external world when servants work on it, which is what masters compel them to do. Servants experience directly the malleability of the external world as they alter it by growing food, digging holes, or building houses. Even though the world resists the servants' actions to modify it, they are able to do so nonetheless,

which has the effect of proving to them its insubstantiality and imperma-
nence, even amid its intransigence. For the servant, the external world's
malleability reveals that it cannot be authoritative.

The fearless masters who don't labor have no contact with this negativity and thus enjoy the fruits of mastery in pure unfreedom. Masters remain
enthralled both to their own identity and to the external world. Both act as
substantial authorities over the master, which the master never has the
opportunity to negate. Masters do not recognize their insubstantiality in
the way that servants do. Through the phenomenology of servitude, Hegel
illustrates that negativity is the occasion for freedom. But his account also
reveals that negativity doesn't have the last word on the subject's freedom.

As Hegel explores the contours of the servant's negative freedom, its
limitations become evident. The problem with pure negativity is that it is
incapable of becoming self-determining, which is why Hegel doesn't end
his exploration of freedom with the servant. Paradoxically, pure negativity
is never negative enough—Hegel calls it incomplete—to negate the external authority that determines it. This becomes clear in the case of the stoic,
the first figure of self-consciousness to appear after the master and servant
in the *Phenomenology*. The stoic locates its freedom in the domain of
thought, which doesn't suffer from the constraint of any external authority.

Stoicism negates the external world in order to grant pure thought an
absolute value. In thought, the stoic is free from all the determinations of
the external world. But when he probes this negative freedom of the stoic,
Hegel finds that the determinations of the external world contaminate it.
Since stoicism provides no guidelines for what to think in one's retreat from
the world, the content of thought can only come from the world, which the
stoic believes itself to have only a negative relation to. The private thoughts
of the stoic have their basis in the public world the stoic rejects as valueless.
Through Hegel's analysis, the negative freedom of stoicism shows itself as
dependent on what it negates. This is the paradigm for all philosophies of
pure negativity or resistance.

Unhappy consciousness, the further development of self-consciousness
in the *Phenomenology*, takes the negativity of stoicism (and skepticism) to
its most extreme expression. This negation is crucial for the establishment
of freedom. The subject must initially turn away from the world to free itself
from the determinants that produce it. For many thinkers following in
Hegel's wake, unhappy consciousness appears as what should be the end

point of the entire *Phenomenology of Spirit*. It is the last form of consciousness that insists on pure negativity in relation to the world. It is the last form
of consciousness that doesn't compromise but insists on constant struggle.
Unhappy consciousness seems free because it refuses to recognize any
attachment. But for Hegel this freedom of pure negativity is an impoverished freedom.

In the domain of unhappy consciousness, freedom is the struggle against
the world. But this struggle cannot be successful. Unhappy consciousness
fights for what it can never attain. It locates its essence in an evanescent
beyond that disappears whenever it is reached. The moment at which
unhappy consciousness would achieve the free act, it betrays itself and
becomes part of the world that it must struggle against and negate. Ending
with unhappy consciousness leaves the subject unable to act freely.

As stoicism, skepticism, and unhappy consciousness reveal, the subject
cannot content itself with negativity if it wants to recognize its freedom.
The attempt to cling to negativity and conceive freedom in opposition produces a hysterical subject, a subject incapable of seeing how its rebellion
actually feeds the authority that it challenges. The stoic's negation of the
external world expands the power of external authority over the stoic, and
this same process occurs whenever the subject fails to recognize that freedom cannot remain purely negative (which is the case with both the servant and the stoic).

What the insistence on negativity misses is that negativity is never free
from all positivity, whether the subject is aware of this or not. If I reject the
social hierarchy and refuse to take part in it, I still have a place within it as
one who refuses it. My negation of the hierarchy manifests itself as a positive position. All forms of freedom, even the freedom of pure negativity,
have a positive correlate. This is the point at which the negation of external determinations becomes the subject's self-determination. This self-
determination does not consist in the subject's ability to do anything at all
or in the multiplicity of choices that the subject has. Instead, the subject's
self-determination is its self-limitation, and this self-limitation becomes, in
my understanding of Hegel, the positive instantiation of freedom.

This becomes apparent in Hegel's turn from self-consciousness to reason in the *Phenomenology*. Whereas the forms of self-consciousness conceive the external world in opposition to self-consciousness, reason sees
itself actualized in externality. This is why Hegel takes reason as the site

where freedom manifests itself. Rather than simply negating the external world and defining itself in opposition to it, reason authorizes the form that the world takes. It finds its freedom there in the midst of that form.

From the perspective of reason, the subject's decision to obey the speed limit while driving ceases to be capitulation to an external authority and becomes the expression of the subject's own freedom. In this act of obedience, the subject follows a law that its investment in the world has authorized. As a result, this limit does not function purely as an external limit for the subject but as an internal one. Or, to put it in Hegel's terms, the *Grenze* (barrier) is also a *Schranke* (limit). The free subject conceives the speed limit as its own self-limitation and thus experiences it as a sign of its own freedom, not as an constraint imposed externally. Though clearly the subject does not establish speed limits itself, they make up the legal order that the subject posits through its daily activity. Recognizing a speed limit as a self-limitation might seem like a minute and even absurd gesture, but it is precisely the type of act that serves as an index of the subject's freedom. The fact that almost everyone disobeys the speed limit indicates our inability to recognize freedom. It is the unfree subject that experiences speed limits solely as a burden imposed by an external authority. The unfree subject constantly experiences its obedience as a constraint that it would like to do away with.

Freedom is the recognition that the subject is the source of its own opposition, that its negation does not rely on any external authority but involves instead its own self-relation. Of course, the subject must negate external figures of authority in order to discover its own freedom, but negation is also a self-relation that these external negations obscure. Once one conceives of the opposition as internal, one recognizes the essence of freedom. As Hegel puts it in the *Science of Logic*, "the idea, because of the freedom which the concept has attained in it, also has the *most stubborn opposition* within it; its repose consists in the assurance and the certainty with which it eternally generates that opposition and eternally overcomes it, and in it rejoins itself."[2] The free subject recognizes that it doesn't require the external authority that it opposes. The opposition that animates freedom—what Hegel calls "the most stubborn opposition"—is ultimately an internal one.

As long as the theorist insists on pure negativity and resistance, what freedom looks like remains mystified. Hegel articulates a philosophy of freedom unburdened of external opposition, a philosophy that requires moving beyond pure negativity and resistance. From the perspective of resistance, one does not see that every authority ultimately suffers from the same inextirpable contradiction that besets the subject itself. The philosophy of resistance has become increasingly popular since Hegel's death. Though resistance to oppressive structures is always necessary, it cannot be the last word if we want to be free. The turn to Hegel reveals freedom beyond resistance, which makes this turn imperative. One must theorize the positive form that freedom takes within the world, or else freedom remains a fetish that covers its absence.

WE OUGHT NOT INVOKE OUGHT

Like so much of his philosophy, Hegel's theory of freedom has its basis in Kant's. As with Kant, Hegel sees freedom as autonomous self-determination that breaks from external constraint. This is why freedom depends on the law. Whereas we acquire the particular aspects of our identity externally from nature or our society, we give the law to ourselves. In Kant's terms, it is the one indication of our autonomy rather than our heteronomy. Though external authorities impose many laws on us, the fact of the law as such marks a disruption in the causal chain that would render us completely determined beings. The turn that Hegel gives to Kant's theory of freedom through the law is that he locates freedom not just in the existence of the law but in its actualization.

By definition, one never fully achieves one's status as a Kantian moral subject. For Hegel, this is the profound limitation that besets Kant's position and that finally renders it untenable for him. And yet Kant does make a significant advance: the revolution of Kantian morality is that it locates freedom within the law rather than in the law's abeyance. In the act of giving itself a moral law, the subject declares its freedom either to obey this law or not to.[3] Even recognizing a law as a law indicates the subject's freedom from the givens of its being insofar as it suggests that the subject could act otherwise. This capacity for acting otherwise emerges with the formulation and recognition of the law.

The law arrives from the subject itself, according to Kant, even though the subject experiences the law as an external constraint. The law does not first come from outside and then become internalized by the subject; instead, the subject's act of giving the law to itself renders it capable of accepting external laws. Kant does not view the existence of the law as part of the subject's ideological manipulation but as the sign that such manipulation must pass through the subject's freedom. But Kant never permits this freedom to become fully actualized. It remains a negative freedom acting against the world as it is without ever assuming a positive form within the world. The Kantian subject fails to see that its free acts constitute the world within which it acts.

Although Hegel finds much to criticize about Kantian morality, he stops to admire the radicality of the moral revolution that Kant inaugurates toward the end of his *History of Philosophy*. He recognizes that the decisive step forward that Kant makes lies in linking morality to freedom rather than to constraint, which is how we typically conceive morality. In his discussion of Kant, Hegel states, "there is no other aim for the will than the one created out of the will itself, the aim of its own freedom. The establishment of this principle was a great advance; human freedom is the ultimate pivot upon which humanity turns, the ultimate and absolutely firm pinnacle that is not open to influence, so that the human being grants validity to nothing, to no authority of whatever form, if it goes against human freedom."[4] Hegel grants that Kant doesn't just postulate but actually proves the subject's freedom and that he does so through the moral law, just as he says.

Kant makes what Hegel calls a "great advance," but his conception of the moral law as what the subject ought to do rather than what the subject already does marks his fundamental misstep. By aligning his philosophical position with the ought (*Sollen*), Kant distances himself from moral success. The Kantian subject constantly struggles to act morally but never fully does so. Morality consists of striving toward moral action, and the incessant failures of the subject force Kant to posit the subject's immortality in order to allow this striving to continue. Because the subject defines itself through unending striving, death does not represent a genuine barrier.

Fichte makes the ought of Kantian morality into the basis of his entire philosophical system. The problem with this is that striving after the good replaces the act. Kantian and Fichtean subjects avoid acting, according to Hegel, because when they do "they enter the sphere of limitedness. They foresee this and therefore fear every contact, remain enclosed within themselves, and revere their inner infinitude."[5] Kantian and Fichtean freedom has the paradoxical effect of creating a subject unable to be certain that it has acted morally and thus freely.

Kant and Fichte's version of morality is that of the rebel. Though they align morality with the law rather than with its transgression, they fail to take this alignment far enough. Hegel pushes it a step further. By identifying ourselves with the achievement of the moral law rather than striving to achieve it, we reveal that freedom is not the absence of limitation but the encounter with an internal limitation that drives us to act.

Though one can assert one's freedom in standing up to an oppressive regime like Malcolm X or Sophie Scholl, one can also do so every time that one acts without any external guarantee for the act. This is why crime is inherently unfree. It treats the law as an external force that it can transgress. Free acts, in contrast, stem from the conviction that the law—even if it is society's law—is one's own. In this sense, freedom implies that the subject is responsible. When Kant and Fichte envision the moral act as what the subject ought to accomplish, they avoid the responsibility that Hegel's version of morality entails.

We should not think of Hegel's philosophy as a rejection of Kantian morality but as the absolute development of it. Kant and Fichte correctly grasp that the subject realizes its freedom in the act of giving itself the law, but they fail to see that this act itself is sufficient. They believe that there is something more to morality, a fulfillment of moral perfection that the subject is yet to achieve. This hysterical view of morality leaves the subject always on this side of moral probity. In doing so, it creates a moral paralysis. The Kantian and Fichtean subject aims at moral perfection and in this way misses the opportunity for the garden-variety ethical act, an act accomplished by recognizing one's morality as actual rather than as potential.

THE INSUBSTANTIALITY OF THE OTHER

For Hegel, the subject is free because there is no substantial Other that can function as a determinative authority for it. The idea of a substance completely divorced from subjectivity—an autonomous and independent entity—functions as the basis for philosophical authority in every modern thinker prior to Hegel, and this hampers efforts at conceiving freedom. As long as the subject believes that an autonomous and independent Other exists, it cannot truly conceive itself as free. This is because the image of a substantial Other that knows its own desire and evinces perfect self-identity has a hypnotic effect on the subject's desire. This image captivates the subject and leads the subject to identify its desire with that of the supposed substantial authority.[6] The subject posits the Other as substantial insofar as the Other remains obscure to it: absence of knowledge creates the illusion of pure substantiality that precludes the emergence of the subject's freedom.

There is an inverse relationship between the obscurity of the Other and the freedom of the subject. The subject interprets this obscurity as an inaccessible hidden truth, and it constitutes itself relative to this otherness, which leaves it enthralled to what it doesn't know. As Hegel points out in the *Philosophy of History*, "The unfree spirit knows truth only as a beyond. The spirit that is free is spirit for itself, is not through an other."[7] The unfree subject remains hypnotized by the spell of an obscure otherness. But overcoming this spell requires more than simply conjuring it away.

The subject is free only when its substantial Other suffers abject humiliation without ceasing to be the expression of authority. This is why, for Hegel, the death of Christ represents the key moment in the unfolding of freedom. The most substantial image of the Other that humanity has ever produced—the infinite God of monotheism that exists beyond the constraints of the physical world—identifies itself with a finite being in an utterly humiliated form. Freedom requires the authority to lose its purely substantial status without losing its authority, so that the subject recognizes that the authority exists for it and through its support rather than independently.

We can see an instance of this freeing effect when a child sees its parent behave foolishly in public and endure mockery from others. The child undoubtedly pities the parent, but the parent loses substantial authority through this humiliation. The parent becomes a lacking figure and yet remains an authority at the same time. The child gains freedom from parental authority in this reconfiguration of authority as still authoritative but not substantial. The point is not simply that authority disintegrates leaving the child on its own. Instead, parental authority remains in force while losing its mysterious secret. This loss enables the child to recognize the role that it has played in the functioning of authority. Freedom emerges from the debris of the Other being deprived of its undisturbed substantiality.[8]

The task of the Hegelian theorist is one of dismantling the forms that the substantial Other takes on as they arise. Though Christianity reveals the substantiality of God as a divided subject through the death of Christ, the idea of a nonsubjectivized substantial Other does not die so easily. It doesn't just have to be defeated twice like Napoleon but time and time again. Though the unknowable God is the most intractable form of the substantial Other, this figure also has many other guises in the contemporary world. We posit it in the secrets of the natural world, the desires of the terrorist, or even the innocence of the child. Substance is the secret truth that we believe we cannot know.

What we posit as an epistemological barrier functions ipso facto as a barrier to our freedom. Though there will always be gaps in our knowledge, these gaps do not contain a hidden truth. The idea that what we don't know is a truth that we are missing obscures the internal limit through which our freedom constitutes itself. Hegel insists on absolute knowing—that is to say, the idea that there is no hidden truth in what we don't know, even though there is always something we don't know—in order to articulate our freedom. The subject who rejects absolute knowing and believes in an ultimate truth that exists elsewhere rejects its freedom through this gesture. Freedom depends on not believing in the substantiality of the Other and on recognizing that every other is in the same existential bind as the subject itself.

WHY WE DON'T REMAIN IN THE PROVINCES

Hegel's critique of the freedom of pure negativity has an analogue with a key decision in his life that provides an instructive contrast with Martin Heidegger, who faced a similar decision and made the opposite choice. Hegel spent ten years of his philosophical career on the outside of the German university system, working first as a newspaper editor and then as a gymnasium rector rather than teaching philosophy at a major university. Hegel never romanticized this outsider position, and, through the publication of the *Science of Logic* and the *Encyclopedia*, he worked to make himself more attractive for a university post. He eventually gained a position at the University of Heidelberg in 1816, which led to the call to Humboldt University in Berlin, which he accepted. Hegel started teaching in this prestigious post in 1817.

Hegel's move from provincial newspaper editor to philosophy professor at the center of the German university system was a move from the margin to the center. When he published the first part of his most important book (the *Science of Logic*) in 1812, Hegel was an anonymous gymnasium rector in the provinces. But when he suddenly died in 1831, he was on the top of the German philosophical world. His thought became the standard against which all other philosophical systems constituted themselves.

Hegel accepts the call to Berlin because he wants to disseminate his philosophy of freedom, and Berlin offers him the largest stage for doing so. By accepting a position at the center of German intellectual life, Hegel exemplifies his own conception of freedom. Freedom does not consist in fighting against some dominant external power but in recognizing that the subject must provide the ground for its own act. When one becomes the supreme philosophical authority in Germany, one recognizes the insubstantiality of this authority because its self-division is directly evident. Of course, one can come to this recognition without actually becoming a supreme philosophical authority oneself, but refusing this position and clinging to an outsider status would have the effect of sustaining the image of authority's substantiality. Had Hegel refused the call to Berlin because he didn't want to compromise himself with the center of power, he would have violated his own philosophy of freedom, which requires such compromises to make itself actual.

Hegel's vision of freedom is certainly possible in the provinces, but it prohibits the philosopher from fetishizing the provinces. Insisting on distance from the center of power or maintaining one's marginality misleads us into constructing a philosophy of opposition, which is, for Hegel, the great danger. When we create a philosophy of opposition, we necessarily posit a substantial authority in the other that we oppose and, in this way, fail to recognize ourselves as free. For philosophical reasons, Hegel has to accept the call to Berlin. This places him in direct opposition to Heidegger, who receives a similar call a little over a century later.

Just as Hegel's acceptance of the call to Berlin offers a personal analogue for his conception of freedom, Heidegger's refusal does the same. Unfortunately, the prevailing conception of freedom today is much closer to Heidegger's than it is to Hegel's. When it comes to the decision to move to the center or remain in the margin, Heidegger makes the contemporary decision. Refusing to heed the call to Berlin that Hegel so eagerly accepts, he opts to remain at the University of Freiburg amid the Black Forest. Leaving his Nazism aside, this decision seems to place Heidegger on higher ethical ground than Hegel. He chooses slow country life where he can spend time thinking and interacting with everyday neighbors rather than hobnobbing with political leaders and famous writers. In short, being a philosopher is more important to Heidegger than being recognized as a philosopher, which is what would draw one to Berlin.[9]

In his defense of the decision to remain in the provinces, Heidegger points out how life at an intellectual hub has a distorting effect on one's thought. He writes, "In the public world one can be made a 'celebrity' overnight by the newspapers and journals. That always remains the surest way to have one's ownmost intentions get misinterpreted and quickly and thoroughly forgotten."[10] During the years that have passed since Heidegger made this pronouncement, the distorting effect of the cult of celebrity has multiplied exponentially. Today, even the retreat into his little hut in Todtnauberg could not keep Heidegger safe from international attention. There might even be an amusement park in Todtnauberg to appeal to the children of Heidegger's many visitors.[11] Fame reaches everywhere, and even philosophers are not immune to becoming celebrities in a way that would have been unthinkable in Heidegger's time.

In today's intellectual universe, there is much more critique leveled against Heidegger's politics than Hegel's. This is due not to the time that Heidegger spent at his hut in retreat from the world but to the moments when he ventured out. Though Heidegger resisted the call to Berlin, he did not refuse the opportunity to become the rector of the University of Freiburg after the Nazis came to power in 1933. As rector and as Nazi party member, Heidegger openly identified himself with figures of authority. If Heidegger had simply remained at his hut in Todtnauberg and continued to philosophize about the dangers of modernity, he would have eliminated *avant la lettre* almost all criticism of his politics. But, in a sense, the rectorship and the public engagement associated with it represent Heidegger's attempt to articulate a positive form of freedom. It fails because he finds the image of rebellion too attractive to resist, and rebellion fundamentally shapes the form that his public engagement took.

The same impulse that leads Heidegger to reject the call to Berlin also moves him in the direction of Nazism. He sees in Nazism a rebellion against modernity, and this spirit of rebellion enthralls Heidegger. He sees modernity as the ruling authority that contemporary philosophy must contest. In the *Introduction to Metaphysics*, Heidegger offers a clear portrait of the danger confronting Europe that Nazism promises to defeat. He writes, "Russia and America, seen metaphysically, are both the same: the same hopeless frenzy of unchained technology and of the rootless organization of the average man."[12] Against this onslaught of enforced conformity coming from both East and West, Nazism, as Heidegger conceives it, offers the possibility of preserving what doesn't fit in modernity—like a philosopher in a hut in the Black Forest.

The unhappy political career of Martin Heidegger offers an object lesson in the inadequacy of rebellion as the form of freedom. The impulse that leads Heidegger to oppose authority leaves him vulnerable to the most despotic authority when it paints itself in the guise of a metaphysical rebellion. Heidegger's commitment to resistance as freedom ironically drives him into the heart of a political system that tolerates no resistance of any kind. Heidegger's great political error stems from a theoretical one concerning the nature of freedom.

The contrast between Hegel and Heidegger is a contrast between two competing ideas of freedom. Hegel's freedom has its basis in the absence of any basis. That is to say, we discover our freedom at the moment when we discover that the Other is not just a pure substance, that what we don't know doesn't hold any secret truths. Our freedom relates to an obstacle, but this is our freedom's own obstacle—an internal stumbling block. The subject realizes Hegel's form of freedom through the abandonment of pure negativity and the acceptance of the subject's self-limitation.

For Heidegger, the free subject does not follow along with the crowd. The crowd is anathema, but, at the same time, Heidegger requires the everydayness of the crowd (what he calls *das Man* or the they) in order to constitute his freedom in relation to. The they must play the role of the villain in Heidegger's thought, and freedom exists through the overcoming of this villain. Hegel's conception of freedom, in contrast, internalizes the villain. He can go to Berlin because he recognizes that the opposition that animates freedom will accompany him there. Hegel's freedom doesn't require an external villain because this form of freedom always brings its own villain along with it.

ESCAPE FROM FREEDOM

In the wake of Hegel's exploration of freedom as the positive manifestation of negativity, two thinkers emerge to challenge directly this conception of freedom. They locate freedom in the pure negativity of history's victims and in the marginalized of history—in the proletariat and in the individual. For Karl Marx and Søren Kierkegaard, Hegel's philosophy of freedom represents a circumscribed conception of freedom that they make more inclusive. But while doing this they reintroduce a substantial Other that has the effect of obviating the subject's freedom that Hegel discovers.

From our contemporary perspective, it is almost impossible not to look on Marx and Kierkegaard collectively as an advance on Hegel. Their expansion of freedom seems much more appropriate to modernity than Hegel's version. What's more, in clear contrast to Hegel, they both give us something to do. Hegel's freedom involves nothing but a change of perspective— seeing oneself in absolute otherness or, in other words, recognizing the insubstantiality of the Other. Marx and Kierkegaard impel us toward political revolution and the leap of faith. These parallel gestures move us toward absolute otherness rather than simply adopting a different perspective on it.

But it is because they give us something to do that we should think twice before going beyond Hegel to Marx and Kierkegaard. To be sure, the proletarian revolution and the leap of faith evince more activity than Hegel's theoretical arrival at the absolute idea. But they both represent a philosophical retreat from Hegel's conception of freedom. In their own specific ways, Marx and Kierkegaard reinstall the image of a substantial Other, which is why we should be skeptical of the advance on Hegel that they offer.

Marx's great achievement involves the revelation that substance is subject in the capitalist economy. Capitalism appeals to its adherents because profit appears substantial, the result of a magical process in which the savvy capitalist buys low and sells high. In volume 3 of *Capital*, Marx introduces subjectivity into this equation in the form of the appropriation of surplus value. As Marx grasps, profit appears substantial only because we don't readily see the production and appropriation of surplus value that generate profit. Once we recognize this substance (profit) also as subject (the appropriation of surplus value), it loses its hold over us. We can escape the reign of the capitalist economy in which profit has the last word.

But Marx's investment in freedom is not as thoroughgoing as that of Hegel: he reintroduces a substantial Other when he turns from economics to politics. For the most part, Marx shrouds his vision of the communist future in silence. He offers only a few vague descriptions of what life in this future will be like, although he does characterize it as a realm of freedom, which seems appealing. Toward the end of volume 3 of *Capital*, he differentiates between the economic realm of necessity and the realm of freedom that exists after the means of production have met all needs. He writes, "The true realm of freedom, the development of human powers as an end in itself, begins beyond [the realm of necessity], though it can only flourish with this realm of necessity as its basis. The reduction of the working day is the basic prerequisite."[13] Because Marx ensconces freedom in an absolute beyond, it is not at all surprising that he does not go on to describe this realm of freedom. It is by definition beyond description and unknown, which gives it the status of a substantial Other uninfected by subjectivity. Marx substantializes freedom in the form of a future to be realized. In doing so he falls victim to the precise trap that Hegel works to avoid throughout his philosophical system. At no point does Hegel point toward an unknown future in which things will be better as Marx does. Operating with this image of the future anchors the subject and provides a guide wire for its actions. This represents an abandonment of the subject's freedom, which is also what occurs with Kierkegaard.

The substantial Other in the case of Kierkegaard is more subtle. In many ways, Kierkegaard, despite his rabid opposition to Hegel, formulates a very Hegelian philosophy that identifies dialectical moments in the structure of belief.[14] But Kierkegaard refuses Hegel's interpretation of Christ's death. For Kierkegaard, God remains utterly distinct from the world of finitude.[15] The humiliation of Christ in the finite world does not manifest God's descent or desubstantialization. This is an impossibility that would eliminate the infinite distance that separates the subject from God, but it becomes everyday theology in the Christendom that Kierkegaard excoriates. This infinite distance is correlative to the subject's freedom. Kierkegaard poses it in opposition to Hegelian absolute knowing as the emblem of freedom.

The subject's freedom, for Kierkegaard, depends on an absence of knowledge about God, who thus acquires a substantial status. Despite God's appearance in the finite form of Christ, Kierkegaard's God is not subjectivized. Kierkegaard's critique of Hegel focuses on how the latter fails to grasp his own inability, as a finite subject, to know God.[16] We can have access to God, but this access is only indirect, which is why Christianity requires the leap of faith on the part of the subject. Unlike Hegel, Kierkegaard gives the subject a task—accomplish the leap and become an authentic Christian—but the cost of this task is prohibitive.

Even though Kierkegaard emphasizes that the existing individual is free to accept Christ or not, he stacks the deck through his characterization of God. No matter how often Kierkegaard proclaims that individuals experience anxiety in their freedom, even this anxiety becomes reassuring because God regains a substantial status in his philosophy (that was lost with Hegel). This becomes clear in *The Concept of Anxiety*, when he states, "Anxiety is freedom's possibility, and only such anxiety is through faith absolutely educative, because it consumes all finite ends and discovers all their deceptiveness."[17] Anxiety is not the horror of experiencing no ground for my freedom (as it would be for Hegel); instead, it has a pedagogical effect on the subject and teaches it the insufficiency of all finite options. The subject benefits from anxiety, according to Kierkegaard's schema, because it attests to the substantiality of God in relation to the subject unsubstantial ends. This is Kierkegaard's version of Marx's retreat from Hegelian freedom.

Both Marx and Kierkegaard turn away from Hegel's philosophy of freedom. They balk at the subjectivization of all substance that Hegel accomplishes and reimagine substantiality in new forms. However much sympathy we might feel for the proletariat and the individual, the philosophies that champion them end up abandoning freedom in their attempt to correct Hegel's theorization of it. For Hegel, there is no freedom in simply negating. Doing so resuscitates the substantiality of the Other that his entire philosophy undermines. The attempt to emend Hegel has the effect of dismantling his philosophy of freedom. If we want freedom, we cannot confine ourselves to negating—which is to say, we cannot simply spend our time in rebellion.

CONFEDERATE FLAGS EVERYWHERE

The ideal ego of the modern subject is that of the rebel. Even if the subject's rebellion is nothing but the guise for a thoroughgoing conformity, the subject clings to it feverishly because it enables the subject to navigate the contradictory imperatives that characterize modernity. The image of the rebel connotes freedom and self-determination, a refusal to conform to the demands of authority, which is what modernity calls for. But while adopting this ideal ego, one can at the same time follow authority's demands without avowing this conformity to oneself. As just an image, rebellion doesn't require acting without the security of an authority figure. One has the security of authority without the embarrassment of open conformity.

Hegel's philosophical project aims to strip away this ideal ego from the modern subject. As he sees it, this image disguises the subject's freedom and causes the subject to misrecognize its relation to authority. It creates a subject incapable of performing a transformative act that nonetheless remains convinced of its own radicality. By demolishing this image that holds sway over the modern subject, Hegel makes his contribution to the project of freedom, the project that he identifies with history itself.

The rebel is an insider who experiences existence as an outsider. This paradox holds the key to the attractiveness of the position. Whenever one would pin the rebel down to a specific position, the rebel is always elsewhere, on the outside of this position. In this way, the rebel's freedom remains a negative freedom that has no positive identity. The rebel is free and never complicit.

Despite his marginal status in the recent theoretical landscape, the paradigmatic thinker of rebellion is Albert Camus. His work devoted to it is entitled *L'homme revolté* (translated as *The Rebel*). This book inadvertently demonstrates the danger that the ideal ego of the rebel poses to the freedom of the modern subject. It is not an accident that the great apostle of freedom in the twentieth century, Jean-Paul Sartre, went out of his way to denounce *L'homme revolté* and break with his former friend over its publication. Though Camus doesn't have many disciples today, his conception of rebellion implicitly informs the investment in resistance that proliferates throughout the contemporary theoretical universe.

In *L'homme revolté*, Camus takes pains to dissociate himself from the winners in history and to side with the losers. This is, according to Camus, what it means to embrace the philosophical stance of rebellion. The tendency to rebellion manifests itself philosophically (in rebellion against the human condition and against God) and historically (in rebellion against concrete domination). In both cases, the urge to rebel, the urge to struggle against an unbeatable opponent, demonstrates humanity at its best. Revolt has value because, for Camus, it embodies the subject's freedom. To rebel is to reject domination—either the domination of God or of a human master—and not simultaneously to participate in domination oneself. Herein also lies the difficulty in sustaining rebellion and why, ultimately, it is always doomed to failure in Camus's eyes. If rebellion were to win—which is to say, if it were to become a successful rebellion—then it would cease to be rebellion and would lose its link to freedom. If rebellion wins, it becomes revolution, and revolution necessarily leads to a conformity that the rebel avoids.

As Camus sees it, the thinker guiltiest of betraying rebellion is Hegel, who was also the first to grasp rebellion's importance. The betrayal consists in Hegel's insistence that the winner is always right, an idea that Camus sees present not just in the final affirmation of the absolute but even in the dialectic of the master and the slave. Though he attacks those who would completely dismiss Hegel's important contribution to the thought of rebellion, Camus nonetheless renders a damning verdict in the end. He writes, "Hegel . . . furnished, on the level of the dialectic of master and slave, the decisive justification of the spirit of power in the twentieth century. The conqueror is always right; that is one of the lessons which can be learned from the most important German philosophical system of the nineteenth century."[18] Oddly enough, Camus locates the idea that "the conqueror is always right" in the dialectic of the master and slave (chapter 4 of the *Phenomenology*), where Hegel shows, in no uncertain terms, that it is the conquered, rather than the conqueror, who is "right."

This profound misreading is doubly significant for its error. It is not just, as Sartre claims, that Camus hadn't bothered to read Hegel before attacking him, but that his commitment to rebellion utterly conditions his reading. For Camus, Hegel's great error—and he can find this error anywhere in Hegel, even in passages that are most opposed to it—lies in Hegel's abandonment of negativity for a positive form of freedom.

For critics Jean-Paul Sartre and Francis Jeanson (who wrote the initial negative review of *L'homme revolté* in *Les Temps Modernes*), Camus's mistake lies in his allergy to revolutionary victory and in his allegiance to rebellious struggle. But neither Sartre nor Jeanson grasp why Camus rejects revolutionary victory. Camus transforms hysteria into a political and philosophical principle. In the face of what Camus considers an absurd world, the subject seemingly has no substantial Other to serve as a ground for its freedom. Rebellion is a strategy for reconstituting the uninterrupted substantiality of the Other in the modern world. This is why Hegel sees such a danger to freedom in the development of the rebel as modernity's ideal ego.

The rebel always has a substantial Other in the form of the authority that the rebel struggles against. This authority is purely substantial because it remains an authority even as its form undergoes a series of complete transformations. It doesn't matter what form the external authority has: external authority as such will endure. The struggle will go on, and freedom will never have to manifest itself in a positive form. Rebels never have to see how their resistance manifests itself without what it resists. Rebellion provides the comfort of being on the outside while imagining that there is a substantial enemy on the other side.

Hegel wants to deprive us of this enemy, which functions as a barrier to freedom. Pure negativity constructs an image of freedom that eliminates the possibility for the recognition of freedom as actual. In contrast, when one compromises one's theoretical position with actuality and when one identifies positive formations of freedom, one is not tainting thought with the scourge of the real world. Instead, through this path one elevates thought to the dignity of actuality.

Hegel pushes negativity to its ultimate point so that it loses its purity and manifests itself in actuality. Without this actualization, negativity cannot serve as the site for freedom. If one wants freedom, one must discover what happens when there are no external authorities left to fight, when the external authorities appear as the mark of our freedom rather than as an obstacle to it. One must denounce, but one must not remain content with just denouncing. The freedom to denounce fails to see that it remains caught up in what it denounces, whereas the freedom that identifies its own limit in the external authority reaches the point of self-determination.

Chapter Nine

ABSOLUTE OR BUST

A TOTALITY THAT UNDERMINES ITSELF

Hegel's insistence on constructing a totalizing system is responsible for much of the hostility that his thought receives, especially during the twentieth century. It seems almost commonsensical that there is a connection, if not a causal relation, between a totalizing philosophical system and the emergence of totalitarian political systems. The fact that Hegel and Nazism arise in the same territory contributes to this wisdom. Though the dispersion of knowledge in the twentieth century might make thinking the totality impossible, the political developments of the century render it ethically reprehensible. While only a few ardent opponents blame Hegel for the Holocaust, most critical thinkers chafe at the construction of a totalizing system in the aftermath of this horror.[1] But the invective against the all-encompassing structure of Hegel's philosophy doesn't wait for the Holocaust.

The fundamentals of the critique originate with Søren Kierkegaard, who mounts it soon after Hegel's death. For Kierkegaard, the problem with the whole is double: it is always only an illusory totality, a conceptual whole that fails to capture the actuality of the particulars, but the very attempt to conceptualize the whole has the effect of violently altering the status of the particulars. For critics of Hegel like Kierkegaard, the conceptual inadequacy of the whole augments rather than mitigates its violence. The thought of all particulars in light of their relationship to the whole distorts their particularity by framing it in terms of an illusion—the totality—and does not do them justice.[2] The whole can never become whole enough to include the variegations of multiplicity that constantly escape it.

In short, Hegel purveys epistemic violence. According to his critics, in the act of identifying the whole, Hegel fails to pay attention to the misalignment between the whole and the particulars that constitute it.[3] The whole is an imaginary illusion constituted out of an assemblage of particulars, and the concept directs our attention away from the disparate entities that make it up. Obviously, one must think beyond the particular if one is to think at all because the particular exists in relation and not in isolation. But relation doesn't necessarily depend on totality: the concept of assemblage has gained traction precisely because it avoids the violent distortion that comes with totality. Discussion about assemblages is implicitly (or explicitly in some cases) a critique of Hegel's constant recourse to the whole.[4]

The construction of a philosophical system was trendy when Hegel came of age as a thinker. Almost every German philosopher felt a compulsion to produce a distinctive system that would function as an individual signature. We can even define German Idealism through the commitment of its adherents to constructing a system. Kant originates German Idealism with a systematic philosophy, but he never formally announces that he is constructing a system and never articulates the foundational principle of that system. It falls to Karl Reinhold and J. G. Fichte to make systematizing explicit in the universe of German Idealism.

The drive to systematize philosophy in the case of Reinhold and Fichte stems from the belief that one can discover a single foundational principle that could act as the starting point for one's philosophy. The system would emerge out of this principle and constantly refer back to it. For Reinhold, this principle is representation. For Fichte, in contrast, it is the self-positing of the I. Even though they establish opposed foundational principles, both thinkers believe that they are simply extracting the principle implicit in Kant's philosophy. From their perspective, Kant's failure is structural rather than theoretical: he didn't see the necessity of the system and thus left the foundational principle in abeyance.

When Hegel comes along in the wake of Reinhold and Fichte, he retains their commitment to a system while abandoning their faith in the discovery of a first principle that would provide the foundation for that system.[5] Hegel's turn away from a first principle marks a key step in his emergence as a distinctive thinker. He comes to believe that any assertion of a first principle would always produce a one-sided and hence incomplete philosophy—a philosophy relying on the reference to some otherness that it doesn't conceptualize but nonetheless requires.

Insisting on a first principle proves an insurmountable barrier to the construction of a system of the whole. In the preface to the *Phenomenology of Spirit*, Hegel clarifies his position on these questions. He states that "the true shape in which truth exists can only be the scientific system of that truth," but he also claims that a "so-called fundamental proposition or first principle of philosophy, if it is true, is for this reason alone also false, just because it is a fundamental proposition or principle."[6] In these two remarks, Hegel both affirms the necessity of a philosophical system and rejects a first principle for that system. He sees that no principle is sustainable as a first principle since it implicitly relies on other principles in order to distinguish itself.

Reinhold and Fichte fail to develop coherent systems not because they don't try but because they remain wedded to deducing the totality beginning with a first principle.[7] The first principle provides the foundation for a system as they believe but actually infects the system with a lacuna that it is impossible to fill because the first principle is a presupposition that the system itself does not justify. Fichte, for instance, cannot deduce the self-positing of the I. He assumes it as the starting point for his system.

In this sense, the two ambitions of German Idealism—constructing a systematic philosophy and discovering a first principle for that philosophy—are irrevocably at odds with each other. The impulse to systematizing precludes the articulation of a first principle that would found the system. The moment that one would articulate the first principle, systematizing would entail locating it within the totality. In this way, the demands of the totality vitiate the possibility of a first principle that would not immediately lose its priority. With the two statements from the preface to the *Phenomenology of Spirit* on the system and on the possibility of a first principle, Hegel preserves the most important legacy of early German Idealism and breaks from the foundational prejudice that hampered its emancipation from early modern philosophy. Hegel owes the idea of the total system to the earlier

German Idealists. My contention is that it is this idea, cleansed of the corresponding first principle, that enables Hegel to reveal the inescapability of contradiction.

Though Hegel constructs a totalizing system, its airtight structure does not produce a perfectly harmonious whole in which nothing is out of place. Instead, the totality renders visible the ontological necessity of contradiction. This is the reason that Hegel insists on thinking the absolute idea. When one pulls up short of the absolute and contents oneself with not thinking systematically, contradiction seems contingent and thus not inevitable. From the perspective of a particular, it appears as if one can eliminate contradiction by revolutionizing the situation. Or it appears that different particulars can coexist without conflict because they seem not to bear on each other. On their own, particulars create the illusion of the possibility of avoiding contradiction. This is, for Hegel, the great danger of the failure to think absolutely.

If I think, for instance, of the problem of a worldwide financial crisis from the perspective a particular bank, the contradictions expressed in the crisis become avoidable. Our bank can get ahead of the curve—foreclosing before other banks, increasing our liquidity sooner, and so on. From the perspective of the particular bank, the crisis is a challenge to overcome, not a contradiction to endure. But when we take the whole of the capitalist system into account, the contradiction becomes necessary. If one bank doesn't fail, others will. In this way, the absolute perspective reveals the deception inhering in the particular.

When Hegel arrives at absolute knowing in the *Phenomenology of Spirit*, he reveals the theoretical radicality inherent in this position. This is not the point at which the subject knows everything that there is to know but rather the point at which the subject recognizes that there are no more conceivable paths out of contradiction. Absolute knowing affirms the necessity of a failure that occurs when the subject collides with the inevitability of contradiction. This is why one might rename absolute knowing the recognition of the inevitability of contradiction.

The absolute does not bring together all prior partial perspectives into a holistic oneness. A close reading of Hegel's discussion reveals that, contrary to the popular understanding, the moment of attaining the whole does not announce the end of all conflict but rather inscribes the necessity of conflict within the system. The sublation (*Aufhebung*) of prior positions occurs through their failure. When we reach the absolute, we have exhausted all possibilities for the elimination of contradiction. At this point we have nowhere else to go. We have come to contradiction in its most intractable form—the internal division within being itself.

In the "Absolute Knowing" section of the *Phenomenology of Spirit*, Hegel articulates the core of his philosophy as he does nowhere else. He proclaims that, when one reaches absolute knowing, "knowing is acquainted not only with itself, but also with the negative of itself, or its limit." This limit is not an external one (which would transform Hegel into Kant) but the internal contradiction of subjectivity. This leads him to add, "to know one's limit is to know how to sacrifice oneself."[8] The link between knowing one's limit and the act of self-sacrifice is found in contradiction. Recognizing oneself as a contradictory entity and recognizing that there is no solution to the problem of contradiction force the subject to give up the dream of pure substantiality—both its own and that of its divine Other. Self-sacrifice is not literal suicide but rather an abandonment of the security that the dream of an actually existing substance provides for the subject.

As long as one pulls up short of the absolute and the universality it entails, one remains invested in some form of nonsubjectivized substantiality, located either in oneself or in some form of the other. The absolute deprives the subject of this escape hatch. It is not, as so many believe, a moment of ultimate mastery over the other but a complete abandonment of the security of all mastery. This is why so many subsequent philosophers have resisted following Hegel to the end of the line.[9] They embrace the dialectical method, while jettisoning the totalizing system and the oppressive absolute, or they critique him for dissolving all otherness within an all-encompassing subject. What all these responses have in common is their retreat from the traumatic implications of acceding to the absolute. It is the only path to freedom, but it costs one all hope for respite from the self-destructiveness of contradiction.

THE REVELATORY WHOLE

Hegel's insistence on the necessity of systematic or totalizing thinking seems difficult to defend today. It is easy to see the epistemic violence that occurs when Hegel constantly refers the particular to the universal. By doing so, his critics argue, he fails to grant the particular its specific difference and conceives that difference only in terms of the universality that determines it. This has disturbing implications that many thinkers have pointed out.

The attack on Hegelian totalization reaches one of its high points at the conclusion of Jean-François Lyotard's influential essay "Answering the Question: What Is Postmodernism?"[10] After identifying Hegel as the theorist who totalizes disparate presentations through a transcendental illusion, Lyotard goes on to identify this illusion with terror and to call for an absolute rejection of any pretensions to totality. He claims, "The nineteenth and twentieth centuries have given us as much terror as we can take. We have paid a high enough price for the nostalgia of the whole and of the one, for the reconciliation of the concept and the sensible, of the transparent and the communicable experience. . . . The answer is: Let us wage a war on totality."[11] As Lyotard sees it, there is a clear through line from Hegel's totalizing philosophy to the mass exterminations of those who didn't fit within the totality in the Soviet Union and Nazi Germany. Though Lyotard doesn't explicitly pin the blame for the Holocaust on Hegel, he does see enough of a connection to issue a warning against the kind of philosophy that Hegel produces. The idea of a totalizing system is anathema to Lyotard and most other thinkers of the late twentieth century.

Not only has the absolute fueled Hegel's opponents like Lyotard, but it has also chagrined many of his adherents. For instance, Robert Solomon, in his otherwise laudatory *In the Spirit of Hegel*, asserts that "'the Absolute' . . . is European cultural imperialism and a historical rationale for murder."[12] Solomon's position is not anomalous, but it does strain his ability to remain within the orbit of Hegel's thought.[13] The problem is that Hegel steadfastly identifies the true with the totality and refuses any attempt to break from the philosophical system.

In the preface to the *Phenomenology of Spirit*, this refusal occasions Hegel's alignment of the true with the whole.[14] On first encountering this claim, it appears as if Hegel envisions a harmonious totality in which each part has its proper place and contributes to the whole. One might imagine this whole on the model of Plato's republic, which has perfect stability because each caste remains in its assigned position without asserting any rights of the particular in relation to the whole. The good of the whole trumps the rights of the particular.

This is the typical reading of Hegel's philosophy and his invocation of the absolute. Even the term *absolute* suggests that this is not a misreading, that Hegel really means that the system contains everything in its proper position. The danger of this type of philosophy has not gone unnoticed. As Solomon (among many others) suggests, it is almost indistinguishable from the history of European cultural imperialism. In response, Hegel's followers have worked diligently to craft a successful apology for the absolute.

To this end, thinkers have begun to recognize the absolute not as a moment that eliminates all difference but as an explosion of it. Catherine Malabou is the chief exponent of this position. For Malabou, when we reach the absolute, we reach a moment of complete openness to transformation or what she terms (following Hegel himself) *plasticity*. By pushing our position to its end point, we open ourselves to the radically new. As Malabou puts it, "Far from enforcing a violent stoppage of the dialectical progress, the advent of Absolute Knowledge will imply instead the exact opposite: its *metamorphosis*. Dialectical sublation will become absolute sublation—its own absolution."[15] When absolute knowing closes a window, it opens a door.

Malabou interprets Hegel's absolute along the lines of the philosophy proposed by Tyler Durden (Brad Pitt) in David Fincher's *Fight Club* (1999). Tyler Durden, the creator of fight club, is a prophet of subjective destitution— the abandonment of all shreds of symbolic identity that connect one to the social order. The fight club, in which one allows oneself to be savagely beaten, is the ultimate expression of this logic. For Tyler Durden, we attain freedom only after an absolute loss. He proclaims, "It is only after you've lost everything that you're free to do anything." The destitution of absolute loss makes visible new possibilities that the chains of symbolic identity had foreclosed. This is the moment of what Malabou would call plasticity. As she sees it, plasticity corresponds exactly to the point of absolute knowing in the *Phenomenology of Spirit*.

Hegel arrives at the absolute after the exhaustion of all other possibilities. We see that no earlier positions are tenable. At this point, openness to unknown possibilities ensues, possibilities that are not prefigured within the dialectic that precedes them. This is why Malabou identifies absolute knowing with the plasticity of the subject. The recognition that all previous possibilities have been exhausted represents the only possible path to novelty.

The radicality of Hegel's absolute is precisely its closure, its refusal to brook additional possibilities. It is only when we see that there are no more avenues that thought can take, no additional possibilities that might portend the possibility of eliminating contradiction, that we reach the absolute. Though Malabou is surely correct to claim that this opens up other hitherto hidden avenues for exploration, the main import of the absolute lies in the fact that it exposes the much more sober truth that any avenue for exploration will encounter: no novel development will overcome the contradiction that defines both thought and being.

PUBLIC MASTURBATION

Hegel's identification of the true with the whole has spawned ironic rejoinders, even among those who are largely sympathetic to Hegel's project. This is the case most famously with Theodor Adorno. In *Minima Moralia*, Adorno proclaims in response to this statement, "The whole is the false."[16] For Adorno, the dialectical method provides the basis for critical social analysis, but the creation of a whole system from this method ultimately results in the betrayal of its critical function. Adorno abandons the systematic whole in order to preserve the emancipatory potential of the method.

The problem is that it is not so easy to avoid the system. Hegel does not simply add the whole to the dialectical method. The whole is operative as soon as the method is. It is possible to assert particular difference, but one always does so through the articulation of universality, even though this universality is not often explicit. In his discussion of individuality in the *Phenomenology of Spirit*, Hegel makes clear that it is impossible for an individual to act without reference to the universal. Without an investment in the universal, the individual would not act at all. Hegel writes that individuals "pretend that their deeds and efforts are something for themselves alone in which they had only *themselves* and *their own essence* as an aim." The problem is, as Hegel sees it, that one's deeds betray one's intentions. He adds, "However, in doing something and thus presenting themselves and showing themselves in the light of day, they immediately contradict by their deed their pretense of wanting to exclude the light of day itself, the universal consciousness, and the participation of all."[17] Acting is having recourse to the universal and abandoning one's private self. Hegel's point here is that individuals cannot act as pure individuals. In the moment of the act, one partakes in the whole by acting rather than remaining idle in one's particularity.

The universal necessarily imposes itself on even the most self-interested act. We can see this in a variety of instances. It is the great lesson of the capitalist economic system, which functions on the basis of the self-interested particular actually working on behalf of the whole. When I try to enrich myself at the expense of everyone else in the society by selling real estate, for example, I inadvertently benefit others by helping them find a place to live and by giving them jobs working for me. What's more, I can only sell real estate within a social system that guarantees the protection of private property. My private act of selling real estate cannot escape involvement with universality. Despite its ultimate betrayal of universality (through its destruction of the public world held in common), the capitalist system reveals universality's triumph. It shows that no matter how we try to avoid it, we make reference to the universal.[18]

Even our most private acts expose our necessary recourse to the universal when we examine them. In the privacy of a diary, I feel as if I hold the universal at bay, which is why I can write things in my diary that I could never say publicly. But even here the force of the universal is evident. Not only do diary writers always imagine someone reading their entries (even if just a future self), but they also use the universal medium of language to communicate their private thoughts. The privacy of the diary does not shelter the subject from the reach of universality. For this reason, masturbation, another essentially private act, presents a more thoroughgoing challenge to Hegel's claim about the role of the universal and the necessity of the absolute.

Masturbators engage in this act for their own pleasure while using their own private fantasies. Unlike writing a diary, typically no one teaches the subject how to masturbate. Furthermore, one doesn't have to have recourse to language in order to do it. It seems private through and through. But the fantasies that enable the masturbatory process are not immune from universality, despite its concealed status. Subjects create their fantasies unconsciously through their interaction with the universal, which is why no fantasy is completely idiosyncratic, even though every fantasy is distinct. When I fantasize about being covered in chocolate, for instance, I dip into the universal to concoct this particular form of enjoyment. My private fantasy includes reference to acts I've witnessed and people I've seen.

What's more, the act of masturbating is a public deed in Hegel's sense because of what it isn't. When we masturbate, we turn away from the public and confine ourselves for a few moments to our private worlds. This confinement is itself revelatory. By turning away from the public, masturbators articulate their negative relationship to the public. Their insistence on their isolated sexual satisfaction indicates their participation in the universal through a conspicuous withdrawal. Someone who only masturbates rather than ever having sex with someone else proclaims their relationship to the social totality as vehemently as someone who has sex in the middle of the street.

The problem with masturbation, however, is that it obscures the reference to the universal that it employs. To masturbate is to experience oneself as a wholly private being, a particular who exists apart from any universality. Most do not even announce to their closest friends that they engage in it. Though it may not lead to blindness, masturbation does mystify the subject's relationship to the universal.

The real estate broker, the diarist, and the masturbator all have recourse to the universal despite their attempts to dwell in their particularity. But perhaps the greatest testament to the necessity of the absolute is one of the most individualistic thinkers who ever lived. Henry David Thoreau proves Hegel's point better than anyone. Thoreau goes to Walden Pond to carve out his own distinct existence away from the influence of others. Not only does he distance himself from other people, but he also avoids most of the accouterments of society. He builds a small cabin by Walden Pond and more or less fends for himself.

Thoreau insists on particularity to such an extent that he doesn't even want others to take his individual project as a model. In *Walden*, he writes, "I would not have any one adopt *my* mode of living on any account; . . . I desire that there may be as many different persons in the world as possible; but I would have each one be very careful to find out and pursue *his own* way, and not his father's or his mother's or his neighbor's instead."[19] No one else should universalize Thoreau's particularity because particularity is what he cherishes. Despite his call for particular diversity, however, Thoreau is actually a partisan of the universal, every bit as much as Hegel. Instead of living on his own in private and quietly dying, Thoreau takes pains to recount his experiences in a book for everyone to read. He gives his two years at Walden Pond a universal form. In Hegel's terms, he ensures that his deed sees "the light of day." Thoreau's emphasis on particularity makes it tempting to interpret him as Hegel's opposite number, but his unabashed recourse to a universal form suggests their hidden kinship.

But it is not enough to recognize the necessity of reference to the universal. Hegel takes the further step of claiming that universals exist within a systematic totality that relates them to each other. One cannot make an isolated truth claim that does not bear on all other possible truth claims. The necessity of the system becomes apparent in Hegel's critique of Kantian morality. When he looks to exemplify the moral law, Kant often has recourse to theft. We know that stealing violates the categorical imperative because it produces a self-contradictory maxim. If my maxim states that I should take what I want regardless of who owns it, this maxim would lead to the destruction of property relations if universalized. It is thus, according to Kant, both contradictory and immoral—or immoral because it is contradictory.

For Hegel, this is a case where Kant's morality runs aground on the basis of his failure to think systematically. Kant treats the subject's maxim— stealing is permitted—in isolation from all the determinations of the social order, including the prevailing property relations. If the society had no private property and everything belonged to people in common, the maxim of taking what I want without regard to ownership would not at all be self-contradictory. One must take the whole into account in order to grasp what is actually at stake, which is what Kantian morality fails to do. One cannot conceive particular maxims in isolation from the whole.

Every claim to a partial truth or a local truth necessarily implies a universal background that this truth relies on.[20] The attempt to avoid the whole leaves one unknowingly implicated in it. This is why Hegel goes through each position leading up to the absolute. If we stopped at the beginning, at sense certainty in the *Phenomenology of Spirit* or at being in the *Science of Logic*, we would simply blind ourselves to the ways in which these apparently simple positions actually imply a totality of relations they refuse to avow. In this sense, the move to the whole is nothing but the expression of what would otherwise be effective but unexpressed. The whole is always operative, and the explication of the system enables us to be aware of it rather than permitting it to work in obscurity. Hegel creates a philosophy oriented around the absolute because he believes that it is impossible not to do so.

While this line of thought does provide a solid ground for Hegel's insistence on the whole, it misses the role that the whole plays in rendering contradiction evident. The problem with the insistence on local truths or particularity is not just that these statements enable the whole to function stealthily. They also have the effect of obscuring the necessity of contradiction. As long as one stops short of the whole, one sustains the illusion that we might discover—or at least that there might exist—a state free of contradiction. This is, for Hegel, the great danger for thought. Reason is our ability to grasp contradiction rather than just being destroyed by it. But the refusal to think in a totalizing way betrays reason and leaves open the possibility for trying to overcome contradiction.

As Hegel recognizes, we don't just arrive at the absolute. We can't avoid it. Though it comes at the end of the *Science of Logic* (and the *Phenomenology of Spirit*) as the final product of the trajectory of Hegel's philosophy, the absolute is at the same time the starting point as well. In the *Phenomenology*, the experience of spirit doesn't begin with sense certainty, perception, and understanding, and then become more and more mediated, finally culminating in absolute knowing. On the contrary, thought begins with Hegel's end point—the absolute—and subsequently makes explicit what was only initially implicit. In the *Science of Logic*, Hegel makes this clear, contending that "one may well say, therefore, that every beginning must be made with the *absolute*, just as every advance is only the exposition of it, in so far as *implicit in existence* is the concept."[21] Even the supposed apprehension of immediacy is always already implicated in the absolute idea. Rather than offering a description of the historical evolution of experience and thought, the *Phenomenology* and the *Logic* recount their mythology, the presuppositions that thought itself posits as its history. From the beginning, we find ourselves immersed in the absolute. As Hegel sees it, we can either attempt to swim through its waters or proclaim to each other that we are actually on dry land.

RIDING TO SINGULARITY

Hegel's investment in the universal was such that he celebrates its triumph even when this means his particular demise. He knows that the sacrifice of particularity on the altar of universality is the only path to an authentic singularity. For Hegel personally, this sacrifice occurs when Napoleon invades the city in which Hegel lives. During the Battle of Jena while Hegel is a young professor at the university there, he famously claims to have seen Napoleon riding on horseback from the window of his house. On October 13, 1806, he writes to his friend Friedrich Niethammer, "I saw the Emperor—this world-soul—riding out of the city on reconnaissance. It is indeed a wonderful sensation to see such an individual, who, concentrated here at a single point, astride a horse, reaches out over the world and masters it."[22] Hegel's description of the event suggests that the encounter with Napoleon awes him and leaves him starstruck, which naturally garners suspicion. No fan of the conquering Napoleon, it seems, can be a philosopher for emancipatory politics.

But what Hegel finds so appealing about Napoleon riding through Jena after the conquest is not the glory of triumph but its status as a positive form of freedom. Though in relation to the French Revolution and to the inhabitants of Haiti Napoleon was not an ambassador of freedom, in Germany it was a different story. Napoleon brings with him the universal and modernity: as he conquers Germany, he also reveals that a thread of universality underlies the various German particular identities asserting themselves at the time. Hegel recoils from the rampant German nationalism and reactionary insistence on traditional identity that predominates in Germany. As Hegel sees it, Napoleon's victory is the victory of universality over particularity, and universality has the effect of laying bare the falsity of the insistence on particularity. One's particular is never as particular as one imagines it to be. The subject always proclaims its particularity from a universal position, though this position often remains mystified. Napoleon's conquest has the happy effect of eliminating the mystification surrounding German particularity.

But for Hegel personally, the conquest is not quite so happy. Napoleon's victory not only implies his own nation's defeat but also the closure of the university where Hegel works, the loss of his job, the possible destruction of the manuscript of the *Phenomenology of Spirit*, and the burning down of his residence. Napoleon's victory basically destroys Hegel's life and condemns him to ten years of teaching at a gymnasium rather than at a university. Though Hegel could not have anticipated how personally costly Napoleon's victory at Jena would be for him, he knows that enemy forces are conquering his own country, and he unconditionally applauds their victory. At few points in the history of philosophy has a thinker cast aside his personal interest for the sake of his philosophical position to the extent that Hegel does during the conquest of Jena. Though it is not quite the equivalent of Socrates drinking hemlock rather than betraying his own thought, it is the embrace of a symbolic death. Hegel does so to escape the trap of thinking like a particular.

The more that we retreat into the particular and refuse the universal, the more we inadvertently rely on it. The most extreme version of the rejection of the universal can never be extreme enough. The particular depends on universality in order to be a particular, which renders the insistence on particularity profoundly misleading. Hegel grasps that any turn away from the universal will have the effect of eliminating rather than sustaining particularity. The path to authentic singularity doesn't lead through the particular but through the universal. It is only by following the universal and attaining the absolute that we discover singularity.

The absolute, for Hegel, is not the assertion of an abstract universality but the point at which authentic singularity can exist. When we think through the absolute, we accede to the necessity of contradiction. At this point, I would suggest, we recognize that the whole always has a hole, that no social whole can achieve a perfect self-identity in which every part has its proper place. This failure is singularity. The singularity of the subject emerges through how the subject doesn't fit in the whole.

Hegel makes a fundamental distinction between particularity and singularity. Unlike particularity that opposes its indeterminate diversity to the universal, singularity emerges out of universality. In the *Science of Logic*, Hegel calls singularity a "*determinate universality*" in order to convey this idea.[23] The singular includes the mediation of the universal within it and becomes unique through how it relates this internal universality. It arises through the recognition of the formative role that the universal plays in determining it, but it is able to articulate its exclusive difference through its relationship to this determination. By going through universality rather than simply ignoring it, we arrive at a determinate singularity rather than an indeterminate and multiple particularity. The explicit connection the universal gives the singular a unique distinctiveness that the particular lacks.

The difference between particularity and singularity manifests itself in the contrast between two American thinkers of the early twentieth century—Booker T. Washington and W. E. B. Du Bois. Slavery and its aftermath is an assertion of white particularity, a white refusal to accede to universal freedom and equality. This occasions various responses by black theorists, but the opposed programs of Washington and Du Bois stand out for their advocacy of particularity versus singularity. Washington proposes a solution to the problem of white racist society by calling for the development of black particularity, whereas Du Bois recognizes that any effective political program must engage the universal.

Though Washington advocates for black freedom, he does so by accepting black particular difference. Rather than challenge the situation of black particularity in early twentieth-century America as an effect of white oppression, he exhorts his comrades not to revolt against this oppression but to "cast down your bucket where you are."[24] As Washington sees it, one should develop one's particularity without insisting on universal aspirations. This insistence on the particular leads directly to the oxymoronic vision of a world in which black and white are separate but united. A few pages later in *Up from Slavery*, he adds, "In all things that are purely social we can be as separate as the fingers, yet one as the hand in all things essential to mutual progress."[25] Though Washington has a vision of social progress, it is not a vision of equality. Championing one's particularity always leaves one where one is, and where one is is necessarily the contingent result of one's social situation. Washington leaves the black subject in an indeterminate particularity rather than allowing for the determination of singularity.

Washington's emphasis on black particularity forms the basis for his politics. But black particularity involves doing activities that whites in charge have historically forced blacks to do—like tilling fields and performing menial labor. In this sense, there is nothing distinct about Washington's vision of black particularity. Black particularity is not singular, and this is its fundamental limitation. It is also the limitation of Washington's political position.

W. E. B. Du Bois presents a clear contrast. Writing contemporaneously with Washington, Du Bois doesn't content himself with black particularity in response to white oppression but instead has recourse to the universal. He recognizes that the same universality that shapes whites also shapes black subjects. But blackness involves a different relationship to this universality. While the white subject can have the illusory solace of an alignment between white particularity and the universal, the black subject inherently recognizes the alienation of particularity in the universal that produces singularity.

Because he pays attention to both universality and its failure to accommodate black identity, Du Bois can articulate black singularity in a way that Washington never approaches. In his most famous statement from *The Souls of Black Folks*, Du Bois claims, "It is a peculiar sensation, this double-consciousness, this sense of always looking at one's self through the eyes of others, of measuring one's soul by the tape of a world that looks on in amused contempt and pity. One ever feels his twoness,—an American, a Negro; two souls, two thoughts, two unreconciled strivings, two warring ideals in one dark body, whose dogged strength alone keeps it from being torn asunder."[26] This statement has gained so much acclaim because it captures both the weight of the universal and its moment of failure in which singularity emerges. Unlike Washington, Du Bois doesn't disdain the universal. He sees that the detour through universality is the only path to actual black singularity. The pure insistence on one's own particularity leaves one stuck within an indeterminate diversity. Du Bois moves through universality and engages it in order to discover the singular as a form of what Hegel calls determinate universality.

Hegel insists on the absolute because he recognizes that we must think absolutely in order to arrive at the singular. The irony of Hegel's philosophy—an irony many have missed—is that, though he seems to serve up individuals for the sake of the systematic whole, the whole exists for the sake of singularity. When we stop short of the totality, we obscure singularity. Hegel recognizes that attempting to isolate ourselves in our immediate particularity and refusing the universal is actually a way of missing the opening for singularity. It is Hegel, not his later antisystematic critics, who is the apostle of the singular.[27]

IS HEGEL A RACIST?

Hegel's commitment to the absolute enables him to resist the traditional form of racism that refuses to see the racial other as a subject and instead treats this other as a substantial entity. This kind of racism emphasizes particular difference that it associates with race, enabling the racist subject to imagine that the denigrated other remains a natural being rather than an alienated subject. This is the position—labeled *orientalism* by Edward

Said—that celebrates Eastern wisdom, fears black animality, and respects the aboriginal bond with nature. Though these attitudes vary widely, each of them stems from a substantialization of the racial other. They treat the other as whole, without the self-division that constitutes the racist subject itself.[28] When racial others are figures of substance rather than alienated subjects, they appear outside the absolute that governs all speaking subjects.

In Hegel's philosophy, no one exists outside the purview of the absolute. As a result, no racial other has a hidden wisdom or a secret bestiality that derives from its connection with nature. In this way, he echoes Said's critique of orientalism. In the most famous instance of this approach, Hegel refuses to grant to the ancient Egyptians a knowledge that outsiders lack, even though Egyptian art is replete with puzzles that suggest the existence of such a knowledge. In the *Aesthetics*, Hegel claims that our lack of knowledge of the solution to the puzzles of Egyptian art is already the solution because not even the Egyptians know. As he says, "The problems remain unsolved, and the solution which *we* can provide consists therefore only in interpreting the riddles of Egyptian art and its symbolic works as a problem remaining undeciphered by the Egyptians themselves."[29] In contrast to European thinkers who find something fascinating about the mystery of Egyptian art, Hegel refuses to posit a solution to the mystery. To do so would be to fall into the racist trap of believing that the racial other somehow bypasses subjectivity and exists as a substantial entity, thereby harboring a secret knowledge. For Hegel, there is no substance, not even God, that avoids the self-division of the subject. Subjectivity is absolute.

But Hegel's commentary on the Egyptians in the *Aesthetics* is not the only indication of his allegiance to the absolute on the question of race. It is through Hegel's embrace of the Haitian Revolution that his racial solidarity through the absolute most stands out. As Hegel composed the *Phenomenology of Spirit*, Haitians engaged in the first successful slave revolt in human history.[30] According to the analysis provided by Susan Buck-Morss in her remarkable *Hegel, Haiti, and Universal History*, Hegel followed the slave revolt closely and used the discussion of "Master and Servant" to comment on the revolt and possible reprisals. Buck-Morss argues, "Beyond a doubt Hegel knew about real slaves and their revolutionary struggles. In perhaps the most political expression of his career, he used the sensational events of Haiti as the linchpin in his argument in *The Phenomenology of Spirit*."[31] The triumph of the servant that Hegel lays out in the

"Master and Servant" section takes the Haitian experience as its inspiration. Haiti is a genuine moment of the universal's triumph, a moment when freedom and equality emerge as not simply particular European values but as universal ones.

Given Hegel's insistence on the necessity of repetition for a transformation to become fully actual, the Haitian Revolution has even more importance than its French precursor.[32] On the basis of the French Revolution alone, the ruling elite around the world could dismiss the assertion of freedom, equality, and solidarity as a contingent blip in human history. The Haitian Revolution forces everyone to reckon with these values as universal through its repetition of the French Revolution. The second revolution is thus more traumatic for the world, and the retreat from it has preoccupied the last two centuries. Hegel, however, remained a supporter of revolutionary Haiti throughout his life.

Later in the *Phenomenology of Spirit*, Hegel envisions how we should respond to the racism that locates the other's otherness in the materiality of the body. In Hegel's epoch, phrenology served as a widespread justification for racist judgments on the intelligence of non-Europeans.[33] Though he recognizes that phrenology stumbles on an insight concerning the necessity of the subject's material being, he nonetheless vehemently attacks it as a theoretical position because he recognizes the role that it plays in the racism of his time. He goes so far as to imagine how one must combat this reactionary philosophy. Since phrenology reduces subjectivity to its natural material manifestation, it is impossible to respond through argument, which presupposes the acceptance the subject's break from nature.

As a result, Hegel contends that one cannot engage in a traditional dispute with the phrenologist. Any argument would fall on deaf ears, so one must have recourse to a response on the level of the phrenologist's own theoretical position. According to Hegel, when someone says to you, "You (your inner being) are this kind of person because your skull bone is constituted in such and such a way," there is only one appropriate response. He claims, "the retort here would really have to go as far as smashing the skull of the person who makes a statement like that in order to demonstrate to him in a manner just as graspable as his wisdom that for a person a bone is nothing *in itself* and is even less *his* true actuality."[34] Here, Hegel envisions a response to the phrenologist that would make the error of this position clear. One must reject it without any debate because the racist attempt to bypass universality in identifying the subject cannot be countered by a convincing argument, which would take place within the universality of language. Hegel's critique of phrenology and the racism inherent in it indicates not only his commitment to the universality of the absolute but also the antiracism that accompanies this commitment.

Unfortunately, Hegel's later comments on race do not uphold the commitment to the absolute of those in the *Phenomenology of Spirit*. It is a commonplace to say that Hegel makes his most indefensible comments as a result of his commitment to an unrelenting totalizing. According to this line of thought, this commitment leads him to forget about the importance of cultural difference and vituperatively condemn those that have no proper place in his schema of history. In his critique of the racism that infects Hegel's philosophy, Peter Park identifies Hegel's insistence on a totalizing system as a culprit. He claims that Hegel's racism has its basis in his belief that "truth is singular" and that "only one philosophy can be true."[35] The fall of Hegel's philosophy into racism, according to Park and others, stems from his failure to grasp the multiplicity of truth, to grant each culture its own particular validity.[36]

Hegel's critics are undoubtedly correct to note that there are moments later in his life when Hegel adopts the traditional racist judgments of his society, though he never wavers from his belief in universal equality. It is certain, for instance, that Hegel accepts popular stereotypes of his epoch concerning Africa, due ironically in large part to the fact that he read almost everything written about Africa at the time. In the *Philosophy of Spirit*, the third part of the *Encyclopedia*, Hegel's denigration of non-Europeans comes to a head. He argues that Africans are at fault for their own slavery, not the white Europeans who enslaved them. He claims, "*Negroes* are to be regarded as a nation of children that has yet to step out of its uninteresting and uninterested impartiality. They are sold and let themselves be sold, without reflecting whether it is right or not."[37] In a similar fashion, rather than blame the European colonists, he sees Native Americans as responsible for their own demise, stating that "with regard to the original inhabitants of *America*, we have to remark that they are a vanishing and weak race."[38] Here, Hegel himself betrays his own philosophy by treating both groups as if they are not fully subjects.[39]

The problem with this judgment is that subjectivity, as Hegel makes clear through his philosophy, comes all at once. This is what Hegel means when he claims that one not only ends with the absolute but also necessarily begins with it. From the moment one becomes a subject, one partakes of the absolute even if one has not fully thought it through. By failing to include Africans and Native Americans fully within the whole, Hegel acts as if one can avoid it, which is what his philosophy absolutely denies.

It is not enough to let Hegel off the hook because he never visited Africa or North America to meet Africans or Native Americans. His own disdain for the revelatory power of experience definitively rules out this line of defense. Hegel errs because he fails to see the particularity of what he reads about these people, that the Europeans writing about them are doing so in order to champion European particularity rather than to get at the participation of Africans and Native Americans in the universal. This error is grievous, but we cannot chalk it up to the dangers of universalizing.

Hegel's failures occur not because of his investment in totalizing but at the moments when he betrays the absolute and falls back into a particularity replete with the rebarbative prejudices of his epoch. It is never Hegel's commitment to the absolute that leads him astray. He falters when he abandons the discipline of absolute knowing for the sake of a particular judgment. This is what critics of Hegel's views on race have missed. He errs not by being too systematic but by forsaking his own commitment to the totality. The problem lies in Hegel's own particularity and his inability to recognize its impact on his judgments. When he adopts stereotypical positions on race, he always does so at moments when he abandons his own philosophy of the absolute.

THE OPPRESSION OF THE PARTICULAR

The problem with the insistence on particular difference is that this insistence, while it often appears in the guise of emancipatory politics, is actually the vehicle for oppressive social relations. Inequality has its basis in the rejection of universality and the celebration of particular difference. Once one abandons the universal for the sake of the particular, one abandons the very terrain on which one might convince others to support one's political program. The result is inevitably a political disaster.

When we first think about particularism, it seems like a leftist position predicated on respect for the difference of the other. We tend to envision particular struggles as those of small farmers against massive agribusiness or a group of immigrants fighting against deportation. But it is fundamentally a conservative philosophy, which is why it functions as the end point of Samuel Huntington's neoconservative bible, *The Clash of Civilizations.* After describing the dangers of the new world composed of opposing civilizations, Huntington writes, "In a multicivilizational world, the constructive course is to renounce universalism, accept diversity, and seek commonalities."[40] According to Huntington, there are no universals binding, for instance, Western civilization and Islamic civilization. They are two competing particulars that can coexist only through accepting the absence of any controlling universal.

The great experiment in the apotheosis of the particular in the modern world is Nazi Germany. In direct contrast to the communist dictatorships that arise alongside it in the twentieth century, Nazism adopts particular difference rather than universality as its point of departure. In this sense, rather than being a manifestation of Hegel's philosophy, as some critics charge, it is a thoroughgoing retreat from that philosophy. Nazism appeals to potential adherents on the basis of their particularity as Germans, while establishing this particularity through its distinction from another particularity—the figure of the Jew. It is not enough to contrast German particularity with French or British particularity. In order to form a genuine particularity, German particularity requires not just difference but a threatening opposition to identify itself.

When one adopts the perspective of the particular concept, Hegel argues in the *Science of Logic,* one unknowingly finds oneself opposed to the universality that appears in the guise of another particular. Hegel contends that "the particular . . . is its difference or reference to an *other,* its *outwardly reflecting semblance*; but there is no other at hand from which the particular would be differentiated than the universal itself."[41] In the attempt to differentiate itself from another particular in order to identify itself, the particular has recourse to the universal because only the universal can provide a path through which the particular can distinguish itself. Another particular considered as particular doesn't suffice. In relation to another particular, the particular has no clearly defined identity. It can only be just one particular among others. This is why the universal is requisite for every affirmation of particularity.

The particular concept is finally nothing but the determination of the universal that emerges in opposition to it. Hegel continues, "The universal determines *itself*, and so is itself the particular; the determinateness is *its* difference; it is only differentiated from itself. Its species are therefore only (a) the universal itself and (b) the particular."[42] The particular concept relies on the determination of the universal through the form of an opposing particular. The case of Nazism perfectly illustrates Hegel's point here. The attempt to assert German particularity establishes an opposition between two particulars (German and Jew), but one of these particulars must take on the form of the universal in order to define the other. In an ironic twist, however, it is not German that takes on this role. The two particular species of the universal are Jew and German, but the opposing particular, Jew, is the one that comes to act as universal because it provides the basis through which one can identify oneself as a German. The oppressed group in a struggle of competing particulars will always represent the universal, even as it is degraded by the oppressor.[43]

Nazism thus exemplifies the logic of the particular and reveals where it always leads. In attempting to affirm the particularity of German identity, Nazism installs the Jew as the universal against which this identity must define itself. The more Nazism promulgates the threat that Jews pose to German identity, the more this identity depends on the Jew as universal, which is why Nazi philosopher Alfred Rosenberg labels Jewishness an "anti-race" without any particularity of its own.[44] Nazi identity depends on the universality of the Jew, but this dependence only augments Nazi hatred. The ultimate end point of the logic of particular difference is the death camp.

In order to sustain itself as a particular, the German requires the Jew to function as the universal that gives an identity to its particularity. As a consequence, Nazi Germany cannot eliminate the Jewish menace without destroying the basis of its own particularity, which is what it seeks to affirm through the annihilation. Nazism is an impossible project. It is not just morally or politically abominable but logically doomed to failure.

Nazism imagines itself as conquering the world, Nazifying every possible territory. This creates the illusion that it is a project linked to the universality of Hegel's absolute idea. Just as Hegel leaves no region out of his universal history, Nazism aims at eliminating all space outside its dominance. The parallel leads some to suggest that absolute philosophy results in the dream of absolute dominance.[45] But, contrary to this superficial relationship, it is actually the absolute that arms us to struggle against Nazism in all its guises.[46]

When we refuse to think absolutely and remain content with some particularity, we create the space in which other particulars that want to impose themselves on the world can arise. The absolute idea reveals the lie at the heart of all such particulars and shatters their fantasy of triumphing over the trauma of contradiction. The risk of fascism doesn't lie in the direction of the absolute but in the turn away from it. The path to universal freedom lies through thinking absolutely.

Chapter Ten

EMANCIPATION WITHOUT SOLUTIONS

WHAT THE FUTURE DOESN'T HOLD

Thinkers turning to Hegel's philosophy for the sake of political action have always faced a seemingly irresolvable dilemma. In multiple statements throughout his works, Hegel makes it perfectly clear that philosophers cannot change the world. For Hegel, philosophy is politically impotent. For instance, in the final pages of the *History of Philosophy*, he proclaims, "The *ultimate* aim and *interest* of philosophy is to reconcile thought or the concept with actuality."[1] According to Hegel, philosophy should not try to change the world because it cannot. It always arrives too late on the scene to offer concrete political proposals.

The name that Hegel gives for the reconciliation of thought with actuality is the absolute, which represents the fundamental barrier to seeing Hegel's philosophy as a political project. As the reconciliation of thought with the actual, the absolute demands that the philosopher give up the possibility of philosophy giving political advice. With the theorization of the absolute, Hegel seems unequivocally to attest to his allegiance to the ruling order. The political energy of his youth, including his investment in the politics of the French Revolution, appears to have fallen by the wayside.[2]

But this verdict on Hegel's politics is not universal. Gillian Rose, for one, contends that the act of theorizing the absolute represents the fullest expression of Hegel's political vision. For her, far from being a retreat from politics, Hegel's commitment to the absolute testifies to his political engagement. This leads Rose to announce that "Hegel's thought has no social import if the absolute cannot be thought."[3] The absolute gives this philosophy its political significance because it marks the point at which Hegel overcomes the split between theory and practice. When we think the absolute, we make clear how reality comes up short politically of our rationality. According to Rose, Hegel believes that the unfreedom of society demands our political act to make the rational actual.[4] Rather than taking the long view in retreat from politics, the perspective of the absolute enmeshes the philosopher in the middle of political contestation. It serves as an indirect political imperative.

In her effort to preserve a politicized Hegel, however, Rose ends up moving too far away from his philosophy when she interprets the absolute as an imperative. Given Hegel's extreme critique of the *ought*, translating the absolute into an imperative constitutes a betrayal of his philosophical project. The absolute cannot function as an imperative if it is genuinely an end point, as Hegel insists that it is. When we attain the absolute, we grasp the irreducibility of contradiction. In this sense, the absolute is, as Rose rightly sees it, the basis for Hegel's politics, but it is not a politics that aims at bringing reality in line with the idea, which is Rose's conception. Instead, we see that there is no possible escape—no matter how much society progresses or technology develops—from the problem of contradiction. Contradiction is the barrier to society's self-identity and the engine behind all political movement. In recognizing the absolute, one recognizes the fecundity of the barrier.

Despite the invective leveled against Hegel's absolute for its apparent political conservatism, the recognition of the inescapability of contradiction that occurs with absolute knowing represents Hegel's key political idea. At the end of the *Phenomenology of Spirit*, Hegel discusses absolute knowing as knowing that abandons its investment in the other as a solution for the subject's own alienation. When it reaches absolute knowing, consciousness "has abandoned the hope of sublating alienness in an external, i.e., alien, manner," which leads it to "turn to itself."[5] With this turn to itself, spirit discovers the impossibility of overcoming its own self-division. All prior modes of thought hold out hope for escape from this self-division that they fantasize in the other. This leads them to treat contradiction externally, as a problem they can eliminate. In this way, these philosophies inadvertently succumb to contradiction by repeating it while trying to overcome it. The absolute, in contrast, doesn't succumb to contradiction because it no longer imagines an escape from it. It is the resolution of contradiction insofar as it is fully reconciled to it.

The political charge of Hegel's philosophy lies in its destruction of every avenue of escape from contradiction. This project occupies the majority of Hegel's time in his works. He explores the viable possibilities for surmounting contradiction in order to show that it cannot be surmounted. Doing so, however, requires a gesture that causes Hegel to appear unabashedly invested in the status quo. In order to reveal our inability to escape contradiction, one must eliminate any conception of a substance external to one's own position, which is what occurs when Hegel thinks the absolute.

The absolute is the complete abandonment of a substantial outside that is not self-divided. In the *Science of Logic*, Hegel states, "in its other [the concept] has *its own* objectivity for its subject matter. All the rest is error, confusion, opinion, striving, arbitrariness, and transitoriness; the absolute idea alone is *being*, imperishable *life, self-knowing truth*, and is *all truth*."[6] Hegel puts his conception of the absolute idea in the most extreme formulation possible. It is as if he wants to give future thinkers something to bristle at. Many are eager to oblige him. Even if one is not a thoroughgoing opponent of Hegel as Karl Popper, it's hard to miss the problematic nature of this statement. Despite how harsh his claim about the absolute sounds, Hegel goes this far solely in order to forestall the subject's attempts to escape into a fantasy of substantial otherness.

Instead of apotheosizing the other as an undivided harmonious entity, the absolute implies an understanding of otherness as itself split and therefore caught up in the same dilemma as the subject itself. The struggle against oppression, for Hegel, does not involve respect for otherness but the ability to see one's own self-division expressed in a different form in the other. One must see the other's alienation as the basis for the shared bond that exists. Without this recognition, one substantializes the other, which is the foundation of the oppressive relation. Recognizing the self-division of the other doesn't reduce everyone to sameness but eliminates the possibility for anyone's hierarchical elevation above another. It is a philosophy of universal equality through the split of every subject from itself.

When we refuse to think absolutely, we imply faith in the self-identity of the otherness that we posit outside our own position. This is why Hegel's philosophical critique of Kant is also a political critique. Kant tries to limit reason, but in doing so he affirms the self-identity of what lies beyond reason. In the preface to the second edition of the *Critique of Pure Reason*, Kant states that the limit he places on the subject's knowledge creates the space for faith in God—that is, a non-contradictory otherness. Kant claims, "I had to deny **knowledge** in order to make room for **faith**; and the dogmatism of metaphysics, i.e., the prejudice that without criticism reason can make progress in metaphysics, is the true source of all unbelief conflicting with morality, which unbelief is always very dogmatic."[7] Every attempt to limit our knowledge makes room for a similar faith, even if it isn't overtly faith in God as it is for Kant. For Hegel, this inaugurates a political disaster.

Though Hegel does not reject God, he decries Kant's version of God as an undivided substantial Other. One cannot have faith in a God of divine substance nor in the harmony of the natural world nor in the noncontradictory existence of an aboriginal people living in peace with their surroundings. All these versions of the substantial Other amount to the same thing, despite their apparent difference. Whenever one limits knowledge, one creates the opening for these political traps. It is only through recognizing that the other is not a solution that one envisions a world of equality.

The absolute provides a path for us to think contradiction without respite. With the absolute, there is no possible reconciliation without the acknowledgment of a fundamental self-division that no amount of struggle can ever overcome. By revealing that there is no external solution to the contradiction of being, the absolute tells us that we can no longer hope for relief from the trauma of history. This is the point when contradiction makes itself manifest as irreducible and when politics becomes unavoidable.

THE POVERTY OF RECOGNITION

The political battle is not for recognition, either of particular identities that seek it or of all subjects reciprocally. The lure of mutual recognition misleads many followers of Hegel seeking to decipher a political program in a philosophy that never makes one explicit. The fact that mutual recognition gains such traction among otherwise astute interpreters stems in all

likelihood from the compelling description that Hegel gives of the struggle for recognition as he recounts the dialectic of master and servant in the
Phenomenology of Spirit.[8] This is the most famous passage in all of Hegel's
works, and its narrative appeal undoubtedly leads to the outsized importance
that the struggle for reciprocal recognition has in the reception of Hegel's
politics.

This discussion in the *Phenomenology of Spirit* and its revival in the third
volume of the *Encyclopedia* (*Philosophy of Spirit*) are Hegel's only elabora-
tions of mutual recognition. In the former work, Hegel implies that mutual
recognition is the only possible solution for the strife stemming from the
struggle for recognition. It is the only way to avoid mastery, servitude, or
death. In the latter work, he predicates freedom on reciprocal recognition
of freedom by the subject and its other.[9] There is thus textual warrant for
the position developed by Robert Pippin, Robert Williams, Robert Brandom, and others (some not named Robert) that sees Hegel's political goal
as the establishment of mutual recognition.[10]

But mutual recognition is never the political end point that Hegel himself formulates. If Hegel were really invested in the politics of mutual recognition, he surely would have written about it in his one published work
devoted to politics—the *Philosophy of Right*.[11] But there is no discussion of
mutual recognition there. Furthermore, its emergence near the beginning
of the *Phenomenology of Spirit* suggests that it cannot function as a political ideal or goal for him.[12] This work doesn't end with two subjects recognizing each other, and, likewise, the *Philosophy of Spirit* doesn't conclude
with free subjects engaged in reciprocal recognition. The end point necessary for adequately expressing the subject's freedom is the modern state or
some similar collective structure, as Hegel makes clear in both the *Philosophy of Spirit* and the *Philosophy of Right*, rather than a community based
on mutual recognition. Pippin's claim that "virtually everything at stake
in Hegel's practical philosophy . . . comes down finally to his own theory
of recognition and its objective realization over time and in modern ethical life" seems a stretch when we consider how slight a role recognition plays
in Hegel's overall philosophy.[13]

Even though the *Philosophy of Spirit* provides ammunition for those who
see Hegel as a philosopher of mutual recognition, the concluding nod to
the state as the prerequisite for the subject's freedom would seem to preclude such an interpretation. At the end of this work, Hegel clearly says,

"Since spirit wills nothing but freedom and has no other end than its freedom, the state is only the mirror image of spirit's freedom, wherein it has its freedom as actual, as a world before itself."[14] It is revelatory that Hegel's text, which plays a vital role in the conception of him as a philosopher of mutual recognition, ends with a panegyric to the state, not to the politics of recognition. Mutual recognition is not a sufficient condition for the subject's freedom, but it is a necessary one.

Pippin and other proponents of mutual recognition put much more faith in recognition than Hegel himself does. For Hegel, mutual recognition fulfills just the basic requirement for the subject's freedom. It is not the ideal end point that Pippin would have it be. Instead, recognition indicates that the subject must leave its immediacy and act publicly. Mutual recognition does not provide a secure identity for the subject nor does it give a sense of belonging to the social order. It serves only to deprive the subject of its illusion of natural being.

The point of mutual recognition, as Hegel sees it, is its destruction of the sense of immediacy that permits the subject to believe in itself as a natural entity. In a key passage from the *Philosophy of Spirit*, one can see precisely how the misinterpretation arises and then how Hegel explains the more modest claims for mutual recognition. He begins, "I am only truly free when the other is also free and recognized by me as free."[15] If one stops after this line, it appears as if Pippin and company must surely be correct. But then Hegel continues, "This freedom of *one* in the *other* unites humans in an inward manner, whereas their *necessity* and *need* bring them together only externally. Therefore, men must will to find themselves again in one another. But this cannot happen so long as they are imprisoned in their immediacy, in their natural being; because it is just this that excludes them from one another and prevents them from being free in regard to each other."[16] Though this is one of the key works that provides the basis for the interpretation of Hegel as a philosopher of mutual recognition, the trajectory of Hegel's argument here actually undermines this image of him. Relative to its champions, Hegel gives an impoverished version of mutual recognition. All that it accomplishes is to strip away need and install desire as what brings us together.

Mutual recognition is not at all valueless. It gives the lie to my belief that I interact with the other only in order to satisfy my natural needs. Without the mediating factor of mutual recognition, I will remain convinced that I go to my neighbor's house merely because I'm hungry or in need of shelter. The self-image of a being controlled by its natural needs will continue to constrain me and blind me to what actually unites me with others. Recognition lifts the subject and the other out of the illusion of natural existence. But this is the starting point for politics, not the end point.

The danger in seeing Hegel as the champion of mutual recognition is that it restores in the political realm the illusion of synthesis. In a world of mutual recognition, we will have overcome contradiction through a dialectical progression. This is a denuded version of Hegel's philosophy that subtracts its radical core—the insistence on the intractability of the subject's conflict with itself and with others. Hegel's value as a political thinker derives from this insistence, not in possibilities for imagining a world in which all subjects experience themselves as recognized. This is what necessitates Hegel's turn to the state.

MOI, C'EST L'ÉTAT

Hegel ends his political philosophy with the state rather than with mutual recognition because he sees in the state a social structure that sustains contradiction. The state is absolute politics—the political equivalent to absolute knowing or the absolute idea. The state form makes freedom actual in a way that mutual recognition does not. Though the content of states differ, the form of the state is universal. The contradiction of the state—it creates the subject's singularity by thoroughly submitting its particularity to a universal law—provides the basis for the subject's freedom. Rather than creating the illusion of eliminating contradiction in the way that mutual recognition does, the state constantly confronts the subject with it.

The state does not just secure the subject's freedom by defending the subject against others that would impinge on this freedom. It rather plays a constitutive role in the modern subject's freedom insofar as it creates a formal structure that divorces the subject fully from its private concerns. The state forces the subject to recognize itself through the mediation of the state structure. As members of the state, it is clear that subjects do not exist on their own apart from their relation to others. The dependence of the subject on the collective becomes evident. Without the state, Hegel believes, the subject has no way to recognize the constitutive role that the whole plays for the assertion of the subject's singularity.

For modern thinkers prior to Hegel, the state is a necessary interruption of the subject's freedom and an interruption of the potential war of all against all that would transpire without it. This is the position of both Jean-Jacques Rousseau and Thomas Hobbes, who see the state as the result of an implicit contract arranged by individual subjects to protect their interests. Hegel vehemently opposes this notion of the state as contractual, a notion that obscures the foundational role the state plays in the freedom of the subject. With Hegel, the state becomes identical with the subject's freedom, a freedom that disappears without the universal structure of the state as its correlate. The state is the basis for freedom because it reveals to the subject the necessity of the obstacle for this freedom to constitute itself.[17] One can imagine freedom without the state but not without some similar structure that functions as a shared obstacle for the collective, which is why Hegel's thought is completely incompatible with any form of anarchism.

When the individual subject conceives itself without reference to the state, it conceives itself initially as a being of pure self-interest, even if it ultimately wishes to subject this self-interest to the interest of the community. One can imagine the subject pursuing its self-interest, but the problem is that this pursuit is not freedom. The subject's interests—even up to its interest in its own survival—are given to it by the society and the natural world in which the subject emerges. Hence, as Hegel sees it, self-interest has nothing to do with the subject's freedom, which depends on the subject alienating itself from the interests that society and nature have given it. The free subject alienates itself from its own givens, and the state is the vehicle for making this alienation explicit to the subject, which is why Hegel insists on it so decisively, in contrast to a loosely bound community, which would not reveal the subject's alienation. It is only through identifying itself with the state or some parallel collective structure that the subject recognizes that its freedom does not lie in the pursuit of its self-interest but rather in the uprooting of that pursuit.

The state doesn't just alienate an isolated subject. It provides a shared obstacle for all the subjects that belong to it that holds them together as a unity. Subjects come together in the state not as an organic whole or an aggregate but as an alienated unity. They are held together through a shared way of being what they are not.

Hegel's celebration of the state in the *Philosophy of Right* has proven the most ignominious aspect of his philosophy since the book's appearance in

1821. Soon after its publication, it becomes the emblem of Hegel's confor-mity to the Prussian monarchy in power at the time.[18] It signals his refusal to use his privileged position as one of the most important philosophers in Germany to challenge authority rather than suck up to it. Even though many disciples of Hegel debunk this interpretation of the *Philosophy of Right* as an exercise in conformity, it has resonates because of Hegel's uncondi-tional embrace of the state, which cannot but strike modern readers as a dangerous moment of capitulation that we would like to strike from Hegel's political philosophy.

Hegel's celebration of the state seems like a relic of the nineteenth cen-tury, given the oppressive abuses of state power that characterize the twen-tieth century. The celebration of the state becomes much more difficult to justify after the state-sponsored murder of millions. But in fact the totali-tarian state arises precisely from the danger that Hegel himself identifies in the *Philosophy of Right*—the state failing to distinguish itself as a state and becoming confused with civil society.[19] When subjects view themselves as private individuals, as nothing but members of civil society, they open themselves to the appeal of the authoritarian leader who promises to har-monize all private relations. The state, in contrast, provides an explicit affir-mation that private relations cannot be harmonious, that they must occur through the alienating mediation of the public world that highlights their unimportance. The authoritarian leader attempts to create harmony by eliminating the singularity that derives from public engagement.

Authoritarian rule is not the evisceration of private life but its apotheo-sis. Under fascist rule, no one is permitted to act as a public being but is rather forced into the cocoon of privacy. The authoritarian regime prohib-its public acts like demonstrations or open debates, even while it tolerates private subterfuges, such as sexual peccadillos or drunkenness. The fact that subjects existing under authoritarian rule view their private lives as a form of resistance to this authority merely testifies to authoritarianism's effec-tiveness in destroying the public world. The sacrifice of the contentiousness of the public sphere produces a social order that seems to run smoothly. This type of rule abridges the constitutive function of the state for subjec-tivity and treats individuals as isolated monads. But the repression of the public sphere ends up suffocating subjects living under authoritarian rule. One must have the public world of the state to be able to endure one's pri-vate life.

Even if it doesn't lead to authoritarianism, the great danger of modernity is not a powerful state that impinges on individual freedom but the failure to recognize the state as a state and to mistake civil society for it. In civil society (Hegel's term for the social bond established through economic exchange), individuals benefit the whole by following their self-interest, such as when the baker profits from selling bread and the customer survives by eating it. The baker doesn't bake for the sake of the customer, and the customer doesn't buy bread to support the baker. Instead, the pursuit of self-interest benefits the whole and unites both parties.[20] As capitalism has developed since Hegel wrote this, civil society has increasingly encroached on the state and placed its own logic over that of the state, so that subjects have completely fallen for the ruse that the state is nothing but the guardian of mutual self-interest. In such a society, freedom becomes increasingly hard to come by. The danger that Hegel foresaw in 1821 has come to fruition.

Though modernity gives birth to the form of the state, it also unleashes an unprecedented development of civil society through the capitalist economy. While the state and civil society develop simultaneously and often work together, their structures are fundamentally at odds with each other. Whereas civil society encourages the subject to immerse itself in its own private concerns, the state demands that the subject recognize itself first and foremost as a public being.

When one conceives of the state as an organization that one joins for the sake of mutual protection, one reduces it to the logic of civil society. Once one thinks that state membership is nothing but an option, one misses completely the constitutive role that the state plays in one's subjectivity. This occurs when the state takes on the hue of civil society, which it has increasingly done since Hegel's death. The state today appears as an oppressive force because it has largely become an arm of civil society, serving as the handmaiden for the forces of capitalism. When this occurs, the state loses its capacity for giving individuals an ethical basis for their existence.[21]

When the capitalist economy displaces the state in this way, it simultaneously disguises our solidarity as subjects. Without a recognition of the necessity of the state, we come to see ourselves as involved in a pitiless war of all against all, in which life is "solitary, poor, nasty, brutish, and short."[22] Once the capitalist economy gains priority over the state form, the fundamental contradiction that defines our political being recedes from view.

Capitalist subjects do not view themselves as political beings. Their individuality simply exists on its own, not through the mediation of the universal. As a result, they experience themselves as private entities. Capitalism's assault on the public world leaves subjects immersed in their own private particularity, unaware of the psychic necessity of the public world to underwrite their privacy.

The more the state appears as an optional encumbrance, the more the subject loses touch with its freedom. Since the state restricts what the subject can do—it passes laws against theft, against drunk driving, and against other enjoyable activities—it seems as if the state has an oppositional relationship to the subject's freedom. By giving priority to the state, Hegel claims that we are public individuals before we are private ones. Our investment in the public sphere is not an option—like the decision to vote or not—but the basis for our private existence. The priority of the state indicates that one must go through the detour of the public in order to be a private individual.[23]

The embrace of the state is not a moment of conformity that Hegel might have avoided but the basis on which he constructs his idea of freedom. As he grants the state a central role in the *Philosophy of Right*, Hegel puts the finishing touch on his philosophy of freedom that begins with the *Phenomenology of Spirit*. This completes the turn from Kant's subjectivist freedom (where Hegel begins) to an objective form, from freedom as pure negativity to freedom as a positive expression of this negativity. As Shlomo Avineri puts it in *Hegel and the Modern State*, "subjectivist philosophy has made it a rule to see freedom only in opposition to the state, overlooking what is to Hegel the immanent truth of the state as the actuality of rational freedom."[24] The state actualizes freedom through making the obstacle to self-interest explicit. When the subject recognizes its essential link to the state, it also recognizes that its freedom doesn't lie down the path of self-interest.

The state reveals to the subject that its freedom is contradictory: the subject becomes free through subjection to the state, not before or outside this subjection. Mutual recognition does not yet make the detour evident in the way the state does. This is the basic contradiction that underlies the modern state: it constitutes the individual subject through its destruction of all the individual's particular attachments. It creates the possibility for privacy by fully submitting the subject to the public world. In the state, individuality must emerge through contradiction. This contradiction of individuality within the state manifests itself, for Hegel, in the figure of the monarch.

MONARCHY OR FASCISM

Hegel's belief that the monarch retains a role in modernity represents yet another of his apparent political missteps. If one can defend the politics of his recourse to the absolute, his retention of the monarch seems beyond the pale. And yet his insistence on constitutional monarchy instead of parliamentary democracy at the end of the *Philosophy of Right* is part of his radical politics, not his purported conservatism. It seems impossible that there could be a serious argument for monarchy in the contemporary world. The idea of constitutional monarchy is itself dated, but Hegel's retention of the monarch in his vision of democracy is not. It is, for him, a way to sustain the place for contradiction. The monarch in Hegel's politics is a form, not a content. Democratic politics must have a position functioning like the monarch in order to avoid being swallowed up by contradiction.

The problem with modern parliamentary democracy is that it leaves no place for the necessity of contradiction. It creates the impression that everyone belongs to the social field, that no one is excluded from the domain of representation. But the dream of universal inclusion always runs up against the barrier that defines any group: in order to define themselves as included, those who belong must define themselves against someone who is excluded. The monarch addresses this problem by embodying exclusion. The monarch has a ruling position within the society but doesn't belong like all the other subjects. The fact that this figure has disappeared in contemporary democracy should be counted as progress, but this progress brings with it a fundamental danger. Without a figure that gives expression to the contradiction of the modern democratic order, the force of contradiction constantly threatens to turn democracy into fascism.

Fascism has an appeal rooted not just in its act of preserving contradiction but also in its transformation of contradiction into opposition. It turns contradiction into the disguised and more palatable form of opposition— German against Jew, American against immigrant, and so on. It has its origin in the tendency of parliamentary democracy to repress contradiction. Political engagement depends on contradiction. Subjects will seek it out in the form of fascism if parliamentary democracy represses it. This is what we have seen play out throughout the twentieth and twenty-first centuries.

In order to avert this danger, Hegel's political philosophy includes the monarch as the mark of the state's insubstantiality. It is the point at which individuality manifests itself in the universality of the state, the point at which the state expresses its own self-division. The monarch lays bare the state's absence of any self-identity. It is thus a moment of failure within the successful state.

Hegel gives the modern monarch a completely circumscribed function. The monarch's gesture of simply proclaiming "I will" subjectivizes the state substance. At this moment, it testifies to individuality within the universality of the state, its dependence on an individual in order to actualize itself. In the *Philosophy of Right*, Hegel states, "This 'I will' constitutes the great difference between the ancient and modern world, and in the great edifice of the state it must therefore have its proper existence. Unfortunately, however, this determination is regarded as only external and arbitrary."[25] Modern democracy fails when it tries to function without the subjectivizing power of the monarch. When it does so, it passes itself off as a self-identical substance, thereby creating the foundation for the rise of fascism as alternate subjectivizing power.

When the monarch recedes from the modern state, the state's contradiction becomes invisible. Subjects lose the sense of themselves as political beings when they do not experience contradiction in the political field. A false consensus takes over, but this consensus never holds. The repression of contradiction in politics always entails its return, usually in the form of a fascist uprising, precisely because as subjects contradiction sustains our desire, which would suffocate without it. Hegel wagers that the presence of the monarch and the contradiction that this figure represents illustrate clearly the lack of any substantial consensus.

Of all Hegel's contemporary champions, Slavoj Žižek stands almost alone for his defense of the monarch in Hegel's political philosophy. Rather than making excuses for the presence of the monarch, Žižek sees it as one of the keys to Hegel's radicality as a thinker. He writes, "The State without the Monarch would still be a *substantial* order—the Monarch represents the point of its subjectivation."[26] For Žižek, the monarch provides a path leading from the illusion of substantiality to subjectivity. He underlines its necessary because he recognizes the image of a substantial state is the primary political danger that we confront today.

The retention of the monarch does not exhaust the political possibilities for expressing contradiction within the modern political order. It is hard to see this figure as tenable today. However, this is only one form the articulation of contradiction within democracy might take. Hegel limits himself to it because it represents the limit of his own epoch, but this in no way precludes the emergence of other possibilities. Whatever form contradiction assumes in today's politics, it must be as explicit as the monarch. Otherwise, the turn to fascism and the erection of enemies will inevitably commence. The expression of contradiction is modern society's bulwark against fascism. When contradiction recedes from view and the promise of social harmony emerges, the fascist leader appears to ensure that contradiction will manifest itself through the comfort of the friend/enemy distinction. This is a path that Hegel's political philosophy cuts off.

DON'T GET INVOLVED

The danger of Hegel's political philosophy is that it will justify the world as it is. Hegel is very clear about what he sees as philosophy's inability to direct how the world will change. In the preface to the *Philosophy of Right*, he announces, "A further word on the subject of *issuing instructions* on how the world ought to be: philosophy, at any rate, always comes too late to perform this function. . . . When philosophy paints its grey in grey, a shape of life has grown old, and it cannot be rejuvenated, but only recognized, by the grey in grey of philosophy; the owl of Minerva begins its flight only with the onset of dusk."[27] As Hegel formulates it, philosophy has a restricted political capacity. Rather than imagining an alternative future, it has the ability to recognize the prevailing structure in force—what he calls the "shape of life." Such a recognition on its own does not create anything new but only exposes the operative contradiction.

For Hegel, the philosopher's task is to interpret the world, not to change it. In the eleventh and final of his "Theses on Feuerbach," Karl Marx targets Hegel more than any other philosopher when he inverts Hegel's unarticulated motto, proclaiming that "the philosophers have only *interpreted* the world, in various ways; the point, however, is to change it."[28] Rather than accepting that philosophy can only make pronouncements after great events have already occurred, Marx enjoins philosophers to thrust themselves into the mix and get their hands dirty. Ironically, it is the materialist philosopher Marx who proclaims that the philosopher can be the prophet of the great event. In the aftermath of Marx's injunction, it seems impossible to philosophize like before. In response, thinkers of all stripes have tried to transform philosophizing itself into offering practical advice, to use theoretical speculation to assist in envisioning a better world. This is what Hegel never does.

For Hegel, attempts to change the world through philosophy will misfire. They will recapitulate what they struggle against. This is because philosophy cannot transcend the material conditions of its own time. When we propose an alternate future, we do so within the terms presently available to us. Even Plato's ideal republic, as Hegel sees it, was not an alternative to Greek society at the time but an expression of its internal logic. The possibilities that we conceive are possibilities determined by the prevailing symbolic structure, not challenges to that structure. Philosophers that give practical political advice almost inevitably express the hidden logic of the system they attempt to contest.

For Hegel, philosophy intervenes politically by making clear the relations that already exist. Philosophical interpretation makes clear how everything within the social order relates. In doing so, however, it also identifies what doesn't fit within the prevailing order—the symptom that expresses the contradiction of the epoch. When interpretation becomes absolute, it doesn't conclude with every piece of the puzzle fitting exactly where it belongs but with the identification of the one piece that doesn't fit at all and that undermines the entire order. One discovers the piece that doesn't fit through the act of interpretation, not by fantasizing a solution to the social order's contradictions.

In the interpretation of civil society in the *Philosophy of Right*, Hegel discovers what he calls the rabble (*Pöbel*) as the piece that doesn't fit. The rabble includes those whom the economy leaves behind—those who are not just unemployed but completely disinvested from the social order as a result of their economic and social exclusion. The rabble expresses the contradiction of civil society because civil society produces it, yet it exists external to its structure.

Rather than proposing solutions that might relieve civil society of this contradictory entity, Hegel shows how imaginary solutions like charity or colonization would fail to eliminate the problem. Within the capitalist economy of Hegel's epoch, there is no solution to the contradiction that the rabble represents. By interpreting civil society absolutely, Hegel exposes this contradiction. This represents the height of the philosopher's political power.

This political power exists only insofar as the philosopher doesn't try to provide a philosophical solution to the contemporary situation. It is always tempting to go further than interpretation, to imagine that philosophy can tell us how society ought to be arranged. But when philosophers propose alternatives, they limit their interpretive power and create the impression that we might overcome contradiction with the proper social arrangements. Nowhere is this clearer than in the case of Marx, who proposes communism as a solution to the contradictions of capitalism.

Marx formulates a precise interpretation of the primary contradiction of capitalist production. According to Marx, capitalist relations of production act as a fetter on the forces of production that capitalism unleashes. As he points out in the *Grundrisse*, "Beyond a certain point, the development of the powers of production becomes a barrier for capital; hence the capital relation [becomes] a barrier for the development of the productive powers of labour."[29] With this interpretation, Marx remains firmly ensconced within Hegel's philosophy of contradiction. Marx's interpretation grasps how capitalism is fundamentally at odds with itself but cannot recognize that it produces the barrier that it struggles against. At this point, Marx might have stopped, identifying the limit as what doesn't belong to the capitalist universe that nonetheless creates it.

But rather than contenting himself with exposing the contradiction of capitalist production, Marx provides a fantasy of overcoming it. This limits his interpretive power since an interpretation looking beyond can never be absolute. For Marx, the contradiction of capitalist production leads to the end of capitalism and the birth of communism. When capitalist relations of production start to act as a barrier to the forces of production, the situation becomes revolutionary. Communism solves this contradiction by removing this brake on the forces of production.

The problem with Marx's solution is that it is a solution. Rather than revealing the irreducibility of contradiction within economics, Marx's fantasy depicts the contradictions on this terrain as soluble. In doing so, he misses the opportunity to reveal that communism or whatever relations of production that replace capitalism would deepen rather than eliminate the contradiction. Marx interprets capitalism from the perspective of the fantasy that "the bourgeois mode of production is the last antagonistic form of social production."[30] Ironically, this fantasy of a noncontradictory alternative evinces the same problem that Marx identifies in capitalism: it cannot recognize that it creates its own barriers despite eschewing them. The fantasy of an alternative that would solve contradiction remains within the logic of what it contests.

In the act of grasping the symbolic structure absolutely, as an ultimate horizon for thought, we can illuminate the contradiction that marks the point of the structure's internal vulnerability. This at once creates the possibility for change and indicates that no change, no matter how revolutionary, will ever heal the wound of the social order. A society can move beyond a specific contradiction, but it will necessarily encounter another one. This is not a recipe for quietism but a call to act. The point of political contestation is to move in the direction of an increasingly resistant contradiction, and philosophy plays a vital role in this movement. This is Hegel's definition of progress: the movement from more easily resolved social contradictions to more intractable ones.

MARX'S RIGHTIST DEVIATION

It is commonly acknowledged that Marx transforms Hegel's idealist dialectic into a materialist one. In doing so, Marx translates Hegel's logical contradictions and the movement they generate into economic contradictions that become the motor for history. It is certainly the case that Marx's identification of contradictions operative within economics provides an important extension of Hegel's philosophy into a realm that Hegel himself didn't address. In this way, Marx represents a genuine advance. But this extension also involves a transformation.

With Marx's materialist turn, it becomes evident that the changes in human society stem from the struggle for basic human needs rather than the realization of abstract ideals like freedom. The claim that material conditions rather than ideals drive us to act has subsequently garnered a lot of traction. This translation seems to politicize Hegel in a way that his own philosophy could not accommodate. The materialist turn is also a turn to an emancipatory politics that laid dormant in Hegel's idealism. Marx predicts revolutionary uprisings while Hegel reconciles thought with the world. The turn from Hegel to Marx, according to many theorists, is the turn from philosophy to politics.[31] As a result, though there are numerous Marxist revolutions in the twentieth century, there are no Hegelian ones.

Hegel himself exhibits extreme political caution, which is why the same system can produce both left-wing and right-wing adherents. Marx throws this caution to the wind, which is why there are no right-wing Marxists. As Sidney Hook puts it, "the political accommodation of Hegel and the revolutionary activity of Marx are acts spread on the pages of history."[32] No one, not even Marx's most fervent opponents, would question that his thought represents an increased politicization of Hegel's and a turn of that philosophy to the left. Marx transforms Hegel's political quietism and ambiguity into an emancipatory political system—or so the common wisdom has it.

But an examination of what happens to Hegel's philosophy of contradiction in the hands of Marx forces us to call this common wisdom into question. Though Hegel never fully grasps it himself, his philosophy provides the basis for an emancipatory political program that might have fueled revolutionary changes in the twentieth century and might do so in the twenty-first. Emancipation, Hegel suggests, occurs through contradiction, not as a result of its overcoming. The free act is the direct avowal of the intractability of contradiction. Marx's translation of this philosophy of contradiction into historical materialism has the effect of betraying this revolutionary program. Marx replaces Hegel's radical political program with a more conservative one. Despite all appearances, Marx represents a rightist deviation from Hegel's radical politics of contradiction.

Hegel's philosophy enables us to articulate a new schema for the divide between emancipatory politics and conservatism or between left and right. Taking this philosophy as the point of reference, we could say that emancipation involves making explicit and embracing contradiction, whereas conservatism aims at repressing or eliminating it. The ultimate right-wing fantasy envisions the elimination of contradiction through the expulsion of the enemy deemed responsible for it. Benign conservatism, however, envisions merely the repression of the contradiction. Benign conservatism will force the poor to work and pass laws making it more difficult for workers to unionize so that capitalism will function without its contradictions coming to the fore. For extremists, the enemy is more intransigent and personalized: it is the Jew, the immigrant, or the minority. Extremists will expel these figures or put them in concentration camps or try to eliminate them. The extreme right fantasizes a return to a mythic moment before contradiction, a moment that rightists believe existed because they interpret contradiction in terms of opposition and deny its constitutive status.

Emancipatory politics, in contrast, refuses to see contradiction as opposition. There is no enemy whose defeat would eliminate contradiction because contradiction is constitutive of subjectivity and society. The point, for the project of emancipation, is sustaining it. One does so by insisting that the society actualizes itself through its failure to be self-identical, not its success. The figure that disrupts social harmony—say, the figure of the Jew or the immigrant—becomes the figure of universality in the emancipatory project. This project doesn't eliminate this figure or create a utopia in which such a figure loses its distinctiveness within universal belonging. Instead, it insists on the irreducibility of this figure of contradiction.

For Hegel and emancipatory politics, one must embrace the excluded rather than shun the symptomatic figure of exclusion. One must accede to the necessity of the failure to solve contradiction. In this sense, Karl Löwith is entirely incorrect when he laments that "success is not only the highest court of appeal for Hegel's historical theory; it is also a constant measure of everyday life, where the assumption is likewise made that the success of something proves its superior right to that which is unsuccessful."[33] This common critique misses the mark because it fails to grasp why Hegel concerns himself with success. If Hegel does pay attention to those who are successful, it is only so that he can expose the failure that inheres in every success. We must not be seduced by the illusory possibility of a future success that would overcome contradiction. Hegel focuses on success in order to reveal, paradoxically, how unsuccessful it is in the face of contradiction. It is Marx, not Hegel, who invests himself in the fantasy of a successful overcoming of contradiction. For Hegel, our failure in the face of contradiction is unavoidable. Recognizing this is the basis for emancipatory politics.

Though contradiction functions as the basis for leftist politics, it can become fodder for the right when the left abandons it. The difference between the leftist and rightist turn to contradiction consists in the promise of a solution. Whereas leftist politics offers contradiction itself as the solution—the problem and the solution become the same thing—right-wing politics points to contradiction in order to announce the need for a solution. Contradiction is present for fascism, but it is only present as an obstacle to be overcome in some fashion—through the social isolation, deportation, or even murder of the figure responsible for the contradiction. For the leftist, in contrast, the enemy is not personalized and thus cannot be killed. The enemy is, instead, nothing but the failure to see the constitutive status of contradiction.

From this perspective, the Marxist political project loses its glint of radicality in relation to Hegel. Rather than accepting the irreducibility of contradiction as Hegel does, Marx theorizes its elimination through the attainment of a communist society. In contrast to Hegel, Marx interprets the development of history not as the furthering and expansion of contradiction but as its progressive overcoming. Capitalism solves the contradictions of feudalism, and communism subsequently solves those of capitalism. History is the arena of successful solutions, not serial failures.

Marx believes that political emancipation does not consist in the collective recognition that we will never achieve a harmonious society but in its successful attainment. Marx's name for emancipation, communism, is the label for success, not for reconciliation with the necessity of failure. Since Marx's political victory over Hegel, the project of emancipation has given up its proper territory—that of intractable contradiction—for the fantasy of harmonious social relations that Marxism promulgates. The problem is not that communism fails to do what Marx claims and is unable to solve the riddle of history but that it actually does so.[34]

The investment in success manifests itself in Marx's conviction that all our problems are solvable. According to Marx, we never bite off more than we can chew in the course of history. In the preface to the *Contribution to the Critique of Political Economy*, he proclaims, "Mankind thus inevitably sets itself only such tasks as it is able to solve, since closer examination will always show that the problem itself arises only when the material conditions for its solution are already present or at least in the course of formation."[35] In this well-known statement, Marx's abandonment of the philosophy of contradiction becomes clear. As Marx sees it, contradiction is nothing but the guise for its solution. It has no enduring power.

Marx's transformation of Hegel's philosophy of failure into a political project of success leaves behind the emancipatory potential of Hegel's philosophy. As a result, our image of Marx as the more politically significant philosopher is due for revision. The turn away from Hegel's politics is a turn away from emancipation and an installation of a fundamentally conservative principle at the heart of the leftist political struggles of the twentieth century. Despite the salience of Marx's critique of capitalism, this was the worst event to occur within the internal history of the project of emancipation. The theoretical turn from Hegel to Marx paved the way for a practical catastrophe.

There are numerous reasons for the catastrophes resulting from the communist victories in the twentieth century. The barbarism of capitalism's defenders and the despotism of communist leaders play crucial roles. But a major factor that goes unmentioned is Marx's own turn away from the emancipatory project that Hegel bequeaths to him, a turn that becomes even more pronounced when Marx becomes Marxism. Of course, Hegel himself didn't recognize entirely the political implications of his own discovery, so one cannot fault Marx too much for his misstep. But once Marx translates Hegel's philosophy of contradiction into a materialist dialectic that aims at overcoming contradiction, all is lost.

Once we imagine this overcoming as a real possibility, any sacrifice becomes justifiable for attaining it. Just as the capitalist will subject workers to untold hours of suffering for the sake of an expanded accumulation that promises the ultimate satisfaction, Marxist regimes will starve millions for the sake of a future free from contradiction.[36] As long as the elimination of contradiction is the goal, one remains within a logic that permits an unlimited sacrifice in the contradictory present. If future society could live without contradiction, one could plausibly argue that the gulag is worth it. But this is the calculus that Hegel's version of emancipatory politics rules out. For this politics, the means is the end because the end, no matter how ideal, never provides a solution. At our historical juncture, the failures of Marx's politics of overcoming contradiction create the opening for Hegel's philosophy that recognizes contradiction as absolute.

CONCLUSION

Replanting Hegel's Tree

The most revelatory event in Hegel's life likely never happened. According to the legend, Hegel, Friedrich Hölderlin, and Friedrich Wilhelm Joseph Schelling—three roommates at the Tübingen Seminary—planted a freedom tree on July 14, 1793, to commemorate their devotion to the French Revolution. This pledge of allegiance was a radical act at the time, an act that indicated their status as partisans of revolutionary upheaval against the established order ruling in Europe. Though Hegel's biographer Terry Pinkard admits that "the story is almost surely false," he also claims that "its believability for those who later told it lay in its adequately capturing the spirit that was undoubtedly animating the three friends."[1] In other words, if Hegel, Hölderlin, and Schelling did not plant a freedom tree in the name of the French Revolution and sing "La Marseillaise" around it, they should have. Hegel's commitment to the event of the French Revolution provides the basis for his entire philosophy.

The French Revolution and its counterpart the Haitian Revolution transform the world by announcing the end of traditional authority. Earthly authority loses its divine support, and divine authority loses its ability to dictate the terms of our existence. After this, all authority becomes subject to the same division as the subject itself. As a result, authority ceases to be authoritative. The French Revolution marks the end of any ontologically justified hierarchy. The values that the revolution promulgates derive from this toppling of authority's self-justification.

These values—*liberté, égalité, fraternité*—are unevenly distributed in Hegel's work. Freedom clearly has pride of place, as Hegel interprets the unfolding of history as the development of freedom in the *Philosophy of History*. Due to this work, Hegel is known as a philosopher of the historical emergence of freedom. But equality and solidarity also underlie the entirety of Hegel's philosophy. As with freedom, equality and solidarity are the political result of an ontology of contradiction. If there is no self-identity and every identity involves what negates it, then all subjects exist equally and in solidarity through this fundamental self-division. It is the isolation of each subject, without even the assurance of its own self, that each subject shares with all others. The isolation of the subject, for Hegel, is the basis of its solidarity. As Hegel sees it, his philosophy reveals what underlies the politics articulated by the French Revolution.

Hegel aims at creating a philosophy that rises to the grandeur of the French Revolution. He does not translate the political revolution into philosophical terms but shows how the destruction of substantial authority enacted during this event has ontological ramifications. As Rebecca Comay notes in *Mourning Sickness: Hegel and the French Revolution*, "Hegel has relentlessly dismantled every attempt to displace or dissolve the traumatic rupture of the French Revolution within a spiritual, philosophical, or aesthetic upheaval."[2] Instead of displacing this traumatic rupture, Hegel makes it the basis of his philosophical enterprise. He does so by creating a philosophy that illustrates why we are free, why we are equal, and why we are in solidarity.

The primary irony of Hegel's commitment to the French Revolution is that he offers one of the most thoroughgoing critiques of the Reign of Terror in the *Phenomenology of Spirit*. He sees the Terror as the result of the French Revolution's failure to see that universality must necessarily include singularity. Without respect for the singularity of the subject, no one can actualize universality. The French Revolution leads to the Reign of Terror because it tries to realize universal freedom without the interruption of singularity. In the course of the *Phenomenology of Spirit*, Hegel shows that the singular is actually not a threat to the universal but its only possible mode of expression. In this way, his critique of the revolution is nothing but a demand that it take the universalization of its own values seriously. At no point does Hegel call these values themselves into question.

Freedom, equality, and solidarity are not just values that the French Revolution invents. Instead, the revolution discovers them. Hegel recognizes that they derive from the structure of being itself, even if it takes modernity for this structure to become evident. But the ontological basis of these values does not ensure their political survival. There are many societies that have had no acquaintance with them, despite the profound reverberations of the French Revolution around the world. Most commonly, societies retreat from these values and accede to regimes of unfreedom, inequality, and self-interest.

Hegel's philosophical intervention marks his effort to install these values in the world by illustrating their ontological basis. His wager is that if we recognize that freedom, equality, and solidarity follow from the nature of being itself we will recognize that they are not just desirable but fundamentally inescapable. No matter how diligently we attempt to abandon them, they return to haunt us. But, on the other hand, Hegel's philosophy also has the benefit of showing why people are so quick to betray these values. Freedom, equality, and solidarity are inherently traumatic values insofar as they require us to confront the absence of any substantial authority. We can only live out these values if we forgo any self-identical other that provides a secure background for our subjectivity.

This is why the predominant uses of the term *freedom* represent its abandonment rather than its enactment. Since freedom is the absence of any substantial authority, there is no such thing as a free market. A market economy establishes the invisible hand of the market as a substantial authority, thereby abandoning freedom in the very effort to realize it. A similar misadventure besets the attempt to create a society of equals in the Soviet Union. Here, the objective laws of history take the place of the substantial authority. In the case of contemporary Christian and Islamic fundamentalism, the substantial figure of otherness is clearer. It is the undivided God that somehow makes known its wishes without suffering from any internal division that would make communication with others possible. In the aftermath of the French Revolution, these betrayals are not exceptional but habitual.

These betrayals don't just cost us freedom, equality, and solidarity. They also fail to deliver on their promises. The free market produces a desolate world with incessant wars; the Soviet Union leaves millions of dead without even realizing a modicum of equality; religious fundamentalism invests itself more in its hatred of secularism than its devotion to God. Trying to sustain the Other as substantial inevitably backfires. In this sense, we have nothing to lose in affirming freedom, equality, and solidarity rather than retreating from them.

Hegel had no illusions about saving the world. He understood that no salvation is possible, that every attempt to overcome contradiction produces a more violent one. But we do have the ability to reconcile ourselves to contradiction. Reconciliation (*Versöhnung*) is the fundamental Hegelian gesture. This is not existential or political salvation but a justification that reveals a divine rupture. It means accepting the insubstantiality of whatever authority we worship. It is only through the strict avowal of the contradictions in all authority that we uphold the values of freedom, equality, and solidarity.

NOTES

INTRODUCTION

1. The leading Left Hegelians were David Friedrich Strauss (author of the *Life of Jesus*), Bruno Bauer, Ludwig Feuerbach (who wrote *The Essence of Christianity*), and Max Stirner. The most prominent Right Hegelians were Johann Eduard Erdmann (primarily known for his history of philosophy), Eduard Gans, Heinrich Hotho (editor of Hegel's *Aesthetics*), and Johann Karl Friedrich Rosenkranz (who wrote *Hegel als deutscher Nationalphilosoph*).

2. In his account of the Young Hegelians (a synonym for the Left Hegelians), William J. Brazill chalks up the quarrel between the Right and Left Hegelians primarily to their divergence on the question of religion. According to Brazill, "The Young Hegelians were not Christians, they were humanists. And that humanism, the product solely of Hegel's influence, formed their essential unity and divided them from the Hegelians of the right." William J. Brazill, *The Young Hegelians* (New Haven: Yale University Press, 1970), 53.

3. One could make the argument that either Lukács's *History and Class Consciousness* or Alexandre Kojève's *Introduction to the Reading of the Phenomenology of Spirit* was the most influential philosophical work of the twentieth century. Lukács not only introduced the concept of reification and thereby led to the formation of the Frankfurt School, but he also theorized the spatialization of originary temporality that influenced Martin Heidegger's landmark *Being and Time*. For his part, Kojève produced an interpretation of Hegel that reverberated through the thought of those who attended his seminar (Jacques Lacan, Maurice Merleau-Ponty, Georges Bataille, and many others) and those who didn't (Jean-Paul Sartre, Michel Foucault, and Judith Butler, just to name a few).

4. See Ludwig Feuerbach, *The Essence of Christianity*, trans. George Eliot (New York: Harper, 1957).

5. In the episode, the repair of the transporter enables Kirk to become singular again. But this restoration leaves him transformed by the recognition of his own self-division. He becomes whole again, but he recognizes, in a Hegelian fashion, that the whole is at odds with itself.

6. G. W. F. Hegel, *Lectures on the Philosophy of Religion*, vol. 3: *The Consummate Religion*, ed. Peter C. Hodgson, trans. R. F. Brown, P. C. Hodgson, and J. M. Stewart (Oxford: Clarendon, 2007), 125 (translation modified). The German reads: "Die höchste Entäußerung der göttlichen Idee als Entäußerung ihrer selbst, d. i. die noch diese Entaußerung ist, drückt sich aus: Gott ist gestorben, Gott selbst ist tot—ist eine ungeheure, fürchterliche Vorstellung, die vor die Vorstellung den tiefsten Abgrund der Entzweiung bringt." G. W. F. Hegel, *Vorlesungen über die Philosophie der Religion*, Teil 3: *Die vollendete Religion*, ed. Walter Jaeschke (Hamburg: Felix Meiner, 1984), 60.

7. Left Hegelianism marks the victory of common sense over philosophy. It seems self-evident that we strive to overcome contradictions that we confront rather than trying to sustain them, but philosophy, as Hegel defines it, is the refusal of what presents itself as self-evident. The more self-evident it is, the more it requires thought to unpack.

8. Aristotle comes closest to formulating the law of identity in the fourth book on the *Metaphysics* where he claims, "it will not be possible for the same thing to be and not to be." Aristotle, *Metaphysics*, trans. W. D. Ross, in *The Complete Works of Aristotle*, vol. 2, ed. Jonathan Barnes (Princeton: Princeton University Press, 1984), 4:4.

9. G. W. Leibniz, *New Essays on Human Understanding*, trans. Peter Remnant and Jonathan Bennett (Cambridge: Cambridge University Press, 1996), 361.

10. Aristotle, *Metaphysics*, 4:3.

11. G. W. F. Hegel, *Science of Logic*, trans. George Di Giovanni (Cambridge: Cambridge University Press, 2010), 360. The German reads: "Solches *identische* Reden *widerspricht sich* also *selbst* . . . es liegt diese reine Bewegung der Reflexion darin, in der das Andere nur als Schein, als unmittelbares Verschwinden auftritt." G. W. F. Hegel, *Wissenschaft der Logik II* (Frankfurt: Suhrkamp, 1986), 44.

12. According to Longuenesse, "It seems to me important in effect to dissipate the threatening misunderstandings concerning Hegelian contradiction by showing that it is neither a refutation of the logical principle of contradiction nor an ontological category defining a relation in being considered as independent from thought." Béatrice Longuenesse, *Hegel et la critique de la métaphysique*, 2d ed. (Paris: Vrin, 2015), 84. Longuenesse's critique of the interpretation of Hegel as a violator of the principle of noncontradiction follows from a deflationist reading that eliminates any ontological implications from his philosophy. In the years since Longuenesse first made this claim (in the first edition of the book in 1981), the deflationist reading has become increasingly popular among interpreters of Hegel.

13. Slavoj Žižek, *The Sublime Object of Ideology* (London: Verso, 1989), 6.

14. Hegel, *Science of Logic*, 745. The German reads: "Es macht sich darüber den bestimmten Grundsatz, daß der Widerspruch nicht denkbar sei; in der Tat aber ist das Denken denkt denselben auch faktisch, nur sieht es sogleich von ihm weg und geht von ihm." Hegel, *Wissenschaft der Logik II*, 562–63.

15. G. W. F. Hegel, *Phenomenology of Spirit*, trans. Terry Pinkard (Cambridge: Cambridge University Press, 2018), 20 (translation modified). The German reads: "Das

bekannte überhaupt ist darum, weil es *bekannt* ist, nichte *erkant*." G. W. F. Hegel, *Phänomenologie des Geistes* (Frankfurt: Surhkamp, 1986), 35.

16. For a contemporary attempt at resuscitating Right Hegelianism, see Roger Scruton, *Conservatism: An Invitation to the Great Tradition* (New York: All Points, 2018). According to Scruton, Hegel's emphasis on the collective origin of individual freedom places him securely within conservative thought.

1. THE PATH TO CONTRADICTION

1. Many who take up Gilles Deleuze's critique of Hegel rely on the image of Hegel as a synthesizing thinker. For instance, Deleuzean Anne Sauvagnargues writes, "no synthesis can get rid of a contradiction by overcoming it. The dialectical movement, which purports to overcome contradiction, does not overcome it." Anne Sauvagnargues, "Hegel and Deleuze: Difference or Contradiction?" in *Hegel and Deleuze: Together Again for the First Time*, ed. Karen Houle and Jim Vernon (Evanston: Northwestern University Press, 2013), 42. Once one characterizes Hegel's dialectics in this way, the line of criticism becomes self-evident and irrefutable. See also Nathan Widder, "Negation, Disjunction, and a New Theory of Forces: Deleuze's Critique of Hegel," in *Hegel and Deleuze,* 18–37.

2. Even Hegel's most thoughtful critics, those not intending to dismiss him, succumb to the allure of the schema of thesis, antithesis, and synthesis. Though he qualifies his endorsement of this schema, Martin Heidegger nonetheless claims, "characterizing the dialectic by the unity of thesis, antithesis, and synthesis is still correct but still only derivative." Martin Heidegger, "Hegel's Concept of Experience," trans. Kenneth Haynes, in *Off the Beaten Track*, ed. Julian Young and Kenneth Haynes (Cambridge: Cambridge University Press, 2002), 138. Alain Badiou, for his part, characterizes Hegel as a thinker of conjunction who cannot think the disjunctive real. He claims that "philosophically Hegel has an absolute thesis that disjunction is unthinkable, inconceivable, not true." Alain Badiou, *Le Séminaire—L'infini: Aristote, Spinoza, Hegel, 1984–1985* (Paris: Fayard, 2016), 258. Conjunction is Badiou's (admittedly kinder) term for synthesis. But both Heidegger's and Badiou's judgments miss the trajectory of Hegel's thought: one must go through conjunction in order to sustain disjunction, not in order to overcome it.

3. Hegel's theory of ideology is never explicitly laid out as such in his philosophy. Though he evinces familiarity with the term (which had recently been coined), he does not devote any time to theorizing it by this name. But at the same time, Hegel tacitly indicates how one could conceive ideology through his understanding our relationship to contradiction.

4. When Hegel describes cognition as synthetic toward the end of the *Science of Logic*, he understands *synthetic* as the involvement with otherness, not as a solution to contradiction or as an all-encompassing unity. Here, he simply follows Kant's distinction between analytic and synthetic propositions.

5. G. W. F. Hegel, *Science of Logic*, trans. George Di Giovanni (Cambridge: Cambridge University Press, 2010), 745. The German reads: "in der Tat aber ist das Denken des Widerspruchs das wesentliche Moment des Begriffes." G. W. F. Hegel, *Wissenschaft der Logik II* (Frankfurt: Suhrkamp, 1986), 563.

6. Hegel, *Science of Logic*, 59. The German reads: "In seiner unbestimmeten Unmittelbarkeit ist es nur sich selbst gleich und auch nicht ungleich gegen Anderes, hat keine Verschiedenheit innerhalb seiner noch nach außen." G. W. F. Hegel, *Wissenschaft der Logik I* (Frankfurt: Suhrkamp, 1986), 82.

7. Hegel, *Science of Logic*, 59. The German reads: "*Das reine Sein und das reine Nichts ist also dasselbe.*" Hegel, *Wissenschaft der Logik I*, 83.

8. G. W. F. Hegel, *Phenomenology of Spirit*, trans. Terry Pinkard (Cambridge: Cambridge University Press, 2018), 40. The German reads: "In der Tat hat auch das nicht spekulative Denken sein Recht, das gültig." G. W. F. Hegel, *Phänomenologie des Geistes* (Frankfurt: Surhkamp, 1986), 61.

9. Alice Graves contends that Hegel accepts the validity of traditional logic's ordinary propositions as long as they remain within their proper domain of finitude and avoid intruding on questions of the infinite. She claims that "such logic should modestly keep within its sphere, and not try to deal with subjects not to be measured by its standards. It should not announce its finite categories and abstractions as though they were all-inclusive, and hence infinite and absolute." Alice Graves, "Hegel's Doctrine of Contradiction," *Journal of Speculative Philosophy* 22, nos. 1/2 (1888): 138. The problem with this otherwise tidy solution to the problem of the relationship between ordinary and speculative propositions is that it transforms Hegel into Kant. He becomes a philosopher who establishes limits on a certain type of thinking. In fact, Hegel recognizes that all attempts to establish limits end up going beyond them, just as the ordinary proposition cannot stay within the proper zone where Graves would like to confine it.

10. There are many significant followers of Hegel who claim that he does not at all reject the principle of noncontradiction. For instance, Karin de Boer argues that "Hegel considers the concept of contradiction to give rise to a particular philosophical principle. Yet this principle has nothing to do with the classical principle of contradiction." Karin de Boer, "Hegel's Account of Contradiction in the *Science of Logic* Reconsidered," *Journal of the History of Philosophy* 48, no. 3 (2010): 364. De Boer is certainly correct to note that Hegel expands the notion of contradiction beyond the confines of the classical principle of noncontradiction and that he obeys the principle in his philosophy. But he does also reveal that it ultimately doesn't hold.

11. Robert Hanna, "From an Ontological Point of View: Hegel's Critique of the Common Logic," *Review of Metaphysics* 40, no. 2 (1986): 331. As Hanna's title suggests, his essay figures Hegel's logic in direct contrast to that of W. V. O. Quine. In the "Two Dogmas of Empiricism" essay in *From a Logical Point of View*, Quine criticizes Kant's distinction between analytic and synthetic judgments. He claims that the judgments Kant holds up as synthetic (like $5 + 7 = 12$) are in fact analytic, insofar as they too are true on the basis of meaning alone and don't provide any explication.

12. Even though it takes what we now know as analytic philosophy a century to emerge in the figures of Gottlob Frege and Bertrand Russell, the real break between analytic and continental philosophy occurs with Hegel. From the analytic perspective, all those who accept Hegel's rejection of the principle of noncontradiction leave the terrain of philosophy. Those after Hegel who don't—that is to say, primarily the neo-Kantians at first, but later Frege, Russell, and Ludwig Wittgenstein—form the beginnings of the analytic tradition. Most historians of philosophy locate the break

much later. As a result, they fail to include the divisiveness surrounding Hegel into their account. See, for instance, Michael Dummett, *Origins of Analytical Philosophy* (Cambridge: Harvard University Press, 1993).

13. George Di Giovanni opts to translate *Schein* as "shine." Though this is a perfectly legitimate translation of the German term, it creates a mystical-sounding *Science of Logic*, which includes sentences like, "Shine is essence itself in the determinateness of being." G. W. F. Hegel, *The Science of Logic*, trans. George Di Giovanni (Cambridge: Cambridge University Press, 2010), 344. The problem with this tendency is that Hegel's philosophy represents an absolute rejection of mysticism. For Hegel, there is no direct pathway to the absolute, which is what the mystic experience promises. One must always arrive at the absolute through the labor of the negative.

14. If one reads a few commentaries on Hegel's works, a peculiar tendency quickly becomes apparent. Commentators spend significantly more time and energy dealing with the beginning of Hegel's works than with their endings. Though many portray Hegel as a philosopher of progress who moves from the unimportant to the important or from the abstract to the concrete, the quantity of attention given to the initial movements in Hegel's philosophy belies this image of progress. Just examining the commentaries and introductions to Hegel, one would imagine that Hegel gives away all his secrets at the beginning and that what follows is merely empty filler. In *The Idea of Hegel's Science of Logic*, for instance, Stanley Rosen devotes over 150 pages each to the first two sections of the *Logic*—the "Doctrine of Being" and the "Doctrine of Essence." But then when he comes to the much more difficult "Doctrine of the Concept," the quantity of pages drops to significantly less than 100 (even though this section is the longest in Hegel's own text). Stephen Houlgate takes this even further, announcing when he arrives at the "Reason" section in his discussion of the *Phenomenology of Spirit*, "Up to this point I have set out Hegel's phenomenological argument in some detail. For reasons of space, however, I will have to omit many details from the following accounts of reason, spirit, religion, and absolute knowing." Stephen Houlgate, *Hegel's "Phenomenology of Spirit": A Reader's Guide* (London: Bloomsbury, 2013). Just when one needs more help because the going gets tougher, the interpreters cut their commentary short. The point is not to single out Rosen or Houlgate for this choice but to indicate its representative status. Interpreters spend more time with the first half of Hegel's books rather than the second half because the latter is always a more unwelcome terrain in which the contradictions are more difficult to resolve.

15. G. W. F. Hegel, *Lectures on the History of Philosophy: Greek Philosophy to Plato*, trans. E. S. Haldane (Lincoln: University of Nebraska Press, 1995), 1:279. The German reads: "Hier sehen wir Land; es ist kein Satz des Heraklit, den ich nicht in meine Logik aufgenommen." G. W. F. Hegel, *Vorlesungen über die Geschichte der Philosophie I* (Frankfurt: Surhkamp, 1986), 320. Though Hegel discusses Heraclitus after Parmenides and Zeno, they were both younger than him.

16. Heraclitus, *Fragments,* ed. and trans. T. M. Robinson (Toronto: University of Toronto Press, 1987), fragment 91.

17. Heraclitus, fragment 49a.

18. Aristotle states, "To punctuate Heraclitus is no easy task, because we often cannot tell whether a particular word belongs to what precedes or to what follows it." Aristotle,

Rhetoric, trans. W. Rhys Roberts, in *The Complete Works of Aristotle*, vol. 2, ed. Jonathan Barnes (Princeton: Princeton University Press, 1984), 3:5.

19. Martin Heidegger vehemently opposes Hegel's characterization of an opposition between Heraclitus and Parmenides, which he attributes to an eagerness to see the history of philosophy as a contest of conflicting opinions. Since all philosophy says the same thing, Heidegger claims, seeing opposition among true philosophers is necessarily misinterpretation.

20. Hegel, *Lectures on the History of Philosophy*, 1:279 (translation modified). The German reads: "Bei ihm ist also zuerst die philosophische Idee in ihre spekulativen Form anzutreffen." Hegel, *Vorlesungen über die Geschichte der Philosophie I*, 320.

21. Despite his attempt to construct an entire system of formal logic that flies directly in the face of Hegel's dialectical logic, Gottlob Frege never mentions Hegel's name in his work. This contrasts him dramatically with fellow exponent of formal logic Bertrand Russell, who is one of Hegel's greatest critics.

22. What is fascinating about Russell's critique is that he does not upbraid Hegel for refusing the principle of noncontradiction but for extending its breadth too far. According to Russell, Hegel's insistence on absolute noncontradiction leads him to believe that one must have a complete system in which everything lines up before one can articulate any particular claim. As Russell sees it, Hegel takes up the principle of noncontradiction and goes haywire. Despite the harshness of Russell's critique, he actually undersells Hegel's audacity and potential for just spouting nonsense.

23. Bertrand Russell, *Our Knowledge of the External World as a Field for Scientific Method in Philosophy* (London: G. Allen and Unwin, 1914), 48–49.

24. This is an argument that Kevin Harrelson formulates in defense of Hegel. He writes, "the metalogical content of positive judgments, 'the individual is universal,' requires not only a previously identified subject, but also a predicative concept with sufficient quantificational status." Kevin J. Harrelson, "Language and Ontology in Hegel's Theory of Predication," *European Journal of Philosophy* 23, no. 4 (2015): 1268. The identity of the subject and the conceptual distinction of the predicate subtends every statement of predication.

25. See Robert Pippin, "Hegel's Metaphysics and the Problem of Contradiction," *Journal of the History of Philosophy* 16 (1978): 301–78.

26. Hegel claims that the problem with the truths of arithmetic is that they are simply analytic, despite Kant's claims to the contrary. Kant holds up $5 + 7 = 12$ as an example of a synthetic truth that Hegel dismisses as an analytic one. During this critique, Hegel implies that there are analytic truths that have a pure self-identity, which would be impossible according to Hegel's own philosophy. But his point is not that there are genuinely analytic truths. Here, Hegel argues that from the perspective of formal mathematical thinking, all truths are ultimately analytic. This is, for him, the limitation of this type of thinking.

27. In this sense, Katherina Dulckeit is correct to note that "for Hegel the distinction between the 'is' of predication and identity ultimately vanishes." Katherina Dulckeit, "Hegel's Revenge on Russell," in *Hegel and His Critics: Philosophy in the Aftermath of Hegel*, ed. William Desmond (Albany: SUNY Press, 1989), 117.

28. At this point, one could turn Russell's critique back on him. Hegel criticizes Russell's theory of descriptions *avant la lettre* for the attempt to reduce identity to a

description. As Hegel conceives it, one will never gather enough descriptions (or predicates) to arrive at identity in this way.

29. Hegel, *Science of Logic*, 358. The German reads: "sie darin besteht, *Trennung* als solche zu sein oder *in der Trennung* wesentlich, d. i. *nichts für sich*, sondern *Moment der Trennung* zu sein." Hegel, *Wissenschaft der Logik II*, 42.

30. Frege breaks with the formal propositional logic and develops an axiomatic predicate logic. Rather than thinking in terms of propositions, Frege avoids the contradictions that emerge through this traditional logic by organizing thought in terms of functions and quantifiers.

31. It is one of the great ironies in the history of philosophy that Bertrand Russell performs the Hegelian gesture of identifying the contradictory point within Frege's new logical system.

32. Songsuk Susan Hahn draws attention to Hegel's extension of the notion of contradiction from logical argumentation to entities in the world. She states, "Rather than locate contradictions merely in subjective reflection, involving logically incorrect relations between propositions and predicates, Hegel locates them in ontological organisms undergoing change in becoming." Songsuk Susan Hahn, *Contradiction in Motion: Hegel's Organic Concept of Life and Value* (Ithaca: Cornell University Press, 2007), 66. Though Hahn rightly sees that Hegel uses the term *contradiction* to describe the natural world, she contends that, for Hegel, nature provides the model for considering thought rather than the other way around. As a result, Hahn believes that we should remodel our thinking on the natural world. This argument goes completely against the spirit of Hegel, for whom the natural world has something to teach us only insofar as we see it through the transcendence of spirit. It is only the subject's break from the natural world that renders its contradiction visible, which mitigates any lesson that this world could offer us for structuring our cognition.

33. Hegel, *Science of Logic*, 382 (translation modified). The German reads: "er aber ist die Wurzel aller Bewegung und Lebendigkeit; nur insofern etwas in sich selbst einen Widerspruch hat, bewegt es sich, hat er Trieb und Tätigkeit." Hegel, *Wissenschaft der Logik II*, 75.

34. Hegel, *Science of Logic*, 95 (translation modified). The German reads: "Das *Sein-für-Anderes* ist in der Einheit des Etwas mit sich, identisch mit seinem *Ansich*; das Sein-für-Anderes ist so *am* Etwas." Hegel, *Wissenschaft der Logik I*, 131.

35. One searches in vain throughout Aristotle's works for the formulation of the principle that Rand attributes to him: A = A. But, that said, many see approximate formulations of this principle at moments in the *Metaphysics*.

36. Galt is not the only character in the novel that rejects the existence of contradiction. It is the shared position of all the novel's producers and distinguishes them from the nonproductive "moochers." For instance, Francisco d'Anconia states, "Contradictions do not exist. Whenever you think that you are facing a contradiction, check your premises. You will find that one of them is wrong." Ayn Rand, *Atlas Shrugged* (New York: Penguin, 1999), 199.

37. To be fair to Whitman, it is likely that his acquaintance with Hegel's thought was minimal and derived primarily from secondary sources.

38. Hegel, *Science of Logic*, 381. The German reads: "Alle Dinge sind an sich selbst widersprechend." Hegel, *Wissenschaft der Logik II*, 74.

39. Hegel follows Ludwig Wittgenstein's dictum from the *Tractatus* that what must be shown cannot be stated straightforwardly. Wittgenstein states, "What can be shown, cannot be said." Ludwig Wittgenstein, *Tractatus Logico-Philosophicus,* trans. D. F. Pears and B. F. McGuinness (Atlantic Highlands, NJ: Humanities Press International, 1961), 4.1212.

40. Hegel, *Science of Logic,* 684. The German reads: "so ist das Lebendige für sich selbst diese Entzweiung und hat das Gefühl dieses Widerspruchs, welches der *Schmerz* ist. Der *Schmerz* ist daher das Vorrecht lebendiger Naturen. . . . Wenn man sagt, daß der Widerspruch nicht denkbar sei, so ist er vielmehr im Schmerz des Lebendigen sogar eine wirkliche Existenz." Hegel, *Wissenschaft der Logik II,* 481.

41. G. W. F. Hegel, *Gesammelte Werke,* Band 6: *Jenaer Systementwürfe I* (Hamburg: Felix Meiner, 1975), 259. The German reads: "die Krankheit des Thiers ist das Werden des Geistes."

2. HEGEL AFTER FREUD

1. Rebecca Comay, *Mourning Sickness: Hegel and the French Revolution* (Stanford: Stanford University Press, 2011), 126.

2. Even Kant himself provides a corrective to the subjectivist reading of his philosophy in the second edition of the *Critique of Pure Reason* when he adds a section entitled "Refutation of Idealism."

3. Heinrich Heine, *Religion and Philosophy in Germany: A Fragment,* 2d ed., trans. John Snodgrass (Albany: SUNY Press, 1986), 123.

4. Daniel Berthold-Bond, *Hegel's Grand Synthesis: A Study of Being, Thought, and History* (Albany: SUNY Press, 1989), 7.

5. Berthold-Bond is explicit about his critique of Hegel for his ambivalence. He notes that "the dilemma he is led into by his ambivalence is not itself necessitated by his philosophic principles, but is more a wayward turn." Daniel Berthold-Bond, *Hegel's Grand Synthesis,* 6. Berthold-Bond writes at length to correct this "wayward turn," but, as a result, he doesn't confront Hegel's obscurity as a problem to be worked through in order to discover his philosophical position.

6. Kant is even worse than Hegel as a prose stylist, and his thought does not labor under the same misunderstandings that plague Hegel's.

7. Peter Singer, *Hegel,* in Roger Scruton, Peter Singer, Christopher Janaway, and Michael Tanner, *German Philosophers* (Oxford: Oxford University Press, 1997), 189.

8. See Frederick Beiser, *Hegel* (New York: Routledge, 2005).

9. Freud makes two passing mentions of Hegel in entire life's work. In *The Interpretation of Dreams,* he cites him indirectly, noting that "Spitta [1882] quotes Hegel as saying that dreams are devoid of all objective and reasonable coherence." Sigmund Freud, *The Interpretation of Dreams,* trans. James Strachey, in *The Standard Edition of the Complete Psychological Works of Sigmund Freud,* ed. James Strachey (London: Hogarth, 1953), 4:55. Later, in the *New Introductory Lectures on Psychoanalysis,* Freud brings up Hegel in the context of a critique of Marx. He states, "I am far from sure that I understand [Marx's] assertions aright; nor do they sound to me 'materialistic' but, rather, like a precipitate of the obscure Hegelian philosophy in whose school Marx graduated." Sigmund Freud, *New Introductory Lectures on Psychoanalysis,*

trans. James Strachey, in *The Standard Edition of the Complete Psychological Works of Sigmund Freud*, ed. James Strachey (London: Hogarth, 1964), 22:177.

10. Mladen Dolar, "Hegel and Freud," *e-flux* 34 (2012): http://www.e-flux.com/journal /34/68360/hegel-and-freud/. Dolar's point in this essay is that Hegel and Freud share precisely the same concern. Both Hegel and Freud engage in a shared effort to expose the crack or rupture as the universal principle.

11. In *The Unconscious Abyss*, Jon Mills argues that Hegel anticipates Freud's discovery of the unconscious through his theorization of the dialectical process. As Mills puts it, "Hegel is a proper precursor of Freud, and although largely unknown to psychoanalytic discourse, Hegel's philosophy contributes to psychoanalytic thought." Jon Mills, *The Unconscious Abyss: Hegel's Anticipation of Psychoanalysis* (Albany: SUNY Press, 2002), 18. Whereas Mills interprets psychoanalysis in the light of Hegel's thought, my strategy is exactly the reverse. The point is to see not how Hegel anticipates psychoanalysis but how the discovery of psychoanalysis enables us retroactively to clarify what is actually at stake in Hegel's philosophy.

12. Positing Hegel's connection to psychoanalytic theory depends on interpreting absolute knowing as the recognition of an absolute gap within self-identity rather than the achievement of self-identity and the closure of the gap between subject and object. Because he interprets absolute knowing in terms of self-identity, Preston Stovall contends that Hegel was not "fettered by the Freudian specters of an id, ego, or unconscious thwarting our ability to be truly self-aware." Preston Stovall, "Hegel's Realism: The Implicit Metaphysics of Self-Knowledge," *Review of Metaphysics* 61 (2007): 98. Stovall misses Hegel's anticipation of psychoanalytic theory because he takes Hegel's philosophy as the articulation of a success rather than the depiction of an inability to succeed. Rather than showing the achievement of self-identity, Hegel reveals how its failure is written into the effort to attain it.

13. Aristotle, *Politics*, trans. B. Jowett, in *The Complete Works of Aristotle*, vol. 2, ed. Jonathan Barnes (Princeton: Princeton University Press, 1984), 1:1.

14. Blaise Pascal echoes Aristotle's claim while giving it a modern twist. For Pascal, even suicide belongs to the acts through which we pursue happiness. He writes, "All men seek to be happy. This is without exception, whatever different means they use. They all strive toward this end. What makes some go to war, and others avoid it, is the same desire in both, accompanied by different perspectives. The will never takes the slightest step except toward this object. This is the motive of every action of every man, even of those who go hang themselves." Blaise Pascal, *Pensées*, ed. and trans. Roger Ariew (Indianapolis: Hackett, 2005), 181. Pascal's interpretation of happiness as the motivation for all acts results from his focus on conscious intentions. Once Freud introduces the unconscious, this interpretation ceases to be tenable.

15. In his *Seminar VII*, dedicated to *The Ethics of Psychoanalysis*, Jacques Lacan claims that the only role of the good is to be sacrificed for the sake of our unconscious desire. He states, "There is no other good than that which may serve to pay the price for access to desire." Jacques Lacan, *The Seminar of Jacques Lacan, Book VII: The Ethics of Psychoanalysis, 1959–1960*, trans. Dennis Porter (New York: Norton, 1992), 321. Our conscious striving for the good hides our satisfaction in its sacrifice.

16. I was once in this situation, and as my new partner became increasingly irate with my slips, I turned to the only possible solution (short of ending the relationship, which unfortunately took a while): I simply stopped using any name at all to refer

to the new partner—a strategy that worked effectively right up to the inevitable collapse of the relationship.

17. G. W. F. Hegel, *Encyclopedia of Philosophical Sciences in Basic Outline, Part I: Science of Logic*, trans. Klaus Brinkmann and Daniel O. Dahlstrom (Cambridge: Cambridge University Press, 2010), 210. The German reads: "der Mensch sich zwar in einzelnen verstellen und manches verbergen kann, nicht aber sein Inneres überhaupt, welches im *decursus vitae* unfehlbar sich kundgibt, dergestalt daß auch in dieser Beziehung gesagt werden muß, daß der Mensch nichts anderes ist als die Reihe seiner Taten." G. W. F. Hegel, *Enzyklopädie der philosophischen Wissenschaften I* (Frankfurt: Suhrkamp, 1986), 278.

18. G. W. F. Hegel, *Phenomenology of Spirit*, trans. Terry Pinkard (Cambridge: Cambridge University Press, 2018), 132 (translation modified). The German reads: "Diese [tierische Funktionen], statt unbefangen als etwas, das in und für sich nichtig ist und keine Wichtigkeit und Wesenheit für den Geist erlangen kann, getan zu werden, da sie es sind, . . . sind sie vielmehr Gegenstand des ernstlichen Bemühens und werden gerade zum Wichtigsten." G. W. F. Hegel, *Phänomenologie des Geistes* (Frankfurt: Surhkamp, 1986), 174.

19. Terry Pinkard, *Hegel's Phenomenology: The Sociality of Reason* (Cambridge: Cambridge University Press, 1996), 2.

20. In "You Can't Get There from Here," Robert Pippin provides the most compelling account of the transitions in the *Phenomenology of Spirit*. Though Pippin focuses on the difficulties of moving from consciousness to self-consciousness and from reason to spirit, his theory covers all the transitions that Hegel makes. As Pippin puts it in his ultimate formulation, "once the mind-world problem is linked to the subject-subject problem, and such subjects are understood in the mutually dependent, self-transforming way they are, the problem of consciousness must become the problem of *Geist*, and *Geist* can only be accounted for by a 'phenomenology' of its collective self-transformations." Robert Pippin, "You Can't Get There from Here: Transition Problems in Hegel's *Phenomenology of Spirit*," in *The Cambridge Companion to Hegel*, ed. Frederick Beiser (Cambridge: Cambridge University Press, 1993), 79–80. Pippin recognizes that the transitions come to make much more sense once we see that our knowledge of objects is implicated in our relations to other subjects and that our relations to other subjects implies a certain relation to objects.

21. Hegel, *Phenomenology of Spirit*, 201. The German reads: "*das Sein des Geistes ein Knochen ist*." Hegel, *Phänomenologie des Geistes*, 260.

22. Jacques Lacan's name for the irreducible symptom that defines subjectivity is the *sinthome*, which stands out from other symptoms because it resists interpretation absolutely.

23. One can see the overlap of aim and object in the case of Kant. Though Kant insists that the thing in itself is unknowable (or corresponds to an illusory way of knowing), he nonetheless conceives of knowledge of the object as the aim of thought. Thought strives to break out of subjective impressions and know objectively. The point of the *Critique of Pure Reason* is to establish the basis for this objective knowledge, which Kant locates in conceiving objects as phenomena rather than as things in themselves.

24. Freud highlights the unimportance of the object for the drive, despite how objects preoccupy the consciousness of subjects who seek them. He writes, "The object

[*Objekt*] of an instinct is the thing in regard to which or through which the instinct is able to achieve its aim. It is what is most variable about an instinct and is not originally connected with it, but becomes assigned to it only in consequence of being peculiarly fitted to make satisfaction possible." Sigmund Freud, "Instincts and Their Vicissitudes," trans. James Strachey, in *The Standard Edition of the Complete Psychological Works of Sigmund Freud*, ed. James Strachey (London: Hogarth, 1957), 14:122.

25. Sigmund Freud, "On the Universal Tendency to Debasement in the Sphere of Love (Contributions to the Psychology of Love II)" (1912), trans. Alan Tyson, in *The Standard Edition of the Complete Psychological Works of Sigmund Freud*, ed. James Strachey (London: Hogarth, 1957), 11:186.

26. Because Freud can imagine someone becoming "free and happy in love" at this point in his career, the situation does not seem as dire as it will with the development of his later theory. As long as the object is repressed, one can imagine overcoming repression and attaining the ultimate satisfaction of obtaining the object. This changes when the site of repression changes in Freud's later thought.

27. Though Freud never rewrote "Instincts and Their Vicissitudes" after the turn to the death drive in 1920, Adrian Johnston did it for him. See Adrian Johnston, *Time Driven: Metapsychology and the Splitting of the Drive* (Evanston: Northwestern University Press, 2005).

28. Freud's distinction between the aim of the drive and the object, when he writes "Instincts and Their Vicissitudes" in 1915, suggests that he already anticipates the revolutionary turn to the death drive that he would make in 1920, even though his theory of the drives remains within the basic structure of the pleasure principle. The turn to the death drive represents the final break from the privileging of the object that haunts the thought of the early Freud. "Instincts and Their Vicissitudes" shows him struggling toward this break.

29. Hegel, *Encyclopedia of Philosophical Sciences in Basic Outline*, 282. The German reads: "Das Gute, das absolut Gute, vollbringt sich ewig in der Welt, und das Resultat ist, daß es schon in und für sich vollbracht ist und nicht erst auf uns zu warten bracht." Hegel, *Enzyklopädie der philosophischen Wissenschaften*, 367.

30. This is what Freud means when he states, "The pleasure principle seems actually to serve the death instincts." Sigmund Freud, *Beyond the Pleasure Principle*, trans. James Strachey, in *The Standard Edition of the Complete Psychological Works of Sigmund Freud*, ed. James Strachey (London: Hogarth, 1955), 18:63.

31. The work of recent writing on Hegel by thinkers indebted to Freud and psychoanalysis shows this to be the case. The writing of theorists such as Rebecca Comay, Mladen Dolar, Adrian Johnston, Slavoj Žižek, and Alenka Zupančič, among others, reveals that interpreting Hegel after engaging the insights of psychoanalysis radically clarifies his thought.

32. Jean Wahl, *Le Malheur de la conscience dans la philosophie de Hegel*, 2d ed. (Paris: Presses Universitaires de France, 1951), 182.

33. Though Lacan's followers have provided much elaboration on what it means, Lacan confines his discussion of traversing the fantasy to the conclusion of his *Seminar XI*. Lacan states that in the traversal of the fantasy "the experience of the fundamental fantasy becomes the drive." He then asks, "How can a subject who has traversed the radical fantasy experience the drive?" Jacques Lacan, *The Seminars of*

Jacques Lacan, Book XI: The Four Fundamental Concepts of Psychoanalysis, trans. Alan Sheridan (New York: Norton, 1977), 273 (translation modified).

34. As Richard Boothby puts it, "To traverse the phantasy in the Lacanian sense is to be more profoundly claimed by the phantasy than ever, in the sense of being brought into in ever more intimate relation with that real core of the phantasy that transcends imaging." Richard Boothby, *Freud as Philosopher: Metapsychology After Lacan* (New York: Routledge, 2001), 275–76.

35. Slavoj Žižek, *The Sublime Object of Ideology* (London: Verso, 1989), 6.

3. WHAT HEGEL MEANS WHEN HE SAYS *VERNUNFT*

1. G. W. F. Hegel, *Elements of the Philosophy of Right*, trans. H. B. Nisbet, ed. Allen W. Wood (Cambridge: Cambridge University Press, 1991), 20. G. W. F. Hegel, *Gundlienien der Philosophie des Rechts* (Frankfurt: Surhkamp, 1986), 24. Referring to this statement, M. W. Jackson claims, "No political theorist has suffered more distortion because of a single sentence than Hegel." M. W. Jackson, "Hegel: The Real and the Rational," in *The Hegel Myths and Legends*, ed. Jon Stewart (Evanston: Northwestern University Press, 1996), 19. Since the 1980s, this famous statement from the *Philosophy of Right* has become known as Hegel's *Doppelsatz*, thanks largely to Dieter Henrich.

2. In recent years, it has become the case that how one interprets this statement indicates where one stands on Hegel himself. Until late in the twentieth century, there were followers of Hegel who took the identification of the rational (*vernünftig*) and the actual (*wirklich*) as a blatantly conservative political claim. Now, however, it is only opponents of Hegel who read the statement in this way.

3. Jean Hyppolite explains the difference between the speculative reading of a proposition and an empirical reading. The empirical reading sustains the subject in an external relation to its predicate and holds the two elements apart. In contrast, a speculative reading recognizes how the subject loses itself in the predicate's otherness. In *Logic and Existence*, he writes, "The speculative proposition's subject is posited completely in its determination or its difference." Jean Hyppolite, *Logic and Existence*, trans. Leonard Lawlor and Amit Sen (Albany: SUNY Press, 1997), 146. The subject of the speculative proposition gains its identity only through the otherness that it encounters in the predicate. There is no identity outside of this encounter.

4. Hegel formulates these oppositions at various points in his works. For instance, in the *Encyclopedic Logic*, he lays out the contrast between the understanding and reason, stating that "reason's battle consists in overcoming what the understanding has rendered rigid." G. W. F. Hegel, *Encyclopedia of Philosophical Sciences in Basic Outline, Part I: Science of Logic*, trans. Klaus Brinkmann and Daniel O. Dahlstrom (Cambridge: Cambridge University Press, 2010), 72. The German reads: "Der Kampf der Vernunft besteht darin, dasjenige, was der Verstand fixiert hat, zu überwinden." G. W. F. Hegel, *Enzykolpädie der philosophischen Wissenschaften I* (Frankfurt: Surhkamp, 1986), 99. In the *Science of Logic*, we can see Hegel clarifying the opposition between actuality and reality. He writes, "we must rather regard everything *as being* actual only to the extent that it has the idea in it and expresses it. . . . [In contrast,] a reality that does not correspond to the concept is mere *appearance*, something

subjective, accidental, arbitrary, something which is not the truth." G. W. F. Hegel, *Science of Logic*, trans. George Di Giovanni (Cambridge: Cambridge University Press, 2010), 671. The German reads: "alles Wirkliche nur insofern *ist*, als es die Idee in sich hat und sie ausdrückt. . . . [Aber] diejenige Realität, welche den Begriffe nicht entspricht, ist bloße *Erscheinung*, das Subjektive, Züfallige, Willkürliche, das nicht die Wahrheit hat." G. W. F. Hegel, *Wissenschaft der Logik II* (Frankfurt: Surhkamp, 1986), 464.

5. Almost all of the defenses of Hegel's claim in the *Philosophy of Right* focus on actuality (*Wirklichkeit*) rather than rationality (*Vernunft*). Steven B. Smith provides the paradigmatic form of this line of thought. He writes, "when Hegel attributes rationality to the actual, he does not mean to encompass by that term everything that is. . . . 'Actuality' in Hegel's technical sense may be understood as the conceptual opposite of what is arbitrary or contingent." Steven B. Smith, *Hegel's Critique of Liberalism: Rights in Context* (Chicago: University of Chicago Press, 1989), 224. While Smith's understanding of what Hegel means by "actuality" certainly hits the mark, his argument responds too well to the problem that Hegel's statement evokes. Smith not only solves the problem, he also eliminates the speculative force of the statement. Rather than being a proposition that articulates the identity of identity and difference, it becomes too much a statement of identity. See also Béatrice Longuenesse, *Hegel et la critique de la métaphysique*, 2d ed. (Paris: Vrin, 2015).

6. G. W. F. Hegel, *Wissenschaft der Logik I* (Frankfurt: Surhkamp, 1986), 217. The German reads: "Kant gibt diesen Begriff von den Antinomien, daß sie nicht sophistiche Künsteleien seien, sondern Widersprüche, auf welche die Vernunft notwendig *stoße* (nach Kantischem Ausdrucke) müsse." George di Giovanni translates this as: "Kant's conception of the antinomies is that they 'are not sophistic artifices but contradictions reason must *run up against.*' This last is a Kantian expression." Hegel, *Science of Logic*, 158.

7. Hegel is not entirely at ease with Kant's arguments in the antinomies, but he believes that the basic point that Kant makes—that metaphysical questions produce contradictory concepts when one attempts to solve them—is totally valid.

8. Kant's attempt to divide knowledge from faith earns him Hegel's particular scorn. As Hegel sees it, locating faith in the gap of knowledge represents a failure to see how knowledge determines the gap. The effort to make room for faith can only be a pretense. Faith must be intrinsic to knowledge, not located in its absence.

9. Kant's limit on the use of reason is not a confession that are no possible answers to metaphysical questions. There are answers, but they are found in faith rather than knowledge. As Kant frames it, the problem with metaphysical questions is that they do tremendous damage to faith and morality. Kant would rather not know in order to preserve the moral universe. This is a position that Hegel cannot abide.

10. Craig Matarrese, "Hegel's Theory of Freedom," *Philosophy Compass* 2, no. 2 (2007): 174.

11. The belief that Hegel redefines reason in the aftermath of Kant occurs across the spectrum of Hegel's interpreters. See, for instance, Robert B. Brandom, *Reason in Philosophy: Animating Ideas* (Cambridge: Harvard University Press, 2009); Hans-Georg Gadamer, *Hegel's Dialectic: Five Hermeneutical Studies*, trans. P. Christopher Smith (New Haven: Yale University Press, 1976); Herbert Marcuse, *Hegel's Ontology and the Theory of Historicity*, trans. Seyla Benhabib (Cambridge: MIT Press,

1987); and Charles Taylor, *Hegel* (Cambridge: Cambridge University Press, 1975). My claim is that, rather than redefining reason after Kant, Hegel accepts Kant's definition while reversing his evaluation of it.

12. In *Glas*, Jacques Derrida points out repeatedly the inability of Hegel to countenance any absolute loss. He writes, "at the end of the operation, the absolute spirit records a profit in any case, death included." Jacques Derrida, *Glas*, trans. John P. Leavey Jr. and Richard Rand (Lincoln: University of Nebraska Press, 1986), 141. From Kierkegaard to Derrida, defenders of the singular find something off-putting about Hegel's transformation of failure to success, for which the model is his rereading of the Kantian antinomies. What neither Kierkegaard nor Derrida sees, however, is how success becomes itself a form of failure in the process of failure's transformation.

13. G. W. F. Hegel, *Philosophy of Nature: Part Two of the Encyclopedia of the Philosophical Sciences* (1830), trans. A. V. Miller (Oxford: Oxford University Press, 1970), 35 (translation modified). The German reads: "Der Begriff . . . ist an und für sich die absolute Negativität und Freiheit, die Zeit daher nicht seine Macht, noch ist er in der Zeit und ein Zeitliches, sondern *er* ist vielmehr die Macht der Zeit, als welche nur diese Negativität als Äußerlichkeit ist. Nur das Natürliche ist darum der Zeit untertan, insofern es endlish ist; das Wahre dagegen, die Idee, der Geist, ist *ewig*." G. W. F. Hegel, *Enzyklopädie der philosophischen Wissenschaften II* (Frankfurt: Surhkamp, 1986), 49–50.

14. Referring to finite things, Hegel claims, "the hour of their birth is the hour of their death." Hegel, *Science of Logic*, 101. The German reads: "die Stunde ihrer Geburt ist die Stunde ihres Todes." Hegel, *Wissenschaft der Logik I*, 140.

15. When it comes to death, the contrast between Hegel and Spinoza reaches its greatest extreme. For Spinoza, death comes to every entity from the outside. There is no self-annihilating entity because there is no subject in Spinoza's universe.

16. Hegel, *Philosophy of Nature*, 56. The German reads: "Ein Mensch kann totgeschlagen werden, dieses Äußerliche ist aber zufällig; das Wahrhafte ist, daß der Mensch durch sich selbst stirbt." Hegel, *Enzyklopädie der philosophischen Wissenschaften II*, 74.

17. Kant's refusal of metaphysical questions leads to the problem of the thing in itself that undermines Kant's philosophy from the moment of its introduction. Very soon after Kant introduced it, followers such as Fichte recognized it as a problem and worked to formulate a new version of the Kantian system that would avoid the thing in itself. Just as the solution to metaphysical questions lies beyond the limit of the understanding, the thing in itself exists beyond appearance.

18. Freud points out that repression creates distortion in the consciousness of the subject because it involves a constant force exerted on consciousness. Consciousness must constantly struggle against the repressed material and form itself around this present absence. The structure of consciousness must actively avoid the repressed material. As a result, what it cannot represent shapes what it can represent.

19. In the *Phenomenology*, Hegel writes, "to receive the plurality of categories again in some way as a discovery, for example, out of the judgments, and thus to acquiesce to them, is in fact to be regarded as a disgrace to science." Hegel, *Phenomenology of Spirit*, 139 (translated modified). The German reads: "Die Vielheit der Kategorien aber auf irgendeine Weise wieder als einen Fund, z. B. aus den Urteilen, aufnehmen und sich dieselben so gefallen lassen, ist in der Tat als eine Schmach der Wissenschaft anzusehen." Hegel, *Phänomenologie des Geistes*, 182.

20. For Aristotle's account of the categories, see Aristotle, *Categories*, trans. J. L. Ackrill, in *The Complete Works of Aristotle*, vol. 1, ed. Jonathan Barnes (Princeton: Princeton University Press, 1984).

21. Phenomenologists focusing solely on conscious experience make the same error in their relegation of the problem of the unconscious to the back burner while we first figure out how consciousness works. This is the position of Eugen Fink, a follower of Edmund Husserl.

22. The connection between Hegel's criticism of the first *Critique* and his criticism of the second is clear. When Kant (and Fichte following him) formulates his morality, he posits morality as a duty that the subject ought to accomplish rather than one that it already accomplishes or has accomplished. Striving toward a better future inheres in Kantian morality. This better future always remains in the beyond, which leaves the subject constantly in the position of striving.

23. Hegel, *Science of Logic*, 26. The German reads: "der Widerspruch eben das Erheben der Vernunft über die Beschränkungen des Verstandes und das Auflösen derselben ist." Hegel, *Wissenschaft der Logik I*, 39.

24. Hegel, *Science of Logic*, 540. The German reads: "Es ist daher in jeder Rücksicht zu verwerfen, Verstand und Vernunft so, wie gewöhnlich geschieht, zu trennen." Hegel, *Wissenschaft der Logik II*, 287. Slavoj Žižek provides a cogent formulation for the relationship between understanding and reason. He writes, "Understanding, deprived of the illusion that there is something beyond it, is Reason." Slavoj Žižek, *The Ticklish Subject: The Absent Centre of Political Ontology* (London: Verso, 1999), 86. Žižek's formulation enables him to reconcile Hegel's critique of understanding with his claim that there is no difference between understanding and reason.

25. Hegel, *Science of Logic*, 538–539. The German reads: "Es ist aber ferner als die unendliche Kraft des Verstandes zu achten, das Konkrete in der abstrakten Bestimmtheiten zu trennen und die Tiefe des Unterschieds zu fassen, welche allein zugleich die Macht ist, die ihren Übergang bewirkt." Hegel, *Wissenschaft der Logik II*, 286.

26. Hegel, *Phenomenology of Spirit*, 20 (translation modified). The German reads: "Die Tätigkeit des Scheidens ist die Kraft und Arbeit des *Verstandes*, der verwundersamsten und größten oder veilmehr der absoluten Macht." Hegel, *Phänomenologie des Geistes*, 36.

27. The fact that the understanding and reason work so perfectly together leads Hegel to refuse to disconnect them. He insists that the separating power of the understanding is intrinsically linked to reason's capacity for grasping contradiction.

28. Hegel, *Phänomenologie des Geistes*, 36. The German reads: "Er gewinnt seine Wahrheit nur, indem er in der absoluten Zerissenheit sich selbst findet." Terry Pinkard's English translation, like A. V. Miller's before, dilutes this key sentence by failing to indicate the violence of "absoluten Zerissenheit." Pinkard writes, "Spirit only wins to its truth by finding its feet in absolute disruption." G. W. F. Hegel, *Phenomenology of Spirit*, trans. Terry Pinkard (Cambridge: Cambridge University Press, 2018), 21. Miller writes, "It wins to its truth only when, in utter dismemberment, it finds itself." G. W. F. Hegel, *Phenomenology of Spirit*, trans. A. V. Miller (Oxford: Oxford University Press, 2018), 19. This is a clear instance where J. B. Baillie's earlier (and more poetic) translation hits the mark much better. Baillie translates it as: "It only wins to its truth when it finds itself utterly torn asunder." G. W. F. Hegel, *The*

Phenomenology of Mind, trans. J. B. Baillie (New York: Harper and Row, 1931), 93. What Baillie captures that Pinkard and Miller miss is that undergoing the violence of being absolutely torn asunder is the necessary condition for spirit to find itself.

29. G. W. Leibniz, *Theodicy*, trans. E. M. Huggard (Chicago: Open Court, 1985), 88.

30. Outside of speech, there is only violence, but communicative rationality rescues us from an unceasing violence, which is why Habermas champions it. Communicative rationality creates a world in which one can have one's mind changed without first having one's arm broken.

31. The supposed barrenness of a rational existence leads to its critique by the thinkers such as Theodor Adorno and the other member of the Frankfurt School. Though Adorno does not want to abandon reason, he sees its instrumentalization as an oppressive constraint on the subject's desire.

32. Hegel, *Phenomenology of Spirit*, 137. The German reads: "alle Wirklichkeit nicht anderes ist als es." Hegel, *Phänomenologie des Geistes*, 179.

33. The way of the world is a paradigmatic moment in the *Phenomenology*. Whereas positions like virtue that privilege ideals always end up betraying them, positions like the way of the world that demand acting without concern about betraying ideals tend to advance the universal in spite of the particular motivations of the subject taking up these positions. For Hegel, the ability to be impure is a necessary condition for being an ethical subject.

34. Bertrand Russell, *A History of Western Philosophy* (New York: Simon and Schuster, 1945), 731.

35. King Friedrich I introduced the new constitution in 1815, but he died in 1816, at which point his son Wilhelm I took up its advocacy amid strident resistance from the Estates Assembly.

36. G. W. F. Hegel, "Proceedings of the Estates Assembly of the Kingdom of Württemberg, 1815–1816," in *Heidelberg Writings: Journal Publications*, ed. and trans. Brady Bowman and Allen Speight (Cambridge: Cambridge University Press, 2009), 42. The German reads: "Wenn landständische Deputierte den Sinn des Privatinteresses . . . mitbringen . . . und sie kommen überhaupt mit dem Willen herbei, für das Allgemeine *sowenig als möglich zu geben* und *zu tun*." G. W. F. Hegel, *Verhandlungen in der Versammlung der Landstände des Königreichs Württemberg im Jahr 1815 und 1816*, in *Nürnberger und Heidelberger Schriften 1808–1817* (Frankfurt: Surhkamp, 1986), 475.

37. Hegel, "Proceedings of the Estates Assembly," 82. The German reads: "um die Sache von keiner anderen Seite zu betrachten als der Erfahrung, so kann man sich auf diese berufen, teils daß Völker selbst, und zwar von den freisinnigsten, ihre Ungeschicklichkeit anerkannt haben, sich eine Verfassung zu geben, und einen *Solon*, *Lykurg* damit beauftragten, welche Männer ferner eine List gebrauchten, um den sogenannten Willen des Volks und die Erklärung dieses Willens über ihre Verfassung zu beseitigen." Hegel, *Verhandlungen in der Versammlung der Landstände des Königreichs Württemberg im Jahr 1815 und 1816*, 530.

38. Lenin famously recognizes the central role that Hegel's *Science of Logic* plays in the structure of Marx's *Capital* in his notebooks on the former work. He writes, "Aphorism: it is impossible completely to understand Marx's *Capital*, and especially its

first chapter, without having thoroughly studied and understood the whole of Hegel's *Logic*. Consequently, half a century later none of the Marxists understood Marx!!" V. I. Lenin, "Conspectus of Hegel's *Science of Logic*," in *Collected Works* (Moscow: Progress, 1969), 38:180.

39. See Germaine Greer, *The Female Eunuch* (New York: Harper, 1970).

40. See Shulamith Firestone, *The Dialectic of Sex: The Case for Feminist Revolution* (New York: Bantam, 1970).

4. THE INSUBSTANTIALITY OF SUBSTANCE

1. James Kreines argues that Kant's discover of the antinomies of pure reason "justifies neither Kant's epistemic limit, nor the impossibility of metaphysics. Rather, the conflicts Kant uncovers can and should be harnessed in the systematic reconstruction of a new form of the metaphysics of reason." James Kreines, *Reason in the World: Hegel's Metaphysics and Its Philosophical Appeal* (Oxford: Oxford University Press, 2015), 5.

2. The fact that Hegel describes his masterpiece the *Science of Logic* as "the exposition of God as he is in his eternal essence before the creation of nature and of finite spirit" certainly gives aid and comfort to Hegel's critics. G. W. F. Hegel, *Science of Logic*, trans. George Di Giovanni (Cambridge: Cambridge University Press, 2010), 29. The German reads: "dieser Inhalt die Darstellung Gottes ist, wie er in seinem ewigen Wesen vor der Erschaffung der Natur und eines endlichen Geistes ist." G. W. F. Hegel, *Wissenschaft der Logik I* (Frankfurt: Suhrkamp, 1986), 44. This statement seems to imply that Hegel is a pre-Critical metaphysician, someone who has nothing to say to those who live in the world after Kant. But when we examine the statement in light of Hegel's ontology, it becomes clear that grasping the "eternal essence" of God involves reconciling it with the most humiliated finite being.

3. Though Hegel accepts an initial divide between thought and being, he does reject Kant's refutation of the ontological proof, despite the flaws that he detects in this proof. Hegel objects to Kant's metaphor. The difference between a hundred real thalers and the idea of a hundred thalers is not the same as the difference between an actually existing God and the idea of God.

4. G. W. F. Hegel, *Phenomenology of Spirit,* trans. Terry Pinkard (Cambridge: Cambridge University Press, 2018), 21 (translation modified). The German reads: "Was außer ihr vorzugehen, eine Tätigkeit gegen sie zu sein scheint, ist ihr eigenes Tun, und sie zeigt sich wesentlich Subjekt zu sein." G. W. F. Hegel, *Phänomenologie des Geistes* (Frankfurt: Suhrkamp, 1986), 39.

5. A look at John McTaggart's *Studies in Hegelian Cosmology* reveals that McTaggart himself recognizes on some level how little evidence he has in Hegel's own work for the panlogical interpretation. With surprise, he states that "Hegel gives a very small part of his writings to Cosmological questions—a curious fact when we consider their great theoretical interest, and still greater practical importance. . . . This peculiarity of Hegel's is curious, but undeniable. I do not know of any possible explanation, unless in so far as one may be found in his want of personal interest in the part of philosophy which most people find more interesting than any other." John

238

McTaggart, *Studies in Hegelian Cosmology* (Cambridge: Cambridge University Press, 1901), 2. McTaggart goes on to conclude that Hegel's system proves both human immortality and the communal nature of God.

6. Slavoj Žižek, *Less Than Nothing: Hegel and the Shadow of Dialectical Materialism* (New York: Verso, 2012), 959.

7. Another version of the amputated Hegel appears in Allen Wood's *Hegel's Ethical Thought*. Wood aims at establishing Hegel as an unparalleled ethical and political thinker, but in order to do so he believes that he must cut away completely "his system of speculative logic" and preserve only "his reflections on the social and spiritual predicament of modern Western European culture." Allen W. Wood, *Hegel's Ethical Thought* (Cambridge: Cambridge University Press, 1990), 5. Though Wood never mentions Kojève in his book, he nonetheless follows Kojève's lead in eliminating Hegel's ontological claims. Wood makes no bones about the necessity of an amputation.

8. Raymond Queneau edited and published Kojève's lecture series in 1947, and an English translation followed decades later. But this translation makes significant cuts to Queneau's edition, with the result that the philosophical originality of Kojève's position is largely lost. He appears as someone who reduces all of Hegel's philosophy to the dialectic of the master and the slave. Even if one doesn't read French, one should stick to the French version. Although one might not understand anything, at least the possibilities for being led astray will be lessened.

9. Alexandre Kojève, *Introduction à la lecture de Hegel,* ed. Raymond Queneau (Paris: Gallimard, 1947), 331. The French reads: "Hegel rejette toute espèce de 'révélation' en philosophie. Rien ne peut venir de Dieu: rien ne peut venir d'une réalité quelconque extra-mondaine, extra-humaine, non temporelle. C'est l'action créatrice temporelle de l'humanité, c'est l'Histoire qui crée la réalité que révèle la Philosophie."

10. Kojève blames Hegel's *Philosophy of Nature* on the influence of Schelling. He notes, "the real (metaphysical) and phenomenal Dialectic of Nature exists only in the (Schellingian) imagination of Hegel." The French reads: "la Dialectique réelle (métaphysique) et phénoménale de la Nature n'existe que dans l'imagination ('schellingienne') de Hegel." Kojève, *Introduction à la lecture,* 490.

11. The theorist who most fully realizes Kojève's project of uniting Hegel with Heidegger and Marx is Walter Davis. Davis makes a compelling case that these projects (along with Freud's) share a common aim—the freedom of the subject—and an acknowledgment of the trauma that this aim entails. See Walter A. Davis, *Inwardness and Existence* (Madison: University of Wisconsin Press, 1989).

12. Rocío Zambrana divides Hegel's thought into an early ontological period and a later period concerned with the norms of intelligibility. She argues that his philosophy undergoes "a shift from an ontological logic to a theory of normative activity." Rocío Zambrana, *Hegel's Theory of Intelligibility* (Chicago: University of Chicago Press, 2015), 36. Zambrana takes a sanguine view of this shift insofar as it saves Hegel from the temptation of pre-Critical metaphysics that he succumbs to in the early *Faith and Knowledge*.

13. See Robert Pippin, *Hegel's Idealism: The Satisfactions of Self-Consciousness* (Cambridge: Cambridge University Press, 1989).

14. According to Robert Brandom, "Hegel's principal innovation is his idea that in order to follow through on Kant's fundamental insight into the essentially normative

character of mind, meaning, and rationality, we need to recognize that normative statuses such as authority and responsibility are at base social statuses." Robert B. Brandom, *Reason in Philosophy: Animating Ideas* (Cambridge: Harvard University Press, 2009), 66.

15. As Adrian Johnston points out, we can easily reverse the usual way of thinking about the privilege of epistemology. Johnston writes, "The real mystery is not that subject can (re)connect with substance, but that subject separated off from substance to begin with—thus creating the very obstacle of separation making possible knowledge as the overcoming of this same separation." Adrian Johnston, "Whither the Transcendental? Hegel, Analytic Philosophy, and the Prospects of a Realist Transcendentalism Today," *Crisis and Critique* 5, no. 1 (2018): 201. Through this reversal, the key question changes from how can we know the world to how can the subject emerge from undifferentiated being.

16. Though this statement is regularly attributed to Hegel, it doesn't appear anywhere in the lectures or writings that have been preserved. The German reads: "Wenn die Tatsachen nicht mit der Theorie übereinstimmen, umso schlimmer für die Tatsachen."

17. The truth of this event is impossible to disentangle from the myth surrounding it, though Bertrand Beaumont makes a valiant effort to do so. He claims that Hegel actually took the side of the empirical evidence and rejected the existence of a planet between Mars and Jupiter that a priori calculations established. See Bertrand Beaumont, "Hegel and the Seven Planets," in *The Hegel Myths and Legends,* ed. Jon Stewart (Evanston: Northwestern University Press, 1996), 285–88.

18. Hegel, *Phenomenology of Spirit,* 12. The German reads: "Es kommt . . . alles darauf an, das Wahre nicht als *Substanz*, sondern ebensosehr als *Subjekt* aufzufassen und auszudrücken. Zugleich ist zu bemerken, daß die Substantialität so sehr das Allgemeine oder die *Unmittelbarkeit des Wissens* selbst als auch diejenige, welche Sein oder Unmittelbarkeit *für* das Wissen ist, in sich schließt." Hegel, *Phänomenologie des Geistes,* 22–23.

19. The struggle between these two visions of subjectivity in Descartes comes to a head in the *Discourse on Method.* There he affirms radical doubt as the principle that divides the subject from itself, but at the same time he sees the subject as being "like the master and possessor of nature." These two visions of subjectivity are not simply two sides of the same coin but are completely incompatible. Descartes turns to the subject of mastery in order to avoid following the implications of the divided subject to their end point. Or one could say that he turns to the subject of mastery so that he doesn't have to become Hegel.

20. The self-identity of substance is what leads Spinoza to insist that there can only be one substance and that God is this substance. Hegel's claim that substance is subject represents what he sees as the only possible way of avoiding Spinozism. The moment one grants the existence of substance that isn't already subject itself, one implicitly declares one's allegiance to Spinoza.

21. G. W. F. Hegel, *Lectures on the Philosophy of Religion,* vol. 3: *The Consummate Religion,* ed. Peter C. Hodgson, trans. R. F. Brown, P. C. Hodgson, and J. M. Stewart (Oxford: Clarendon, 2007), 127. The German reads: "Daß ich einen Apfel esse, ist, daß ich seine organische Selbstständigkeit vertilge und ihn mir assimiliere. Daß ich dies tun kann, dazu gehört, daß der Apfel an sich—schon vorher, ehe ich ihn

anfasse—in seiner Natur diese Bestimmung habe, ein zu Zerstörendes zu sein und zugleich ein solches, das an sich eine Homogeneität mit meinen Verdauungswerkzeugen hat, daß ich ihn mit mir homogen machen kann." G. W. F. Hegel, *Vorlesungen über die Philosophie der Religion,* Teil 3: *Die vollendete Religion,* ed. Walter Jaeschke (Hamburg: Felix Meiner, 1984), 62–63.

22. In his commentary on the first *Critique,* Graham Bird points out that Kant wants to privilege appearances rather than malign them. He notes, "for Kant the world of appearances is not a second-best substitute for 'real' knowledge but an expression of the real world of possible experience and science." Graham Bird, *The Revolutionary Kant: A Commentary on the "Critique of Pure Reason"* (Chicago: Open Court, 2006), 175. To read Kant any other way is to equate him with George Berkeley, an equation that Kant specifically rejects in the "Refutation of Idealism" that he adds to the second edition of the *Critique of Pure Reason.*

23. Hegel, *Science of Logic,* 201. The German reads: "Es ist dies eine zu große Zärtlichkeit für die Welt, von ihr den Widerspruch zu entfernen, ihn dagegen in den Geist, in die Vernunft zu verlegen und darin aufgelöst bestehen zu lassen. In der Tat ist es der Geist, der so stark ist, den Widerspruch ertragen zu können, aber er ist es auch, der ihn aufzulösen weiß. Die sogennante Welt aber (sie heiße objeketive, reale Welt oder, nach dem tranzendentalen Idealismus, subjektives Anschauen und durch die Verstandeskategorie bestimmte Sinnlichkeit) entbehrt darum des Widerspruchs nicht und nirgends, vermag ihn aber nicht zu ertragen und ist darum dem Enstehen und Vergehen preisgegeben." Hegel, *Wissenschaft der Logik I,* 276.

24. Hegel's ontology has nothing to do with recent calls for bypassing the subject and making direct claims about objects, like that of object-oriented ontology. This line of thought rejects the possibility of the object's self-contradiction. The refusal of contradiction is not simply the point at which object-oriented ontology finds itself at odds with Hegel. It also represents its fundamental ontological presupposition. The assumption that objects are isolated and self-identical appears throughout the works of the object-oriented ontologists, though the philosophical ground for this assumption is absent.

5. LOVE AND LOGIC

1. Though he grasps the theoretical importance of Hegel's later work, György Lukács provides the paradigmatic Marxist account of his intellectual trajectory, charging Hegel with an "abandonment of the revolutionary ideas of his youth." Georg Lukács, *The Young Hegel: Studies in the Relations Between Dialectics and Economics,* trans. Rodney Livingstone (Cambridge: MIT Press, 1976), 72. To be clear, Lukács believes that this abandonment enabled Hegel to gain philosophical insight that he otherwise would not have had. In the end, however, this remains a critique and statement of where Hegel veered off course.

2. As Dieter Henrich puts it, "From Hegel's incorporation of 'love' as the grounding term of his reflection the system emerged without a break." Dieter Henrich, *Hegel im Kontext* (Frankfurt: Suhrkamp, 2010), 27.

3. Though Spinoza's philosophy concludes with the intellectual love of God, this is not its starting point or its motivating force, as love is for the early Hegel.

4. In the *Philosophy of Right*, Hegel makes clear the relationship between love and contradiction. He states, "Love is . . . the most immense contradiction; the understanding cannot solve it, because there is nothing more intractable than this punctiliousness of the self-consciousness which is negated and which I ought nevertheless to possess as an affirmative." G. W. F. Hegel, *Elements of the Philosophy of Right*, trans. H. B. Nisbet, ed. Allen W. Wood (Cambridge: Cambridge University Press, 1991), 199 (translation slightly modified). The German reads: "Die Liebe ist daher der ungeheuerste Widerspruch, denn der Verstand nicht lösen kann, indem es nichts Härteres gibt als diese Punktualität des Selbstbewußtseins, die negiert wird und die ich doch als affirmativ haben soll." G. W. F. Hegel, *Grundlinien der Philosophie des Rechts: Hegels Werke 7* (Frankfurt: Suhrkamp, 1986), 308. Even though at this point in his philosophy trajectory the concept plays the role that love once did, Hegel continues to identify love with the structure of contradiction.

5. See G. W. F. Hegel, *Lectures on Natural Right and Political Science: The First Philosophy of Right, Heidelberg 1817–1818*, trans. J. Michael Stewart and Peter C. Hodgson (Berkeley: University of California Press, 1995). G. W. F. Hegel, *Gesammelte Werke, Band 26,1: Vorlesungen über die Philosophie des Rechts* (Hamburg: Felix Meiner, 2013).

6. G. W. F. Hegel, *Science of Logic*, trans. George Di Giovanni (Cambridge: Cambridge University Press, 2010), 532. The German reads: "es ist es selbst und greift über sein Anderes über; aber nicht als ein *Gewaltsames*, sondern das vielmehr in demselben ruhig und *bei sich selbst* ist. Wie es die freie Macht genannt worden, so könnte es auch die *freie Leibe* und *schrankenlose Seligkeit* genannt werden." G. W. F. Hegel, *Wissenschaft der Logik II* (Frankfurt: Suhrkamp, 1986), 277.

7. Hegel, *Science of Logic*, 384. The German reads: "es für sich noch sozusagen kein Schaden, Mangel oder Fehler einer Sache ist, wenn an ihr ein Widerspruch aurgezeigt werden kann. Veilmehr jede Bestimmung, jedes Konkrete, jeder Begriff ist wesentlich eine Einheit unterschiedener und unterscheidbarer Momente, die durch den *bestimmten, wesentlichen Unterschied* in widersprechende übergehen." Hegel, *Wissenschaft der Logik II*, 79.

8. Hegel, *Science of Logic*, 178. The German reads: "Sie [die Arithmetik] enthält nicht nur den Begriff und damit die Aufgabe für das begreifende Denken nicht, sondern ist das Gegenteil desselben. Um der Gleichgültigkeit des Verknüpften gegen die Verknüpfung." G. W. F. Hegel, *Wissenschaft der Logik I* (Frankfurt: Suhrkamp, 1986), 244.

9. Alain Badiou seems to disprove the claim that the mathematician cannot be a great lover. He holds both that mathematics is ontology and that the love event has the ability to rupture our historical situation. But even Badiou does not place mathematics and love in the same realm. Unlike love, mathematical ontology has nothing to do with truth because there are no ontological events. Events occur only in the truth procedures—science, art, politics, and love.

10. G. W. F. Hegel, "The Positivity of the Christian Religion," in *Early Theological Writings*, trans. T. M. Knox (Philadelphia: University of Pennsylvania Press, 1975), 68. The German reads: "der Zweck und das Wesen aller wahren Religion und auch unserer Religion Moralität der Menschen sei." G. W. F. Hegel, "Die Positivität der christlichen Religion," in *Frühe Schriften: Hegels Werke 1* (Frankfurt: Suhrkamp, 1986), 105.

11. Hegel does not completely let Christ off the hook. Some of his acts—such as limiting his disciples to twelve and thereby consecrating an elite—plant the seeds for the centuries of positivity that would follow. Still, Christ's culpability pales in comparison with that of the church that he founds.

12. Hegel, "The Positivity of the Christian Religion," 138. The German reads: "bürgerliche und politische Freiheit hat die Kirche als Kot gegen die himmlischen Güter und den Genuß des Lebens verachten gelernt, und so wie die Entbehrung der Mittel, die physischen Bedürfnisse zu befriedigen, den tierischen Teil des Menschen des Leben berauben, so bringt auch die Beraubung des Genusses der Freiheit des Geistes der Vernunft den Tod, in welchem Zustand die Menschen den Verlust, [mangelden] Gebrauch derselben, Sehnsucht nach ihr so wenig fühlen werden, als der töte Korper sich nach Speise und Trank sehnt." Hegel, "Die Positivität der christlichen Religion," 182.

13. He writes, "What will stand in the way of your being understood and your considerations being accepted is, I imagine, that in general people simply will not want to give up their not-self. Morally speaking, they fear illumination." G. W. F. Hegel, Letter to Schelling, 30 August 1795, in Hegel: The Letters, trans. Clark Butler and Christiane Seiler (Bloomington: Indiana University Press, 1984), 41 (translation modified). The German reads: "Was Dir im Wege stehen wird, verstanden zu werden und Deinen Betrachtungen, Eingang zu finden, wird, stelle ich mir vor, überhaupt das sein, daß die Leute schlechterdings ihr Nicht-Ich nicht werden aufgeben wollen. In moralischer Rücksicht fürchten sie Beleuchtung." G. W. F. Hegel, Brief an Schelling, 30 August 1795, in Briefe von und an Hegel, vol. 1 (Hamburg: Felix Meiner, 1952), 29–30.

14. As Allen W. Wood puts it, "For the Frankfurt Hegel, Jesus's teaching is no longer a version of Kantian morality. Now it is an antinomian religion that goes beyond morality." Allen W. Wood, Hegel's Ethical Thought (Cambridge: Cambridge University Press, 1990), 129.

15. Only the fragment entitled "Love" has been translated and published in English. See G. W. F. Hegel, "Love," in Early Theological Writings, trans. T. M. Knox (Philadelphia: University of Pennsylvania Press, 1975), 302–8.

16. G. W. F. Hegel, "Liebe und Religion," in Frühe Schriften, 244. The German reads: "Die Religion ist eins mit der Liebe."

17. G. W. F. Hegel, "Religion, eine Religion stiften," in Frühe Schriften, 243. The German reads: "Leibe kann nur stattfinden gegen das Gleiche, gegen den Spiegel, gegen das Echo unseres Wesens." The title—the only title of these short texts provided by Hegel himself and not by editors—suggests that Christianity has the effect of a rupture. Stiften indicates the founding of a new religion.

18. G. W. F. Hegel, Letter to Nanette Endel, 9 February 1797, in Hegel: The Letters, trans. Clark Butler and Christiane Seiler (Bloomington: Indiana University Press, 1984), 57. The German reads: "so habe ich mich nach reiflicher Ueberlegung entschlossen, an diesen Menschen nichts bessern zu wollen, im Gegenteil mit den Wölfen zu heulen." G. W. F. Hegel, Brief an Nanette Endel, 9 Februar 1797, Briefe von und an Hegel, vol. 1 (Hamburg: Felix Meiner, 1952), 49.

19. The wild materialist interpretation of Endel's role would turn things around and see Hegel's philosophical turn to the religion of love as the fruit of his lovemaking with her.

20. G. W. F. Hegel, "The Spirit of Christianity and Its Fate," in *Early Theological Writings*, trans. T. M. Knox (Philadelphia: University of Pennsylvania Press, 1975), 292. The German reads: "in dem Auferstandenen und dann gen Himmel Erhobenen fand das Bild wieder Leben und die Liebe die Darstellung ihrer Einigkeit; in dieser Wiedervermählung des Geistes und des Körpers ist der Gegensatz des Lebendigen und des Toten verschwunden und hat sich in einem Gotte vereinigt; das Sehnen der Liebe hat sich selbst genießen." G. W. F. Hegel, "Der Geist des Christentums und sein Schicksal," in *Frühe Schriften*, 408.

21. Terry Pinkard, *Hegel: A Biography* (Cambridge: Cambridge University Press, 2000), 684.

22. Hegel, "The Positivity of the Christian Religion," 69–70. The German reads: "er rief die moralischen Prinzipien, die in der heiligen Büchern seines Volkes lagen." Hegel, "Die Positivität der christlichen Religion," 106.

23. Yirmiyahu Yovel, *Dark Riddle: Hegel, Nietzsche, and the Jews* (University Park: Penn State University Press, 1998), 99.

24. Hegel, "The Spirit of Christianity and Its Fate," 241. The German reads: "Versöhnung in der Liebe ist statt der jüdischen Rückkehr unter Gehorsam eine Befreiung." Hegel, "Der Geist des Christentums und sein Schicksal," 357.

25. Kant writes, "the moral law is given, as it were, as a fact of pure reason of which we are a priori conscious and which is apodictically certain, though it be granted that no example of exact observance of it can be found in experience." Immanuel Kant, *Critique of Practical Reason*, in *Practical Philosophy*, trans. and ed. Mary J. Gregor (New York: Cambridge University Press, 1996), 177.

26. Though Kant formulates the categorical imperative in the *Groundwork of the Metaphysics of Morals* in 1785, it is not until writing the *Critique of Practical Reason* in 1788 that Kant grasps that the moral law itself entails our freedom. The Kantian revolution occurs between the writing of these two works.

27. As Kant puts it in the aptly titled brief essay "On a Supposedly Right to Lie from Philanthropy," "Truthfulness in statements that one cannot avoid is a human being's duty to everyone, however great the disadvantage to him or to another that may result from it." Immanuel Kant, "On a Supposedly Right to Lie from Philanthropy," in *Practical Philosophy*, ed. and trans. Mary J. Gregor (New York: Cambridge University Press, 1996), 612.

28. Hegel, "The Spirit of Christianity and Its Fate," 247. The German reads: "Erst durch die Liebe ist die Macht des Objektiven gebrochen, denn durch sie wird dessen ganzes Gebiet gestürzt; die Tugenden setzen durch ihre Grenze außerhalb derselben immer noch ein Objektives, und die Vielheit der Tugenden eine um so größere unüberwindliche Mannigfaltigkeit des Objektiven; nur die Liebe hat keine Grenze." Hegel, "Der Geist des Christentums und sein Schicksal," 363.

29. *Casablanca*, like almost every commercial romantic film, attempts to obscure the contradiction of love in its conclusion. After Rick sends Ilsa away with Victor, we see him along with Louis (Claude Rains), the French prefect of police who has assisted him, walking together into the fog to join the French Resistance. This final coupling diminishes the impact of love's disruptiveness on the spectator, though this disruptiveness nonetheless remains visible through Rick's displacement. Rather than using the guise of friendship to hide a homoerotic bond, the film uses the homoerotic ending to deflect the trauma of the love relation between Rick and Ilsa.

30. In the language of Hegel's mature philosophy, love enables the subject to recognize as for-itself what it already was in-itself.
31. In *The Metaphysics of Morals*, Kant argues that one cannot command love, and thus he translates the Christian injunction into the command to do good to one's neighbor, an act that will produce love. See Immanuel Kant, *The Metaphysics of Morals*, in *Practical Philosophy*, ed. and trans. Mary J. Gregor (New York: Cambridge University Press, 1996), 530–31.
32. Hegel, "The Spirit of Christianity and Its Fate," 247. The German reads: "liebe deinen Nächste als dich selbst heißt nicht, ihn so sehr lieben als sich selbst; denn sich selbst leiben ist ein Wort ohne Sinn." Hegel, "Der Geist des Christentums und sein Schicksal," 363.
33. Alice Ormiston argues that "the philosophical system, while it does provide a higher form of knowing than Hegel had earlier conceived as possible, does not thereby seek to replace the knowledge of love. Rather, the deep antagonism between love and reason with which Hegel tries to come to grips in this early essay points towards his mature system as an attempt to protect and preserve love against the divisive and eclipsing effects of a narrower, abstract rationality." Alice Ormiston, "'The Spirit of Christianity and Its Fate': Towards a Reconsideration of the Role of Love in Hegel," *Canadian Journal of Political Science* 35, no. 3 (2002): 503–4. Though Ormiston sees the early Hegel's investment in love, she misses the extent to which this investment enables him eventually to see the concept differently and to view love as a model for it. Far from Hegel positing an antagonism between love and reason, he comes to see them as functioning in precisely the same way.

6. HOW TO AVOID EXPERIENCE

1. Kant makes this argument in the Transcendental Aesthetic of the *Critique of Pure Reason*. He divides space and time into the forms of outer sense and inner sense, though they work together to constitute our representations. See Immanuel Kant, *Critique of Pure Reason*, trans. Paul Guyer and Allen W. Wood (Cambridge: Cambridge University Press, 1998), 155–92.
2. Louis Althusser, the most celebrated theorist of ideology, also argues that we can never get rid of ideology, though he conceives ideology in radically different terms and in a basically anti-Hegelian way.
3. Brian Greene, *The Fabric of the Cosmos: Space, Time, and the Texture of Reality* (New York: Random House, 2004), 5.
4. G. W. F. Hegel, *Science of Logic*, trans. George Di Giovanni (Cambridge: Cambridge University Press, 2010), 745 (translation modified). The German reads: "in Raum und Zeit herabfallen, worin das Widersprechende im Neben- und Nacheinander *außeneinander* gehalten wird." G. W. F. Hegel, *Wissenschaft der Logik II* (Frankfurt: Suhrkamp, 1970), 563.
5. See David Hume, *A Treatise of Human Nature* (New York: Oxford University Press, 2000).
6. Hegel's insistence on the material base of all thinking leads him to proclaim again and again the impossibility of a philosophy transcending its own epoch.

7. Hegel, *Science of Logic*, 519 (translation modified). The German reads: "der Begriff *aus ihrer Dialektik* und *Nichtigkeit* als ihr *Grund* hervorgeht, nicht aber, daß er durch ihre *Realität* bedingt wäre. Das abstrahierende Denken ist daher nicht als bloßes auf-die-Seite-Stellen des sinnliche Stoffes zu betrachten, welcher dadurch in seiner Realität keine Eintrag leide, sondern es ist veilmehr das Aufheben und die Reduktion als bloßer *Erschiennung* auf das *Wesentliche*, welches nur im *Begriff* sich manifestiert." Hegel, *Wissenschaft der Logik II*, 259.

8. Tom Rockmore contends that Hegel didn't concern himself with experience because "he thought that it is more important to devote oneself to theory than to more practical pursuits since in the long run ideas tend to realize themselves." Tom Rockmore, *Before and After Hegel: A Historical Introduction to Hegel's Thought* (Berkeley: University of California Press, 1993), 43. The problem with this claim is Hegel's steadfast conviction that our deeds reveal who we are, not our ideas. He turns his philosophy away from experience because it misleads us, not because it always realizes the ideas that inform it.

9. Simon Lumsden focuses not on the role of contradiction in Hegel's version of experience but on the change that the object undergoes. He writes, "Experience is for Hegel the process in which our knowledge of an object is transformed." Simon Lumsden, "Satisfying the Demand of Reason: Hegel's Conceptualization of Experience," *Topoi* 22 (2003): 46. While this is undoubtedly correct as far as it goes, it doesn't capture the full extent of Hegel's revision of what constitutes experience. Experience isn't just the transformation of the object but the act of undergoing contradiction.

10. G. W. F. Hegel, *Phenomenology of Spirit*, trans. A. V. Miller (Oxford: Oxford University Press, 1977), 57 (translated modified). The German reads: "An dieser Darstellung des Verlaufs der Erfahrung ist ein Moment, wodurch sie mit demjenigen nicht übereinzustimmen scheint, was unter der Erfahrung verstanden zu werden pflegt. Der Übergang nämlich vom ersten Gegenstande und dem Wissen desselben zu dem anderen Gegenstande, *an dem* man sagt, daß die Erfahrung gemacht worden sei, wurde so angegeben, daß das Wissen wom ersten Gegenstande, oder das *Für*-das-Bewußtsein des ersten Ansich, der zweite Gegenstand selbst werden soll." G. W. F. Hegel, *Phänomenologie des Geistes* (Frankfurt: Surhkamp, 1986), 79.

11. Despite his suspicions about Hegel's interpretation of experience through the absolute, Martin Heidegger provides an instructive account of what experience is for Hegel. He writes, "Every experience is, essentially understood, a dis-illusionment. It lets what was hitherto held fast come out as that which is untenable. The so-called good experience that we undergo with something is a dis-illusionment as well." Martin Heidegger, "Elucidation of the 'Introduction' to Hegel's *Phenomenology of Spirit*," in *Hegel*, trans. Joseph Arel and Niels Feuerhahn (Bloomington: Indiana University Press, 2015), 102.

12. In his commentary on the *Phenomenology of Spirit*, Jean Hyppolite provides a pithy account of the contradiction that undoes perception. He states, "If these matters interpenetrate, their independence disappears, and there remains only one unique thing without determinations; if they are juxtaposed, their independence is saved, but the unique thing is lost and we return to objective essence, a dust cloud made up of parts that are not the parts of anything and that are themselves infinitely divisible

into parts." Jean Hyppolite, *Genesis and Structure of Hegel's Phenomenology of Spirit*, trans. Samuel Cherniak and John Heckman (Evanston: Northwestern University Press, 1974), 112. Every solution that the subject of perception attempts leads back to contradiction. Thus, the *Phenomenology* must abandon perception for the sake of understanding, which avoids these contradictions (while giving birth to new and more obstinate ones).

13. Hegel has a unique position within Deleuze's philosophy. He is the one philosopher whom Deleuze discusses but sees only in antagonistic terms. Even Freud, who receives a hostile critique in *Anti-Oedipus*, plays a positive role in Deleuze's formulation of repetition in *Difference and Repetition*. Hegel is the only one who is always an enemy because his critique of difference leaves no room for compromise.

14. Deleuze's apotheosis of the power of sensation becomes clearest in his book on Francis Bacon. There, he writes, "It is the nature of sensation to envelope a constitutive difference of level, a plurality of constituting domains." Gilles Deleuze, *Francis Bacon: The Logic of Sensation*, trans. Daniel W. Smith (Minneapolis: University of Minnesota Press, 2004), 33. It is as if conceptual thinking must aspire to the difference that sensation enjoys, which is why Deleuze sees the task of philosophy not as one of discovering the concepts that we are already employing (which would be Hegel's position) but as one of producing concepts (which Hegel would dismiss as an utterly fantasmatic project).

15. Deleuze never addresses the fact that identity for Hegel is nothing but the failure of identity to fully constitute itself. An entity becomes what it is through its failure to be what it is, not through its success. If one must label Hegel a philosopher of identity, one must grapple with this conception of identity that directly defies the law of identity. The rejection of the law of identity runs throughout Hegel's philosophy.

16. Gilles Deleuze, *Difference and Repetition*, trans. Paul Patton (New York: Columbia University Press, 1994), 51.

17. Deleuze himself doesn't avow his reliance on induction. The priority of difference remains, to his mind, a self-evident truth, not the result of an inductive proof.

18. Alain Badiou points out the tension between the univocity of being and the insistence on pure difference that runs throughout Deleuze's thought. For Badiou, Deleuze is a philosopher of the one before he is a philosopher of difference. See Alain Badiou, *Deleuze: The Clamor of Being*, trans. Louise Burchill (Minneapolis: University of Minnesota Press, 2000).

19. One might claim that the rise of pragmatism illustrates the turn from the concept to experience even more than that of phenomenology. Though there are clear connections between pragmatism and phenomenology, the latter's focus on how objects come into being for the subject indicates a more thoroughgoing commitment to the priority of experience. For the phenomenologist, pragmatism remains too oriented around the concept in its acceptance of objects as given to consciousness.

20. Martin Heidegger lays out clearly the opposition between his version of phenomenology and Hegel's philosophy. He states, "For *Hegel*, being (infinity) is also the essence of time. For *us*, time if the original essence of being." Martin Heidegger, *Hegel's Phenomenology of Spirit*, trans. Parvis Emad and Kenneth Maly (Bloomington: Indiana University Press, 1988), 146. According to Heidegger, Hegel's fundamental error concerns the obfuscation of our originary temporality.

21. Edmund Husserl, *Logical Investigations*, vol. 2, trans. J. N. Findlay (New York: Routledge, 2002), 343.

22. As Husserl puts it in *Ideas*, "we take our start from what lies *prior to* all standpoints: from the total realm of whatever is itself given intuitionally and prior to all theorizing, from everything that one can immediately see and seize upon." Edmund Husserl, *Ideas Pertaining to a Pure Phenomenology and to Phenomenological Philosophy, First Book*, trans. F. Kersten (Dordrecht: Kluwer, 1998), 38–39.

23. Edmund Husserl, *Cartesian Meditations: An Introduction to Phenomenology*, trans. Dorion Cairns (Boston: Kluwer, 1991), 151.

24. It is not surprising that the project of phenomenology gives birth to the deconstruction of Jacques Derrida. Even though Derrida extends the project of deconstruction to the rest of Western philosophy, it begins with Derrida pointing out Husserl's inability to theorize a pure original experience. In his early works, Derrida correctly sees that the phenomenological ideal of pure experience does not exist.

25. Hegel's position on the necessary role that the concept plays in experience explains the link to Wilfrid Sellars that informs the approach of the Pittsburgh school of Hegelianism. Sellars famously attacks the myth of the given—the notion that our concepts derive from our experience of objects immediately present to us.

26. Hegel, *Science of Logic*, 715. The German reads: "allenthalben muß das Abstrakte den Anfang und das Element ausmachen, in welchem und von welchem aus sich die Besonderheiten und die reichen Gestalten des Konkreten ausbreiten." Hegel, *Wissenschaft der Logik II*, 522–23.

27. This is the point that Sally Sedgwick makes in *Hegel's Critique of Kant*. According to Sedgwick, Hegel demonstrates that the Kantian categories lack the purity from sensible intuition Kant assumes they have. Both the categories and the intuition are involved in each other through a reciprocal determination. See Sally Sedgwick, *Hegel's Critique of Kant: From Dichotomy to Identity* (Oxford: Oxford University Press, 2012).

7. LEARNING TO LOVE THE END OF HISTORY

1. Benedetto Croce, *What Is Living and What Is Dead in the Philosophy of Hegel*, trans. Douglas Ainslie (London: Macmillan, 1915), 140.

2. G. W. F. Hegel, *Lectures on the Philosophy of World History*, vol. 1: *Manuscripts of the Introduction and Lectures of 1822–3*, ed. and trans. Robert F. Brown and Peter C. Hodgson (Oxford: Clarendon, 2011), 150. The German reads: "der Mensch als Geist nicht ein Unmittelbares ist, sondern wesentlich ein in sich Zurückgekehrtes. Diese Bewegung der Vermittlung ist so das wesentliche Moment der geistigen Natur; dadurch wird der Mensch selbstständig und frei." G. W. F. Hegel, *Vorlesungen über die Philosophie der Weltgeschichte: Berlin 1822/1823, Nachschiften von Karl Gustav Julius von Griesheim, Heinrich Gustav Hotho und Friedrich Carl Hermann Victor von Kehler*, ed. Karl Heinz Ilting, Karl Brehmer, and Hoo Nam Seelmann (Hambug: Felix Meiner, 1996), 30.

3. In "Hegel's Logic of Freedom," William Maker argues the converse. He claims that the structure of the *Science of Logic* depends on the idea of freedom as its initial

precondition. According to Maker, "Freedom is the form and content of logic. It is not difficult to see why logic as philosophical science must begin in and as pure freedom, in the self-determination of self-determination, if it is going to be absolutely unconditioned. Independently of a modern practical interest in worldly freedom, Hegel shows that philosophy itself requires freedom as its innermost *theoretical* core." William Maker, "Hegel's Logic of Freedom," in *Hegel's Theory of the Subject*, ed. David Grary Carlson (New York: Palgrave, 2005), 6. While I agree completely with Maker's alignment of logic with freedom, his position requires him to insert a presupposition into Hegel's logic, a logic structured on the avoidance of any presupposition.

4. G. W. F. Hegel, *Science of Logic*, trans. George Di Giovanni (Cambridge: Cambridge University Press, 2010), 745. The German reads: "Es macht sich darüber den bestimmten Grundsatz, daß der Widerspruch nicht denkbar ist; in der Tat aber ist das Denken des Widerspruchs das wesentliche Moment des Begriffes." G. W. F. Hegel, *Wissenschaft der Logik II* (Frankfurt: Suhrkamp, 1986), 563.

5. G. W. F. Hegel, *Vorlesungen über die Geschichte der Philosphie III* (Frankfurt: Suhrkamp, 1986), 367. The German reads: "Aber für den Willen ist kein anderer Zweck als der aus ihm selbst geschöpfte, der Zweck seiner Freiheit. Es ist ein großer Fortschritt, daß dies Prinzip aufgestellt ist, daß die Freiheit die letzte Angel ist auf der der Mensch sich dreht, diese letzte Spitze, die sich durch nichts imponieren läßt, so daß der Mensch nichts, keine Autorität gelten läßt, insofern es gegen seine Freiheit ist." E. S. Haldane and Frances H. Simson translate the passage as follows: "For the will, however, there is no other aim than that derived from itself, the aim of its freedom. It is a great advance when the principle is established that freedom is the last hinge on which man turns, a highest possible pinnacle, which allows nothing further to be imposed on it; thus man bows to no authority, and acknowledges no obligations, where his freedom is not respected." G. W. F. Hegel, *Lectures on the History of Philosophy 3: Medieval and Modern Philosophy*, trans. E. S. Haldane and Frances H. Simson (Lincoln: University of Nebraska Press, 1995), 459. The only major difference between this translation and Hegel's text is the word *imposed*, which the translators use to make sense of the unusual term *imponieren*. Hegel's point toward the end of this passage is not that the subject that recognizes its freedom refuses to allow anything to be imposed on it (though this is undoubtedly the case) but that it is not *impressed* by anything, which is the significance of *imponieren* in this context.

6. Hegel's commitment to this position and to the revolutionary nature of modernity led him to champion every revolution he encounters. As Domenico Losurdo notes, "every revolution in human history was supported and celebrated by Hegel, despite his reputation as an incorrigible defender of the established order." Domenico Losurdo, *Hegel and the Freedom of Moderns*, trans. Marella Morris and Jon Morris (Durham: Duke University Press, 2004), 99.

7. The idea that free subjects give duties to themselves rather than receiving them from an Other is, of course, the primary contribution of Kant's moral philosophy. Kant's discovery of his moral philosophy marks, for Hegel, the end of history. All that is left for us to do after Kant's moral revolution is to recognize that Kant has made the decisive step in the history of freedom.

8. Many observers have described Hegel as the inventor of history in philosophy. For instance, Joseph McCarney claims, "For he is, beyond all comparison, the histori-

cal philosopher, the one for whom history figures most ambitiously and elaborately as a philosophical category." Joseph McCarney, *Hegel on History* (London: Routledge, 2000), 7.

9. In this sense, Hegel's theorization of the end of history represents a direct riposte to Spinoza, who insists on our ability to abstract ourselves from a historical perspective and take up the perspective of eternity.

10. Slavoj Žižek, *Less Than Nothing: Hegel and the Shadow of Dialectical Materialism* (New York: Verso, 2012), 218.

11. See Francis Fukuyama, "The End of History?," *National Interest* 16 (1989): 3–18. Fukuyama subsequently developed this thesis in a book-length work entitled *The End of History and the Last Man* (New York: Free Press, 1991). More recently, Fukuyama has qualified his claims, though he has not retracted them.

12. Others attempt to cut out the dead idea of the end of history from the rest of the Hegelian corpus. This is the position of Steven B. Smith, who, in an otherwise sympathetic interpretation of Hegel's political philosophy, argues, "Hegel's thesis about an end of history could not but become another stifling orthodoxy that would generate its own antithesis, namely, an end to the end of history." Stephen B. Smith, *Hegel's Critique of Liberalism: Rights in Context* (Chicago: University of Chicago Press, 1989), 230–31. Though Smith articulates several justifications for Hegel's claim about history coming to an end, he ultimately believes that one must reject it in order to stay true to the core of Hegel's philosophy.

13. Jean Hyppolite published the first translation of the *Phenomenologie des Geistes* in 1941 as *Phénoménologie de l'esprit*, two years after the end of Kojève's lectures.

14. Kojève translates Hegel's *Herr* and *Knecht* into *maître* and *esclave* in French, which would be *master* and *slave* in English. Most translators and interpreters of Hegel avoid the term *slave* as misleading, though some retain *master*. The two translators who rendered the *Phenomenology* into English in the twentieth century, J. B. Baillie and A. V. Miller, opt for *bondsman* rather than *slave,* for instance.

15. The problem with Kojève's account should become evident with the invocation of a prehistorical state of nature. For Hegel, we have absolutely no insight into the state of humanity prior to history because the emergence of spirit so dramatically distorts what precedes it. When we look at the state of nature, we see only the fantasy of the state of spirit.

16. Alexandre Kojève, *Introduction à la lecture de Hegel*, ed. Raymond Queneau (Paris: Gallimard, 1947), 25. The French reads: "Le Maître a lutté et risqué sa vie pour la reconnaissance, mais il n'a obtenu qu'une reconnaissance sans valeur pour lui. Car il ne peut être satisfait que par la reconnaissance de la part de celui qu'il reconnaît être digne de le reconnaître. L'attitude de Maître est donc une impasse existentielle."

17. There are commentators on Hegel who take up and develop Kojève's reading of Hegel. See, for instance, Reinhart Klemens Maurer, *Hegel und das Ende der Geschichte: Interpretationen zur "Phänomenologie des Geistes* (Stuttgart: Kohlhammer, 1965); and Barry Cooper, *The End of History: An Essay on Modern Hegelianism* (Toronto: University of Toronto Press, 1984).

18. Kojève did not simply take over Koyré's thesis about the end of history in Hegel's philosophy. He also took over the course on Hegel that Koyré was giving when Koyré sought a replacement.

19. Philip Grier, "The End of History and the Return of History," in *The Hegel Myths and Legends*, ed. Jon Stewart (Evanston: Northwestern University Press, 1996), 186. Grier makes clear the fundamental break between Kojève's philosophy and Hegel's, even though Kojève poses his philosophy as merely a commentary. Grier writes, "No serious reader of Hegel could fail to recognize that Kojève is as much creator as interpreter of the system he ascribes to Hegel." Grier, 185.

20. Hegel, *Lectures on the Philosophy of World History*, 168. The German reads: "Geist . . . ist bei keinem anderen mehr, sondern bei sich, bein seinem Wesen, nicht bei einem Zufälligen, sondern in absoluter Freiheit. Dies also wäre der Endzweck der Weltgeschichte." Hegel, *Vorlesungen über die Philosophie der Weltgeschichte*, 59.

21. Toward the end of the introduction to the *Philosophy of History*, Hegel says, "World history goes from east to west; because Europe is the end of world history as such, Asia is the beginning." G. W. F. Hegel, *Philosophy of History*, trans. J. Sibree (New York: Dover, 1956), 103 (translation modified). The German reads: "Die Weltgeschichte geht von Osten nach Western, denn Europa ist schlechthin das Ende der Weltgeschichte, Asien der Anfang." G. W. F. Hegel, *Vorlesungen über die Philosophie der Geschichte* (Frankfurt: Suhrkamp, 1986), 134.

22. Despite Constantine's conversion to Christianity in 312 CE, he did not name Christianity the state religion of the Roman Empire but did end the persecution of Christians.

23. As Emil Fackenheim puts it, "Modern Christian faith has moved from external, Catholic authorities into an inward Protestant heart. Modern states have smashed slavery and feudalism and recognized the rights and duties of men as men, i.e., belonging to them simply because they are human." Emil L. Fackenheim, *The Religious Dimension in Hegel's Thought* (Bloomington: Indiana University Press, 1967), 37. For Hegel, Christianity had to undergo this transition in order for it to provide an articulation of free subjectivity.

24. If we compare the iconography of Protestantism with that of Catholicism, it would seem that Hegel makes the wrong choice for the form of Christianity that embraces divine humiliation. Catholicism's crucifix gives us a vision of a devastated God suffering on the cross, while the empty Protestant cross appears to spare us from this confrontation. For Hegel, however, the absence is crucial for the freedom of the subject. As long as God remains on the cross in a particular form, we do not yet have the moment of the Holy Spirit, the moment when individual subjects can come together through God's absence.

25. Hegel, *Lectures of the Philosophy of World History*, 449. The German reads: "Hat der Mensch die Wahrheit der christlichen Religion nicht, hat er gar keine Wahrheit; denn dies ist die alleinige Wahrheit." Hegel, *Vorlesungen über die Philosophie der Weltgeschichte*, 421.

26. Hegel, *Lectures of the Philosophy of World History*, 449. The German reads: "Daran war zu erinnern, damit man nicht an ein gemeintes Christentum, wie jeder es sich macht, zu denken habe." Hegel, *Vorlesungen über die Philosophie der Weltgeschichte*, 422.

27. Karl Popper, *The Open Society and Its Enemies*, vol. 2: *The High Tide of Prophecy: Hegel, Marx, and the Aftermath* (Princeton: Princeton University Press, 1966), 27.

28. For discussions of the similarity of the cunning of reason to Adam Smith's invisible hand, see John B. Davis, "Smith's Invisible Hand and Hegel's Cunning of Rea-

son," *International Journal of Social Economics* 16, no. 6 (1989): 50–66; and Edna Ullmann-Margalit, "The Invisible Hand and the Cunning of Reason," *Social Research* 64, no. 2 (1997): 181–98. The problem with these comparisons is that they follow from a traditional reading of the cunning of reason derived entirely from the *Philosophy of History* and failing to take into account the more developed elaboration of the idea in the *Science of Logic*. Once one does this, the similarity with Smith lessens considerably.

29. Jacques Lacan critiques the cunning of reason as a denial of the unconscious. He writes, "The 'cunning of reason' means that, from the outset and right to the end, the subject knows what he wants." Jacques Lacan, "The Subversion of the Subject and the Dialectic of Desire in the Freudian Unconscious," in *Écrits: The First Complete Edition in English*, trans. Bruce Fink (New York: Norton, 2006), 679. Despite his theoretical debt to Hegel, Lacan's direct references to Hegel tend to miss the mark, as is evident here, due to his reliance on Kojève, who introduced him to Hegel's work.

30. Hegel, *Philosophy of History*, 33 (translation modified). The German reads: "die *List der Vernunft* . . . sie die Leidenschaften für sich wirken läßt . . . die Individuen werden aufgeopfert und preisgeben. Die Idee bezahlt den Tribut des Daseins und der Vergänglichkeit nicht aus sich, sondern aus der Leidenschaften der Individuen." Hegel, *Vorlesungen über die Philosophie der Geschichte*, 49.

31. Hegel, *Science of Logic*, 663. The German reads: "Dass der Zweck sich aber in die *mittelbare* Beziehung mit dem Objekt setzt und *zwischen* sich und dasseble ein anderes Objekt *einschiebt*, kann als die *List* der Venunft angesehen werden." Hegel, *Wissenschaft der Logik II*, 452.

32. Hegel, *Science of Logic*, 663. The German reads: "Insofern ist das *Mittel* ein *Höheres* als die *endlichen* Zwecke der *äußeren* Zweckmäßigkeit; — der *Pflug* ist ehrenvoller, als unmittelbar die Genüsse sind, welche durch ihn bereitet werden und die Zwecke sind." Hegel, *Wissenschaft der Logik II*, 453.

33. Richard Dawkins, *The Selfish Gene*, rev. ed. (Oxford: Oxford University Press, 2006), 62.

8. RESISTING RESISTANCE

1. G. W. F. Hegel, *Phenomenology of Spirit*, trans. Terry Pinkard (Cambridge: Cambridge University Press, 2018), 115 (translation modified). The German reads: "Dieses Bewußtsein . . . hat die Furcht des Todes, des absoluten Herrn, empfunden. Es ist darin innerlich aufgelöst worden, hat durchaus in sich selbt erzittert, und alles Fixe hat in ihm gebebt. Diese reine allgemeine Bewegung, das absolute Flüssigwerden alles Bestehens, ist aber das einfache Wesen des Selbstbewußtseins, die absolute Negativität, *das reine Fürsichsein*, das hiermit *an* diesem Bewußtsein ist." G. W. F. Hegel, *Phänomenologie des Geistes* (Frankfurt: Suhrkamp, 1986), 153.

2. G. W. F. Hegel, *Science of Logic*, trans. George Di Giovanni (Cambridge: Cambridge University Press, 2010), 674. The German reads: "die Idee hat um der Freiheit willen, die der Begriff in ihr erreicht, auch den *härtesten Gegensatz* in sich; ihre Ruhe besteht in der Sicherheit und Gewißheit, womit sie ihn ewig erzeugt und ewig überwindet und in ihm mit sich selbst zusammengeht." G. W. F. Hegel, *Wissenschaft der Logik II* (Frankfurt: Suhrkamp, 1986), 549.

3. In *Opus Dei*, Giorgio Agamben wrongly identifies the Kantian moral law with external constraint rather than with freedom because he sees morality as the result of an internalization of the external law. Agamben posits external constraint instead of self-constraint because he takes the *Metaphysics of Morals* rather than the earlier *Critique of Practical Reason* as his starting point for understanding the relationship between the moral law and external constraint. In the Second *Critique*, Kant makes it clear that the moral law has priority and cannot derive from any externality at all. See Giorgio Agamben, *Opus Dei: An Archaeology of Duty*, trans. Adam Kotsko (Stanford: Stanford University Press, 2013), 114.

4. G. W. F. Hegel, *Lectures on the History of Philosophy, 1825–1826*, vol. 3: *Medieval and Modern Philosophy*, ed. Robert F. Brown, trans. Robert F. Brown and J. M. Stewart (Oxford: Clarendon, 2006), 190–91 (translation modified). The German reads: "für den Willen ist kein anderer Zweck als der aus ihm selbst geschöpfte, der Zweck seiner Freiheit. Es ist dies ein großer Fortschritt, daß dies Prinzip aufgestellt ist, daß die Freiheit des Menschen die letzte Angel ist, auf der der Mensch sich dreht, die letzte, absolut feste Spitze ist, welche auf sich nicht einwirken läßt, so daß der Mensch nichts, keine Autorität, welche Form es sei, gelten läßt, wenn sie gegen seine Freiheit geht." G. W. F. Hegel, *Vorlesungen über die Geschichte der Philosophie*, Teil 4: *Philosophie des Mittelalters und der neueren Zeit*, ed. Pierre Garniron and Walter Jaeschke (Hamburg: Felix Meiner, 1986), 168.

5. G. W. F. Hegel, *Lectures on Natural Right and Political Science: The First Philosophy of Right, Heidelberg 1817–1818 with Additions from the Lectures of 1818–1819*, trans. J. Michael Stewart and Peter C. Hodgson (Berkeley: University of California Press, 1995), 127. The German reads: "so kommen sie in die Sphäre der Beschränktheit, sie sehen dies voraus, fürchten deßwegen jede Berührung, bleiben in sich zurückgekehrt, verehren ihre innere Unendlichkeit." G. W. F. Hegel, *Gesammelte Werke*, Band 26,1: *Vorlesungen über die Philosophie des Rechts* (Hamburg: Felix Meiner, 2013), 71.

6. In the case of Spinoza, it is not a question of aligning his desire with the substantial Other because, for him, there is nothing but this one substance. Spinoza himself becomes swallowed up in the substance of God, which is why his philosophy can leave no place for the subject and must conceive of freedom merely as the reconciliation with necessity.

7. Hegel, *Lectures on the Philosophy of World History* (translation modified), 1:353. The German reads: "Der unfreie Geist weiß das Wahre nur als ein Jenseits; der freie Geist ist für sich Geist, nicht bei einem anderen." G. W. F. Hegel, *Vorlesungen über die Philosophie der Weltgeschichte: Berlin 1822/1823, Nachschriften von Karl Gustav Julius von Griesheim, Heinrich Gustav Hotho und Friedrich Carl Hermann Victor von Kehler*, eds. Karl Heinz Ilting, Karl Brehmer, and Hoo Nam Seelmann (Hambug: Felix Meiner, 1996), 291.

8. The classic cinematic instance of the parent's humiliation in front of the child occurs in Vittorio De Sica's *Bicycle Thieves* (1948). After helping his father Antonio (Lamberto Maggiorani) search for his stolen bicycle, Bruno (Enzo Staiola) watches him attempt to steal someone else's and then endure the public humiliation of being caught. This moment represents freedom for Bruno as a subject, but not simply because he no longer has any attachment to his father as an authority. Despite his tears, Bruno's look up at his father shows that his father remains an authority even

at the moment of his desubantialization. In one of the concluding shots of the film, De Sica focuses on Bruno grasping his father's hand, indicating his identification with his father at this moment. This is the positive manifestation of freedom, as Hegel conceives it. Just as the speed limit sign continues to exist in the external world when the subject recognizes this sign as its own limit, so does the father. What changes is that Bruno now sees his own role in the father's authority. I am indebted to Richard Boothby at Loyola University Maryland for this point.

9. To be fair, the situations of Hegel and Heidegger before they received the call to Berlin were not identical. Hegel had just spent ten years unable to find an academic post, while Heidegger had a nice academic position at the University of Freiburg. The call to Berlin likely meant more to Hegel than it did to Heidegger.

10. Martin Heidegger, "Why Do I Stay in the Provinces?," trans. Thomas Sheehan, in *Heidegger: The Man and the Thinker*, ed. Thomas Sheehan (Piscataway, NJ: Transaction, 2009), 27–30.

11. When I visited Todtnauberg in 1998, the infamy of Heidegger's Nazism had almost resulted in its erasure as a tourist attraction. I went expecting great fanfare and even Heidegger memorabilia, but I had to traverse long fields, interact with wandering cows, and finally find myself only able to look in the window of an unmarked hut. That said, the uneventfulness of the hut made seeing it all the more epochal for me.

12. Martin Heidegger, *Introduction to Metaphysics*, trans. Gregory Fried and Richard Polt (New Haven: Yale University Press, 2000), 40.

13. Karl Marx, *Capital: A Critique of Political Economy*, trans. David Fernbach (New York: Penguin, 1981), 3:959.

14. One might speculate that without Hegel's friend-become-enemy Schelling as his teacher, Kierkegaard would have built upon the philosophical edifice that Hegel created rather than struggling against its caricature. Schelling's tendentious and ultimately preposterous version of Hegel's thought rendered this impossible.

15. If he had had the chance to read Kierkegaard, Hegel would have seen him as a thinker whose vision of God remains at times pre-Christian. Kierkegaard is often stuck in the Jewish universe with a God that has not fully manifested itself.

16. See Søren Kierkegaard, *Concluding Unscientific Postscript to Philosophical Fragments*, vol. 1, trans. Howard V. Hong and Edna H. Hong (Princeton: Princeton University Press, 1992).

17. Søren Kierkegaard, *The Concept of Anxiety: A Simple Psychologically Orienting Deliberation of the Dogmatic Issue of Hereditary Sin*, trans. Reidar Thomte (Princeton: Princeton University Press, 1980), 155.

18. Albert Camus, *The Rebel: An Essay on Man in Revolt*, trans. Anthony Bower (New York: Vintage, 1991), 136–37.

9. ABSOLUTE OR BUST

1. Though Theodor Adorno acknowledges a profound debt to Hegel, he nonetheless provides a representative critique of Hegel's invocation of the whole. Adorno writes, "By specifying, in opposition to Hegel, the negativity of the whole, philosophy satisfies, for the last time, the postulate of determinate negation, which is a positing. The ray of light that reveals the whole to be untrue in all its moments is none other

than utopia, the utopia of the whole truth, which is still to be realized." Theodor W. Adorno, *Hegel: Three Studies*, trans. Shierry Weber Nicholsen (Cambridge: MIT Press, 1993), 87–88. We know after Auschwitz, Adorno argues, where the insistence on totality leads and thus must offer a corrective for Hegel's gravest error if we are to sustain his philosophical importance.

2. The particular for Kierkegaard is the existing subject, which is what the system necessarily misses. In *Concluding Unscientific Postscript*, he writes, "In a logical system, nothing may be incorporated that has a relation to existence, that is not indifferent to existence." Søren Kierkeggard, *Concluding Unscientific Postscript to Philosophical Fragments*, trans. Howard V. Hong and Edna H. Hong (Princeton: Princeton University Press, 1992), 1:110. Though Hegel includes existence (*Dasein*) as a category within his logical system, this category cannot include existence in its individual manifestation without distorting it beyond recognition.

3. For instance, Ranajit Guha takes Hegel to task for his failure to give each particular its due. According to Guha, absolute knowledge assumes the top position in the epistemological hierarchy and subsumes all particulars within it. He writes, "the last term, *absolute knowledge*, emerges hierarchically as the highest in which all the others are dissolved and affirmed at the same time." Ranajit Guha, *History at the Limit of World-History* (New York: Columbia University, 2002), 3. Here, Guha misses the key to absolute knowing: rather than being at the top of the hierarchy, it dismantles all hierarchies because it bespeaks the absence of any substantial authority that is not also subject.

4. For an account of the philosophy of assemblages in contrast to that of totality, see Manuel DeLanda, *A New Philosophy of Society: Assemblage Theory and Social Complexity* (New York: Bloomsbury, 2006).

5. Gérard Lebrun insists vehemently on Hegel's rejection of any fixed starting point for his philosophy. Lebrun states, "every beginning is without fail non-true, inasmuch as it is *lived* as a beginning and not *understood* as a moment, but this understanding, in order to be authentic, must dissipate this inevitable first impression. One must pass by this fiction of a fixed and dated beginning; but in the end, it is only a fiction, and one must finish by recognizing it." Gérard Lebrun, *La Patience du concept: Essai sur le discours hégélien* (Paris: Gallimard, 1972), 166.

6. G. W. F. Hegel, *Phenomenology of Spirit*, trans. Terry Pinkard (Cambridge: Cambridge University Press, 2018), 5, 15. The German reads: "Die wahre Gestalt, in welcher die Wahrheit existiert, kann allein das wissenschaftliche System derselben sein"; "ein sogenannter Grundsatz oder Prinzip der Philosophie, wenn er wahr ist, schon darum auch falsch ist, insofern er nur als Grundsatz oder Prinzip ist." G. W. F. Hegel, *Phänomenologie des Geistes* (Frankfurt: Surhkamp, 1986), 14, 27.

7. Schelling's *System of Transcendental Idealism* of 1800 comes closest to jettisoning a foundational principle, but it doesn't quite get there because he starts with the idea of the coincidence of subject and object. At the beginning of this work, Schelling proclaims, "All knowledge is founded upon the coincidence of an objective with a subjective." F. W. J. Schelling, *System of Transcendental Idealism*, trans. Peter Heath (Charlottesville: University Press of Virginia, 1978), 5.

8. Hegel, *Phenomenology of Spirit*, 466 (translation modified). The German reads: "Das Wissen kennt nicht nur sich, sondern auch das Negative seiner selbst oder seine

Grenze. Seine Grenze wissen heißt, sich aufzuopfern wissen." Hegel, *Phänomenologie des Geistes*, 590.

9. Vehement hostility to Hegel emerges in England among Bertrand Russell and Karl Popper, in France among Louis Althusser and Gilles Deleuze, and in Germany among Friedrich Nietzsche and Martin Heidegger, just to name a few. Though many of these thinkers have almost nothing in common, they nonetheless share a suspicion about the Hegelian absolute and its violence to the singular.

10. Lyotard's essay dramatically increased in influence when the editors of the English translation of *The Postmodern Condition* decided to include it as an appendix to the seminal book. See Jean-François Lyotard, *The Postmodern Condition: A Report on Knowledge*, trans. Geoff Bennington and Brian Massumi (Minneapolis: University of Minnesota Press, 1984).

11. Jean-François Lyotard, "Answering the Question: What Is Postmodernism?," in *The Postmodern Condition: A Report on Knowledge*, trans. Geoff Bennington and Brian Massumi (Minneapolis: University of Minnesota Press, 1984), 81–82.

12. Robert C. Solomon, *In the Spirit of Hegel* (Oxford: Oxford University Press, 1983), 27.

13. In his book on the *Phenomenology of Spirit*, Fredric Jameson takes a similar tack. He contends that absolute spirit is "a most sketchy and disappointing anticlimactic conclusion for so intricate a work." Fredric Jameson, *The Hegel Variations: On the "Phenomenology of Spirit"* (New York: Verso, 2010), 116.

14. Hegel famously claims, "The true is the whole." Hegel, *Phenomenology of Spirit*, 13. The German reads: "Das Wahre ist das Ganze." Hegel, *Phänomenologie des Geistes*, 24.

15. Catherine Malabou, *The Future of Hegel: Plasticity, Temporality, and Dialectic*, trans. Lisabeth During (New York: Routledge, 2005), 155.

16. Theodor Adorno, *Minima Moralia: Reflections from Damaged Life*, trans. E. F. N. Jephcott (New York: Verso, 1978), 50.

17. Hegel, *Phenomenology of Spirit*, 241 (translation modified). The German reads: "Sie geben ihr Tun und Treiben für etwas aus, das nur für sie selbst ist, worin sie nur *sich* und *ihr eigenes* Wesen bezweckten. Allein indem sie etwas tun und hiermit sich darstellen und dem Tage zeigen, widersprechen sie unmittelbar durch die Tat ihrem Vorgeben, den Tag selbst, das allgemeine Bewußtsein und die Teilnahme aller ausschließen zu wollen; die Verwirklichung ist vielmehr eine Ausstellung des Seinigen in das allgemeine Element, wodurch es zur *Sache* aller wird und werden soll." Hegel, *Phänomenologie des Geistes*, 309.

18. For Jean-Joseph Goux, Hegel learns the lessons of capitalism too well. He writes, "what would best coincide with this political economy would be a philosophy of negativity teaching that all value is produced by pain: none other than Hegel's." Jean-Joesph Goux, *Symbolic Economies: After Marx and Freud*, trans. Jennifer Curtiss Gage (Ithaca: Cornell University Press, 1990), 210. Goux challenges Hegel's claim that the ability to feel pain attests to the priority of the organic world relative to the inorganic by linking this idea to Adam Smith and David Ricardo's labor theory of value.

19. Henry David Thoreau, *Walden* (New York: Penguin, 1983), 114.

20. Though the universal blocks any articulation of pure particularity, this does not imply that the universality has the purity that it denies to particularity. The

universal does not operate above particularity but must form itself through the expression of the particular. The attempt to assert the priority of the abstract universal necessarily ends up swallowing itself just like the Reign of Terror in the French Revolution.

21. G. W. F. Hegel, *Science of Logic*, trans. George Di Giovanni (Cambridge: Cambridge University Press, 2010), 740. The German reads: "Man kann daher wohl sagen, daß mit dem *Absoluten* aller Anfang gemacht werden müsse, so wie aller Fortgang nur Darstellung dieselben ist, insofern das *Ansichseiende* der Begriff ist." G. W. F. Hegel, *Wissenschaft der Logik II* (Frankfurt: Suhrkamp, 1986), 555.

22. G. W. F. Hegel, Letter to Friedrich Niethammer (October 13, 1806), in *Hegel: The Letters*, trans. Clark Butler and Christiane Seiler (Bloomington: Indiana University Press, 1984), 114. The German reads: "den Kaiser—diese Weltseele—sah ich durch die Stadt zum Rekognoszieren hinausreiten; —es ist in der Tat eine wunderbare Empfindung, ein solches Individuum zu sehen, das hier auf einen Punkt konzentriert, auf einem Pferd sitzend, über die Welt übergreift und sie beherrscht." G. W. F. Hegel, Brief an Niethammer, 13 October 1806, in *Briefe von und an Hegel* (Hamburg: Felix Meiner, 1952), 1:120.

23. Hegel, *Science of Logic*, 546. The German reads: "bestimmte Allgemeinheit." Hegel, *Wissenschaft der Logik II*, 298.

24. Booker T. Washington, *Up from Slavery* (New York: Penguin, 1986), 219.

25. Washington, 221–22.

26. W. E. B. Du Bois, *The Souls of Black Folks* (New York: Library of America, 1990), 8–9.

27. One could contrast Hegel with Friedrich Nietzsche on the question of singularity. While the latter appears to celebrate singularity in a way that Hegel does not, his failure to think systematically ends up undermining his conceptualization of singularity. In *Beyond Good and Evil,* Nietzsche writes, "the concept of greatness will include: being noble, wanting to be for yourself, the ability to be different, standing alone and needing to live be your own fists." Friedrich Nietzsche, *Beyond Good and Evil: Prelude to a Philosophy of the Future,* trans. Judith Norman (New York: Cambridge University Press, 2002), 107. What Nietzsche fails to recognize is that the noble spirit living on its own requires the herd from which it distinguishes itself. The singularity of Nietzsche's noble spirit has its basis in a failure to recognize its unconscious investment in the universal.

28. The racist subject's substantialization of the racial other leads this subject to believe that the other is awash in an enjoyment that the subject itself cannot access. The racist subject recognizes its own lack but cannot see this lack in the racialized other.

29. G. W. F. Hegel, *Aesthetics: Lectures on Fine Art,* trans. T. M. Knox (Oxford: Clarendon, 1975), 1:354. The German reads: "Die Aufgaben bleiben ungelöst, und die Lösung, die wir geben können, besteht deshalb such nur darin, der Rätsel der ägyptischen Kunst und ihrer symbolischen Werke als diese von den Ägyptern selbst unentzifferte Aufgabe aufzufassen." G. W. F. Hegel, *Aesthetik I* (Frankfurt: Suhrkamp, 1986), 456–57.

30. Because Europe did like not the precedent of a successful slave revolt, Haiti paid the price for this victory for a long time—and is still paying.

31. Susan Buck-Morss, *Hegel, Haiti, and Universal History* (Pittsburgh: University of Pittsburgh Press, 2009), 59.

32. In the *Philosophy of History,* Hegel formulates his theory of historical repetition. He states, "in general a political revolution is sanctioned in the opinion of humans, when it repeats itself. Thus Napoleon was twice defeated, and the Bourbons twice expelled. By repetition that which at first appeared only as contingent and possible becomes actual and validated." G. W. F. Hegel, *Philosophy of History,* trans. J. Sibree (New York: Dover, 1956), 313. The German reads: "überhaupt eine Staatsunwaltzung gleichsam im Darfürhalten der Menschen sanktioniert wird, wenn sie sich wieder-holt. So ist Napoleon zweimal unterlegen, und zweimal vertrieb man die Bourbonen. Durch die Wiederholung wird das, was im Anfang nur als zufällig und möglich erschien, zu einem Wirklichen und Bestätigen." G. W. F. Hegel, Vorlesungen über die Philosophie der Geschichte (Frankfurt: Suhrkamp, 1986), 380.
33. See Stephen Jay Gould, *The Mismeasure of Man* (New York: Norton, 1996).
34. Hegel, *Phenomenology of Spirit,* 198. The German reads: "du (dein Inneres) bist dies, weil dein Knochen so beschaffen ist, so heißt es nichts anderes als . . . hier mußte die Erwiderung eigentlich so weit gehen, einem, der so urteilt, dan Schädel einzuschlagen, um gerade so greiflich, als seine Weisheit ist, zu erweisen, daß ein Knochen für den Menschen nichts an sich, viel weniger seine wahre Wirklichkeit ist." Hegel, *Phänomenologie des Geistes,* 256–57.
35. Peter K. J. Park, *Africa, Asia, and the History of Philosophy: Racism in the Formation of the Philosophical Canon, 1780–1830* (Albany: SUNY Press, 2013), 117.
36. In perhaps the most compelling indictment of Hegel's treatment of race, Robert Bernasconi contends that "Hegel is self-conscious in his Eurocentrism. He does not simply append his views about non-European peoples to his philosophy; these views are elevated above the level of mere prejudice by the logical framework which helps sustain them and to which they in turn lend support." Robert Bernasconi, "With What Must the Philosophy of World History Begin? On the Racial Basis of Hegel's Eurocentrism," *Nineteenth-Century Contexts* 22 (2000): 172. The fundamental problem with Bernasconi's critique is that it transforms Hegel into a thinker for whom the beginning of history is decisive and determinative, whereas in fact Hegel theorizes that the beginning is nothing but the effect of history's end point. Bernasconi also minimizes the importance of Hegel's explicit statements rejecting racial hierarchies. See also Robert Bernasconi, "Hegel at the Court of the Ashanti," in *Hegel After Derrida,* ed. Stuart Barnett (London: Routledge, 1998), 41–63.
37. G. W. F. Hegel, *Philosophy of Mind,* trans. William Wallace and A. V. Miller (Oxford: Clarendon, 1971), 42 (translation substantively modified). The German reads: "Die Neger sind als eine aus ihrer uninteressierten und interesselosen Unbefangenheit nicht heraustretende Kindernation zu fassen. Sie werden verkauft, und lassen sich verkaufen, ohne alle Reflexion darüber, ob dies recht ist oder nicht." G. W. F. Hegel, *Enzyklopädie der philosophischen Wissenschaften III* (Frankfurt: Suhrkamp, 1986), 59.
38. Hegel, *Philosophy of Mind,* 45 (translation modified). The German reads: "In betriff aber endlich der ursprünglichen Amerikaner haben wir zu bemerken, daß dieselben ein verschwindendes schwaches Geschlecht sind." Hegel, *Enzyklopädie der philosophischen Wissenschaften III,* 63.
39. For a thorough summary of the contending positions on Hegel and race, see Rocío Zambrana, "Hegel, History, and Race," in *The Oxford Handbook of Philosophy and Race,* ed. Naomi Zack (Oxford: Oxford University Press, 2017), 251–60.

40. Samuel P. Huntington, *The Clash of Civilizations and the Remaking of World Order* (New York: Simon and Schuster, 1996), 318.
41. Hegel, *Science of Logic,* 534–35 (translation modified). The German reads: "Das Besondere . . . ist dessen Unterschied oder Beziehung auf ein *Anderes,* sein *Scheinen nach außen*; es ist aber kein Anderes vorhanden, wovon das Besondere unterschieden wäre, als das Allgemeine selbst." Hegel, *Wissenschaft der Logik II,* 281.
42. Hegel, *Science of Logic,* 535. The German reads: "Das Allgemeine bestimmt *sich,* so ist es selbst das Besondere; die Bestimmtheit ist *sein* Unterschied; es ist nur von sich selbst unterschieden. Seine Arten sind daher nur a) das Allgemeine selbst und b) das Besondere." Hegel, *Wissenschaft der Logik II,* 281.
43. Though the dialectic of the master and servant from the *Phenomenology of Spirit* functions as a starting point for most revolutionary thinkers, the discussion of the particular concept in the *Science of Logic* is actually more fecund territory. Here, Hegel shows how the oppressed particular becomes the bearer of universality, which can serve as the basis for revolutionary action.
44. Alfred Rosenberg, *The Myth of the Twentieth Century: An Evaluation of the Spiritual-Intellectual Confrontations of Our Age,* trans. Vivian Bird (Newport Beach, CA: Noontide, 1982), 301.
45. Karl Popper famously attempts "to show the link of Hegelian historicism and the philosophy of modern totalitarianism." Karl Popper, *The Open Society and Its Enemies 2, the High Tide of Prophecy: Hegel, Marx, and the Aftermath* (Princeton: Princeton University Press, 1962), 78.
46. Nazi thinkers themselves understand that Hegel is their mortal enemy. Rosenberg, the leading Nazi philosopher (and only philosopher executed at Nuremberg), sees Hegel as responsible for turning Germans away from the particularity of blood connections.

10. EMANCIPATION WITHOUT SOLUTIONS

1. G. W. F. Hegel, *Lectures on the History of Philosophy,* vol. 3: *Medieval and Modern Philosophy,* trans. E. S. Haldane (Lincoln: University of Nebraska Press, 1995), 545 (translation modified). The German reads: "Das *letzte* Ziel und *Interesse* der Philosophie ist, den Gedanken, den Begriff mit der Wirklichkeit zu versöhnen." G. W. F. Hegel, *Vorlesungen über die Geschichte der Philosophie III* (Frankfurt: Surhkamp, 1986), 455.
2. György Lukács offers the canonical critique of politics of Hegel's turn to the absolute. In *The Young Hegel,* he writes, "history does not contain its own real autonomous laws of motion, but on the contrary, the latter only really exist and come into their own in the science that comprehends and annuls history, i.e., in absolute knowledge. But this annuls the whole scheme of history elaborated by objective idealism. The spirit which is supposed to make history and whose very essence is supposed to be the fact that it is the actual driving force, the motor of history, ends up by turning history into a mere simulacrum." György Lukács, *The Young Hegel: Studies in the Relations Between Dialectics and Economics,* trans. Rodney Livingstone (Cambridge: MIT Press, 1976), 546–47. As Lukács conceives it, the reconciliation that occurs with absolute knowing is a betrayal of what leads up to it. For another famous

259

10. EMANCIPATION WITHOUT SOLUTIONS

version of this critique, see Jürgen Habermas, *The Philosophical Discourse of Modernity: Twelve Lectures*, trans. Frederick G. Lawrence (Cambridge: MIT Press, 1987).
3. Gillian Rose, *Hegel Contra Sociology* (London: Humanities, 1981), 208.
4. Herbert Marcuse takes a similar tack when he interprets Hegel as saying, "The realization of reason is not a fact but a task." Herbert Marcuse, *Reason and Revolution: Hegel and the Rise of Social Theory*, 2d ed. (New Jersey: Humanities, 1983), 26. In contrast to Rose, however, Marcuse believes that later in his life Hegel betrays his own insistence on the rationality of the actual when he praises the existing state in the *Philosophy of Right*.
5. G. W. F. Hegel, *Phenomenology of Spirit*, trans. Terry Pinkard (Cambridge: Cambridge University Press, 2018), 463 (translation modified). The German reads: "Erst nachdem es die Hoffnung aufgegeben, auf eine Äußerliche, d. h. fremde Weise das Fremdsein aufzuheben, wendet es sich . . . an sich selbst." G. W. F. Hegel, *Phänomenologie des Geistes* (Frankfurt: Surhkamp, 1986), 586.
6. G. W. F. Hegel, *Science of Logic*, trans. George Di Giovanni (Cambridge: Cambridge University Press, 2010), 735. The German reads: "in seinmen Anderen *seine eigene* Objektivität zum Gegenstande hat. Alles Übrige ist Irrtum, Trübheit, Meinung, Streben, Willkür und Vergänglichkeit; die absolute Idee ist *Sein*, unvergängliches *Leben, sich wissende Wahrheit*, und ist *alle Wahrheit*." G. W. F. Hegel, *Wissenschaft der Logik II* (Frankfurt: Suhrkamp, 1986), 549.
7. Immanuel Kant, *Critique of Pure Reason*, trans. Paul Guyer and Allen W. Wood (Cambridge: Cambridge University Press, 1998), 117.
8. Henning Ottmann argues that the interpretation of Hegel suffers from the "measureless overestimation of the dialectic of master and servant concerning what constitutes its meaning for Hegel's phenomenology and his philosophy." Henning Ottmann, "Herr und Knecht bei Hegel: Bermerkungen zu einer Missverstandenen Dialektik," *Zeitschrift für philosophishe Forschung* 35 (1981): 365.
9. In the 1827–1828 lecture series on the *Philosophy of Spirit*, Hegel states, "I know that the other is an I, but in its appearance it confronts me like a thing, like something completely external to me. This is the highest contradiction—the most complete indifference towards each other, and the most complete identity. The suspension of the contradiction—for it cannot remain a contradiction—is the process of recognition." G. W. F. Hegel, *Lectures on the Philosophy of Spirit, 1827–8*, trans. Robert R. Williams (Oxford: Oxford University Press, 2007), 187 (translation modified). The German reads: "So weiß ich, daß das andere ein Ich ist, aber wie es erscheint, ist es mir gegenüber ebenso wie ein Ding, ein vollkommen Äußerliches für mich. Das ist der höchste Widerspruch, die vollkommenste Gleichgültigkeit gegeneinander und die vollkommene Identität. Das Aufheben dieses Widerspruchs—er kann nicht so bleiben—ist der Prozeß des Anerkennens." G. W. F. Hegel, *Vorlesungen über die Philosophie des Geistes: Berlin 1827/1828*, eds. Franz Hespe and Burkhard Tuschling (Hamburg: Felix Meiner, 1994), 167.
10. See, for instance, Robert Williams, *Hegel's Ethics of Recognition* (Berkeley: University of California Press, 2000); and Sybol Anderson, *Hegel's Theory of Recognition: From Oppression to Ethical Liberal Modernity* (London: Bloomsbury, 2009).
11. In clear contrast to the silence with which the *Philosophy of Right* greets mutual recognition, it speaks voluminously on the state, which indicates where Hegel's political investment actually lies.

12. The location that a position has in Hegel's work provides a shorthand for insight into what he thinks of it. If it comes at the beginning, this indicates a profound lack of enthusiasm, not a full-throated embrace. As the philosophy moves onward, Hegel's enthusiasm increases.

13. Robert Pippin, *Hegel's Practical Philosophy: Rational Agency as Ethical Life* (Cambridge: Cambridge University Press, 2008), 29.

14. Hegel, *Lectures on the Philosophy of Spirit,* 264. The German reads: "Indem der Geist nichts will als frei sein und keinen anderen Zweck hat als seine Freiheit, so its Staat nur der Spiegel seiner Freiheit, worin er seine Freiheit als ein Wirkliches, als eine Welt vor sich hat." Hegel, *Vorlesungen über die Philosophie des Geistes,* 263.

15. G. W. F. Hegel, *Philosophy of Mind*, trans. William Wallace and A. V. Miller (Oxford: Clarendon, 1971), 171. The German reads: "so bin ich wahrhaft frei nur dann, wenn auch der andere frei ist und von mir als frei anerkannt wird." G. W. F. Hegel, *Enzykopädie der philosophischen Wissenschaften III* (Frankfurt: Suhrkamp, 1986), 220.

16. Hegel, *Philosophy of Mind,* 171 (translation modified). The German reads: "Diese Freiheit des *einen* im *anderen* vereinigt die Menschen auf innerliche Weise, wogegen das *Bedürfnis* und die *Not* dieselben nur äußerlich zusammenbringt. Die Menschen müssen sich daher ineinander wiederfinden wollen. Dies aber kann nicht geschehen, solange dieselben in ihrer Unmittelbarkeit, in ihrer Natürlichkeit befangen sind; denn diese ist eben dasjenige, was sie voneinander ausschließt und sie verhindert, als freie füreinander zu sein." Hegel, *Enzykopädie der philosophischen Wissenschaften III,* 220.

17. In *Hegel's Philosophy of Freedom*, Paul Franco points out that Hegel was the first thinker to grant the state a positive role in the formation of the subject's freedom. The state does not just provide a milieu in which the subject can act freely without constantly fearing for its life. Much more than this, it forces the subject to undergo an explicit and necessary alienation for its interests, which enables the subject to disentangle its freedom from the advancement of its interest. See Paul Franco, *Hegel's Philosophy of Freedom* (New Haven: Yale University Press, 1999), 343.

18. One of the primary culprits of this interpretation of the *Philosophy of Right* is Rudolf Haym, who was one of the chief propagators of this critique. In his account of Hegel's life and thought, he claims, "The Hegelian system has become the scientific dwelling of the spirit of the Prussian restoration." Rudolf Haym, *Hegel und seine Zeit* (Berlin: Rudolf Gärtner, 1857), 359.

19. If we think about the two authoritarian horrors of the twentieth century—Stalinist Russia and Nazi Germany—it seems as if Hegel misses the real danger. The problem is not imagining the state in terms of civil society but the excessive power of the state to curtail individual freedom. But ironically, both of these totalitarian enterprises avoided complete identification with the state. In each case, a party apparatus adjacent to state structure pulled the strings. This party apparatus arose out of an implicit recognition that the state alone is the realization of freedom.

20. Hegel reads Adam Smith and derives his conception of civil society in part from Smith's description of the laws that govern economic interaction. But, unlike Smith, he sees that unbridled capitalist interactions necessarily would produce a realm of intractable poverty that no economic strategy could remedy. Hegel would call this

realm of intractable poverty the "rabble." For more on Hegel's theorization of the rabble, see Frank Ruda, *Hegel's Rabble* (London: Bloomsbury, 2011).

21. In the *Philosophy of Right*, Hegel states, "The state in and for itself is the ethical whole, and actualization of freedom, and it is the absolute end of reason that freedom should be actual. The state is the spirit which is present in the world and which *consciously* realizes itself therein, whereas in nature, it actualizes itself only as the other of itself, as dormant spirit." G. W. F. Hegel, *Elements of the Philosophy of Right*, trans. H. B. Nisbet, ed. Allen W. Wood (Cambridge: Cambridge University Press, 1991), 279. The German reads: "Der Staat an und für sich ist das sittliche Ganze, die Verwicklung der Freiheit, und es ist absoluter Zweck der Vernunft, daß die Freiheit wirklich sei. Der Staat ist der Geist, der in der Welt steht und sich in derselben mit *Bewußtsein* realisiert, während er sich in der Natur nur als das Andere seiner, als schlafender Geist verwirklicht." G. W. F. Hegel, *Gundlienien der Philosophie des Rechts* (Frankfurt: Surhkamp, 1986), 403.

22. Thomas Hobbes, *Leviation*, ed. Edwin Curley (Indianapolis: Hackett, 1994), 76.

23. What is unique about the modern state in relation to the ancient polis is that it doesn't drown the subject within the collectivity that it forms. For the subject in ancient Greece, there is no principle of singularity operative, which is why Socrates is such a subversive figure in this world. As a champion of individual questioning, he challenges the basic structure of the polis. Through his execution, the polis attempts to defend itself from the modern principle of individual singularity that would be its undoing. But the principle that Socrates embodies ultimately triumphs in the modern state, which privileges singularity. In modernity, one can express one's individuality as a result of one's subjection to the state, not in opposition to it.

24. Shlomo Avineri, *Hegel's Theory of the Modern State* (Cambridge: Cambridge University Press, 1972), 124.

25. Hegel, *Elements of the Philosophy of Right*, 321 (translation modified). The German reads: "Dieses 'Ich will' macht den großen Unterschied der alten und modernen Welt aus, und so muß es in dem großen Gebäude des Staats seine eigentümliche Existenz haben. Leider wird aber diese Bestimmung nur als äußere und beliebige angesehen." Hegel, *Gundlienien der Philosophie des Rechts*, 449.

26. Slavoj Žižek, *The Sublime Object of Ideology* (London: Verso, 1989), 221–22.

27. Hegel, *Elements of the Philosophy of Right*, 23. The German reads: "Um noch über das *Belehren*, wie die Welt sein soll, ein Wort zu sagen, so kommt dazu ohnehin die Philosophie immer zu spät. . . . Wenn die Philosophie ihr Grau in Grau malt, dann ist eine Gestalt des Lebens alt geworden, und mit Grau in Grau läßt sie sich nicht verjüngen, sondern nur erkennen; die Eule der Minerva beginnt erst mit der einbrechenden Dämmerung ihren Flug." Hegel, *Gundlienien der Philosophie des Rechts*, 27–28.

28. Karl Marx, "Theses on Feuerbach," in *The Marx-Engels Reader*, ed. Robert C. Tucker (New York: Norton, 1978), 145 (emphasis in the original).

29. Karl Marx, *Grundrisse*, trans. Martin Nicolaus (New York: Penguin, 1993), 749.

30. Karl Marx, *A Contribution to the Critique of Political Economy*, trans. S. W. Ryazanskaya (New York: International, 1970), 21.

31. In addition to Étienne Balibar, Frank Ruda celebrates Marx for revealing that philosophy can never escape the domain of politics and thereby eliminating its illusion of autonomy. See Ruda, *Hegel's Rabble*.

32. Sidney Hook, *From Hegel to Marx: Studies in the Intellectual Development of Karl Marx* (New York: Columbia University Press, 1994), 19.

33. Karl Löwith, *From Hegel to Nietzsche: The Revolution in Nineteenth-Century Thought*, trans. David E. Green (New York: Columbia University Press, 1964), 218.

34. In a sense, Marx is correct to proclaim, "Communism is the riddle of history solved, and it knows itself to be this solution." Karl Marx, *The Economic and Philosophic Manuscripts of 1844*, trans. Martin Milligan (New York: International, 1964), 135. Marx's communism, unlike Hegel's absolute, announces the end of contradiction rather than entrenching it as unsurpassable.

35. Marx, *A Contribution to the Critique of Political Economy*, 21.

36. If he did not have the fantasy of a future free from contradiction, Maurice Merleau-Ponty would not have been able to write *Humanism and Terror*, which is his defense of Stalinism. From Merleau-Ponty's perspective, the oppressiveness of the Stalinist regime receives its justification from the future in which we will have overcome the burden of contradiction.

CONCLUSION

1. Terry Pinkard, *Hegel: A Biography* (Cambridge: Cambridge University Press, 2000), 24.

2. Rebecca Comay, *Mourning Sickness: Hegel and the French Revolution* (Stanford: Stanford University Press, 2011), 149.

INDEX